# HOW CARRIERS FOUGHT

*To my daughter.*

# HOW CARRIERS FOUGHT

## Carrier Operations in World War II

LARS CELANDER

CASEMATE

*Philadelphia & Oxford*

Published in the United States of America and Great Britain in 2018 by
CASEMATE PUBLISHERS
1950 Lawrence Road, Havertown, PA 19083, USA
and
The Old Music Hall, 106–108 Cowley Road, Oxford OX4 1JE, UK

Hardcover Edition: ISBN 978-1-61200-621-5
Digital Edition: ISBN 978-1-6120-062-2 (epub)

A CIP record for this book is available from the British Library

Printed and bound in the United States of America

Typeset in India by Versatile PreMedia Services. www.versatilepremedia.com

For a complete list of Casemate titles, please contact:

CASEMATE PUBLISHERS (US)
Telephone (610) 853-9131
Fax (610) 853-9146
Email: casemate@casematepublishers.com
www.casematepublishers.com

CASEMATE PUBLISHERS (UK)
Telephone (01865) 241249
Email: casemate-uk@casematepublishers.co.uk
www.casematepublishers.co.uk

# Contents

# Preface

It all started as an itch. Having read many books and articles on the big carrier battles of World War II, there were still a number of things I did not understand. Things like what actually went on and why things happened the way they did. I looked for books that told me not so much about the "what," "why," or "when" but about the more elusive "how." From time to time, some interesting and useful tidbits of information showed up but never a complete description.

There are many excellent books detailing what happened in those battles, how the events unfolded, what led up to them, and their significance in various ways. But that was not what I was looking for. I wanted something written more from the perspective of a commander, a tactician, a systems engineer, or an analyst, not a traditional historian. How did they do it? Why did they do it like that? Could they have done it a better way?

Not finding any book on the topic, I started digging around on the Internet. Gradually I started to get a decent understanding of how a carrier battle really was fought. The best way to understand something is often to try to explain it to someone else. By writing things down as an essay, I forced myself to structure my understanding and to clarify my thinking. It also identified the gaps in my knowledge, forcing me to go searching for what I had not yet understood.

Having done that, I found myself with an essay that I then posted on my personal website. This led to some very encouraging feedback; the essay seemed to fill a need. Nothing like it appeared to exist, at least not in the open literature. Similar analyses might well have been done by military professionals but perhaps not in a form intended for a wider audience.

In short, not finding the book I wanted to read, I wrote it myself.

Lars Celander

# Glossary of Terms

| | |
|---|---|
| AA | Anti-Aircraft |
| AEW | Airborne Early Warning |
| AP | Armor Piercing |
| ASW | Anti-Submarine Warfare |
| CAP | Combat Air Patrol |
| CIC | Combat Information Center |
| HE | High Explosive |
| IFF | Identification Friend or Foe |
| IJN | Imperial Japanese Navy |
| RN | Royal Navy |
| USN | United States Navy |
| Albacore | Fairey Albacore biplane torpedo bomber |
| Avenger | Grumman TBF Avenger torpedo bomber |
| Barracuda | Fairey Barracuda dive/torpedo bomber |
| Bearcat | Grumman F8F Bearcat fighter |
| Betty | Mitsubishi G4M "Betty" twin-engine medium bomber |
| Catalina | Consolidated PBY Catalina twin-engine flying boat |
| Corsair | Vought F4U Corsair fighter |
| Dauntless | Douglas SBD Dauntless scout/dive bomber |
| Devastator | Douglas TBD Devastator torpedo bomber |
| Emily | Kawanishi H8K "Emily" four-engine flying boat |
| Fulmar | Fairey Fulmar two-seat reconnaissance/fighter |
| Hellcat | Grumman F6F Hellcat fighter |
| Helldiver | Curtiss SB2C Helldiver dive bomber |
| Jake | Aichi E13A "Jake" floatplane |
| Jill | Nakajima B6N "Jill" torpedo bomber |
| Judy | Yokosuka D4Y "Judy" dive bomber |
| Kate | Nakajima B5N "Kate" torpedo bomber |
| Kingfisher | Vought OS2U Kingfisher floatplane |
| Liberator | Consolidated PB4Y Liberator long-range patrol bomber |

| | |
|---|---|
| Martlet | Grumman F4F Wildcat fighter (in British service) |
| Mavis | Kawanishi H6K "Mavis" four-engine flying boat |
| Sea Hurricane | Hawker Hurricane fighter (naval version) |
| Seafire | Supermarine Spitfire fighter (naval version) |
| Skua | Blackburn Skua two-seat fighter/dive bomber |
| Swordfish | Fairey Swordfish biplane torpedo bomber |
| Val | Aichi D3A "Val" dive bomber |
| Wildcat | Grumman F4F Wildcat fighter |
| Zero | Mitsubishi A6M "Zero" fighter |

# Introduction

## A New Form of Naval Warfare

On November 13, 1921, the first purpose-built carrier was launched. It was the Japanese *Hosho*, which displaced 7,590 tons and had a design speed of 25 knots. The British would follow a year later with the launch of the *Hermes*, slightly larger and also capable of 25 knots.

Back in 1920, the USN had done the first experiments with take-off-and-landings cruisers with temporarily erected wooden decks but it was the British that during the war years did most of the development. One approach was seaplanes launched from catapults and then landing on water. Another was wheeled planes taking off and landing on flat decks built on converted ships. The first such functional carrier was the British *Argus*. It was the first to have the key characteristics of a flat deck, a hangar, and elevators to transport planes between the two decks.

The American carrier *Langley*, a converted collier, was not the first in ship design but was used to develop many of the methods that are still being used. It was the first to use a Landing Signals Officer (LSO) to help pilots with landing, and also the first to use arresting wires and to have planes parked forward and a barrier to protect them from a plane that had missed the arresting wires. This way of doing flight operations quadrupled the number of planes that could be carried. With that many planes came the need for faster flight operations which meant developing a new set of skills. *Langley* was a slow ship, however, unable to generate much wind over the deck, which made it less useful. It was also small, limiting the number of planes that could be carried.

After World War I, for various reasons, all major navies began converting battlecruisers to aircraft carriers. Battlecruisers had always been intended as the scouts of the fleet and it was now clear that by carrying aircraft they could do it much better. The guns were removed and replaced with a flight deck. The USN built the *Lexington* and *Saratoga*, the IJN built the *Akagi* and *Kaga*, while the RN built the *Furious*, *Glorious*, and *Courageous*. These were large, fast, and powerful ships, the first "fleet" carriers. They were larger than many battleships of the day, clearly indicating that the aircraft carrier had become something that mattered and that major navies were ready to invest large sums of money in them. They were still very much subordinate to the battleship, however, an adjunct to the battle fleet with the role limited to scouting and perhaps raiding.

The torpedo had become a major weapon. The problem with the torpedo was always how to get close enough to the enemy battleships. The torpedo carrying bomber presented a solution to that problem. The aircraft carrier now threatened the battleship.

In a fleet exercise in 1929, *Saratoga* was detached from the main fleet and launched a surprise attack against the Panama Canal. The attack was a success. It was now obvious that naval aviation was something to be reckoned with even at the strategic level.

Before Pearl Harbor, the Japanese pioneered the concept of using all the carriers together as one large force, intended for massive strikes with strategic implications. They became the first to have their carriers steaming together as one large formation.

## A Very Technologically Complex Form of Warfare

This new type of naval warfare gave rise to a whole new set of problems involving a range of evolving technologies including navigation techniques suitable for aircraft, radio communications, landing on and taking off from a small flight deck, managing large numbers of aircraft on the flight deck and in the hangar. There were also the very considerable issues involved with formation flying and executing coordinated attacks. Torpedoes and torpedo bombing techniques were developed, as were dive bombing techniques, initially seen as a very radical form of attack. Simply finding the enemy was a major issue; it was revolutionized by the introduction of radar.

All this development went on for many years without any opportunity for testing within a battle situation. Every time a new and more powerful aircraft type was introduced, the goalposts moved.

When the war started, nobody really knew what would happen. Nobody really knew anything about carrier operations. There were lots of theories and opinions, sometimes strongly expressed, but at the end of the day, nobody could know for sure how it would all work out in actual combat.

## Short but Interesting Lives

As aircraft engine development continued, striking power and range increased dramatically. As a carrier needed to be fast, both for its intended role as a scout and to facilitate flight operations, protection did not keep pace. Carriers evolved into "eggshells armed with hammers," destined for short but interesting lives.

A battleship action was fairly simple: pound away at the enemy line until one side withdraws. The only complication was the desire to cross the other fleet's T. It had been like that for centuries. A carrier battle was different. It was less of a slugging match and much more of a game of poker.

The enemy was never seen. Everything depended on the scouting report. These were often unreliable. Commanders often had to make their decisions based on fragmentary information. Then there was the considerable time it took from when a decision was made until something actually happened. Preparing and launching a strike took time. There was also a long time to wait until a strike actually reached its target, if any was found. A strike that successfully engaged the enemy carriers was almost certain to cause heavy damage, in many cases sinking most of them.

Adding all these elements together, we have a very deadly game indeed. Let us say the commanders involved occasionally had some very stressful days at the office.

## Differently and Better?

This book starts out by examining the tools and building blocks of carrier operations. It then examines major carrier battles with a focus on how these tools were employed in those engagements.

We then have a good understanding of how carrier battles were fought. Then comes that nagging little question of what if…

What if they had done it differently in this or that battle? Would that have changed anything? Would the battles have turned out any differently? We can see that carrier operations changed in major ways during the war years. How much of that change was due to changing technology and how much was due to a better understanding of how to wage this new type of warfare? Answering these questions will provide us with a deeper understanding of carrier warfare.

The point about these what-ifs is not to speculate about a different outcome of the entire war. That is quite useless, we know what happened. The point is simply a better understanding of the dynamics.

One such topic is concentration versus dispersion. A prime example is the battle of Midway and the way the Japanese divided their forces while the Americans concentrated theirs. Inside the USN there was also intense debate on whether carriers should steam together for mutual protection or separately, to not have all the eggs in one basket. A poker player can play loose or tight—it depends on the chip count.

Another topic is the best balance between fighters and bombers. The combatants started the war with only about 20 percent fighters. The US ended the war with more like 80 percent while the Japanese stayed largely the same. Why?

An old and at times rather heated debate concerns whether or not armored flight decks were worth the cost in other areas like size of air group. The answer was quite unexpected for the author.

One of standard truths when writing about naval warfare of World War II is that the carrier had superseded the battleship. Is that really true or was it perhaps more complicated than that? To answer these questions I have used a model for combat between carriers. This combat model is based on the historical battles, on actual hit percentages and losses. All major carrier battles are therefore described, with a focus on the flow of flight operations and on the number of hits and losses. How searches were made is described, how many planes were used, and the range and coverage of the search. Strikes are detailed, how many planes were launched, how many hits were scored and losses suffered.

With the understanding gained from answering these questions, we can then describe and explain how carrier operations evolved during the war. Finally, we can then put this evolution in the context of the requirements and goals of the major navies and of their overall conduct of the war.

This book then has a certain flow to it. It starts with the tools, then how these tools were used in the battles, and then how well these tools were used. Having done that, this book will examine what happened and why in carrier battles, in order to answer the question "how?"

PART I

# Carrier Operations

# CHAPTER I

# Navigation and Communication

## Life in the Cockpit

Life in the cockpit of a World War II single-engine carrier-borne aircraft was most of all noisy. That big engine only a few feet away created a loud drone. Radial engines have a rather deep, slightly muffled roar to them, while inline engines have a sharper and more aggressive sound that tends to be more tiring. Those leather helmets were there for a reason. The earphones provided as part of the helmet assisted in using the radio, despite the noise. The microphone was a boom or throat microphone or integrated into the oxygen mask. Radio operators typically had a handheld microphone.

Cockpits were generally roomy. Radial engines, common on carrier aircraft, have a relatively large frontal area which makes it easier to fit more spacious cockpits. Fighters with inline engines, like the Spitfire or the Bf 109, tended to have cockpits that were much more cramped.

Cold temperature at altitude was generally not a problem for the pilot; warmth was provided by the closeness of the engine. For the rear gunner, or anyone sitting in an open cockpit, it was a different matter. Depending on altitude and climate it could be very cold. Sitting on the deck in tropical waters, waiting for take off, the breeze over the flight deck provided some cooling.

Cockpits were not pressurized. Oxygen masks had to be used above 12,000–14,000 feet. The oxygen tank was mounted in a fixed position, as the crew sat in their seats and did not move around. The prewar continuous flow type masks allowed operation up to 20,000–25,000 feet but had to be adjusted as the altitude changed and tended to waste oxygen. The more sophisticated demand-type masks allowed operation up to about 40,000 feet. For the latter type, a leak-proof fit for the mask was essential. The wearer had to be freshly shaven but might have a mustache. The fit around the nose was the most difficult part, as human noses vary greatly in shape and size. To get a good fit, the mask tended to put considerable pressure around the nose which could rub it raw and make the mask quite painful to wear. If high-g maneuvers were expected, likely exacerbated by the pilot sweating heavily, the mask had to very tightly secured indeed. Oxygen starvation (hypoxia) is a particularly insidious condition, as the first symptom is often a sense euphoria and not caring about what is happening. It then continues with disorientation, loss of consciousness, and death. Many pilots and aircrew were killed by a badly adjusted or leaking mask or any other problem with the oxygen supply. It was not unusual to see a plane drop out of the sky for no apparent reason. When using oxygen, it was common for aircrew to periodically check on each other. Cruising altitude was usually at around 12,000 feet to save on the limited oxygen available, as well as to avoid the discomfort and dangers of using oxygen. Dive bombers liked to climb to about 20,000 feet to get above the defenders before the attack and CAP had to be prepared to meet them at that altitude. Cockpits of modern fighters are only weakly pressurized and issues with the oxygen supply are a persistent and major danger.

No food or beverage was generally brought on missions despite these lasting upwards of 4–5 hours. Several battle accounts mention that the crews were quite hungry and thirsty after a mission and that the lack of food indeed had an effect on pilot endurance. As an LSO said to a pilot after he finally managed to land after five unsuccessful attempts: "You had to land here son, this is where the food is."

Aircrew often had some emergency ration with them to be used if shot down. This could take the form of stuffing something in pockets or somewhere in the plane. If accessible, it could be dipped into on a long mission. The heavy bombers of the bombing campaigns carried food and (hot) beverages for the crews but carrier aircraft did not, at least not on combat missions. Training missions were more relaxed and food and water was sometimes brought on long flights.

Smoking was generally not permitted in the cockpit but it went on anyway from time to time. Given how common smoking was at the time, this was unavoidable. Most soldiers and sailors smoked, the same in all militaries. Cigarettes were used as a way to relax from the stress of combat and some pilots were inveterate smokers. Some types of heavy bombers had lighters and ashtrays in the cockpit but carrier-borne aircraft generally did not have such amenities. On board a carrier, smoking was generally allowed but was restricted on flight and hangar decks or where gasoline was handled, for obvious reasons. Smoking was facilitated and encouraged by the military, with active support from the tobacco industry, particularly on the Allied side.

A Hellcat in the elevator well onboard USS *Monterey*. No smoking was allowed inside the hangar (at least the sign says so on this carrier; in practice it varied).

Modern-day statisticians have calculated that the increase in smoking habits during World War II, due to so many men being in the military, cost more man-years of life lost than did combat.

A relief tube was fitted for each crew in case there was a need to urinate. The flight suit zipper went far down but there was still a fair amount of digging out and then careful aiming to be done for successful completion of the task, often while busy keeping station in a formation. The relief tube was quite unpopular, if nothing else because it tended to freeze and become blocked at cruising altitude (air temperature goes down about 3°C per 1,000 feet of

altitude). Adult diapers were an alternative but do not appear to
used by carrier pilots. Female pilots had trouble using the relief t
used diapers instead, for example while doing long delivery flights o
from where they were manufactured in Bethpage, New York, to the West
Coast. Pilots sometimes simply landed with a "damp" or even "smelly" flight
suit. Heavy bombers generally used a chemical toilet, a bucket with a lid, or
a cardboard box. Here the crew had room to move about but then a co-pilot
was required and, if at altitude, portable oxygen bottles. To avoid dealing with
these problems, urinating before a mission was standard. Pilots often resorted
to not drinking any liquids before a mission ("tactical dehydration"). This was
not a good solution as dehydration affected performance, sometimes as much
as being intoxicated, something which was not really understood at the time.

Amphetamine pills were widely available among all major combatants during
World War II. They increase wakefulness for an additional 2–10 hours beyond
what could be considered typical endurance. In those days it did not have the
connotation of drug addiction it has today. The Germans used them during
the campaigns against Poland and France but quickly became aware of how
they impaired judgment and more or less stopped using them. Side effects
included aggressiveness, irritability, anxiety, paranoia, hallucinations, and
general confusion. After use, it would take a day or two to return to normal.
Allied heavy-bomber crews were routinely issued with amphetamines to stay
alert on long missions, as were crews of long-distance naval patrol planes.
The common brand name was Benzedrine or "Bennies." Carrier crews with
their relatively short missions of up to 4–5 hour did not use these pills much
at all. Still, there are reports of amphetamine pills having been taken by US
pilots before landing back on the carrier. Japanese carrier pilots have also been
described as taking "vitamin pills" to stay alert.

G-suits were experimented with from 1943 and onwards. The British
used a system with water-filled bladders around the legs which would fill
automatically as the g-suits were applied. Americans used a suit that would
be filled with compressed air. Both systems worked as advertised; pilots could
now handle and additional 1–1.5 g. Fighter pilots could be more aggressive in
turns and had an advantage in combat. Early suits were uncomfortable to wear
for extended periods though. G-suits could have been used by dive-bomber
pilots during the pull-out but that appears to not have been done. The Ju-87
had a different solution to this: it had an autopilot that handled the pull-out
if the pilot blacked out.

Formation flying was an essential part of combat. Much time was spent
training on it. Flying in a formation, the pilot had to constantly keep the

correct position. On the way to and from the target area, the formation was loosened up to reduce the workload on the pilots. Approaching the target area the formation was tightened up and required more attention.

Flying over vast stretches of open water with nowhere to land put a constant psychological pressure on navigation and on conserving fuel. There was also the constant worry about some kind of engine problem. Little confidence was placed on radios and various electronic navigation aids; both were prone to breakdowns and there had not always been time for proper training. Being a radio operator was not only about operating the radio, how to use it correctly, and to understand its limitations; it was also about giving the radio the tender loving care it needed to stay functioning well (like keeping it properly tuned, fixing a loose connection, or coaxing along a recalcitrant vacuum tube somewhere).

Combat missions were often long and boring, followed by a few minutes of sheer terror. The danger of AA fire was something one could not do much about—who got killed and who survived was just a matter of luck. Being powerless in that regard was something that just had to be accepted. Toward the end of the war missions consisted mostly of a daily grind of ground support with the ever-present danger from AA taking a psychological toll.

Search missions were better appreciated. There was more of a sense of serenity and peace, more time to enjoy the beauty of flying, watching the clouds and the slowly changing weather conditions.

Carriers were free of mosquitoes and sundry other nasty critters, as well as of most tropical diseases. Pilots of all navies preferred carrier duty to being stationed on a tropical island.

## Bailing Out and Ditching

All pilots and aircrew had a parachute. They spent their time in the cockpit sitting on it. It was not a very comfortable seat—a parachute is a parachute and not a wonder of ergonomics.

Bailing out required sufficient altitude to give the parachute time to open. It meant opening the canopy, usually by sliding it backwards—a simple thing to do in normal circumstance but with the plane shot up and perhaps the crew member being injured himself, it could easily become a major operation. Sometimes it was simply not possible to get out. Carrier combat was often at low level, so using a parachute was not always an option.

Bailing out at a high altitude meant disconnecting from the oxygen supply. The pilot then had to do a free fall and not pull the rip cord until he had reached an altitude where there was enough oxygen in the air. The time for the free fall was short enough so that hypoxia would not cause the pilot to lose consciousness.

Ditching was dangerous in planes with liquid-cooled inline engines. The problem was the air scoop for the cooling radiator, typically placed on the belly somewhere. It would scoop water, forcing the plane to a very rapid stop, often knocking the pilot unconscious as well as flipping the plane over. Scooping water, it would also make the plane sink very fast. The very short time to get out forced the pilot to unbuckle himself before the ditching, further increasing the risk of being knocked unconscious. The recommended procedure was therefore to dip one of the wings and as it touched the water the plane would cartwheel to a stop with less scooping of water. Cartwheeling is obviously not a controlled procedure and ditching with an inline engine was often fatal. This was one more reason why radial engines were almost always used for carrier-based aircraft. With a radial engine, ditching was likely a survivable event. Most of the danger came from being knocked unconscious and/or trapped and unable to get out of the sinking plane. A fixed landing gear does not seem to have precluded ditching; there are several accounts of Val dive bombers ditching and the aircrew surviving to be picked up.

The Zero was different in that pilots in many situations elected not to wear the parachute harness, using the parachute only as a seat cushion. The reason for this was that the parachute harness restricted movement in the cockpit. Another reason was that bailing out in combat would often mean capture, at least in wartime, something that was not really an option for pilots. On the other hand, the Zero had excellent ditching characteristics, including sealed flotation compartments in the wings and a flotation bag inside the rear fuselage that could be inflated by the pilot. Early war USN types like the Wildcat, Dauntless, and Devastator also had flotation gear but soon had them removed. In the case of the Devastator, the express purpose was that the plane would indeed sink, quickly and reliably, taking the top-secret Norden bomb sight with it (and presumably the aircrew as well). In the case of the Wildcat it was due to reliability problems—the large inflatable bags in the wings had a habit of inflating at inopportune moments which lead to some fatal accidents. The RN did not use flotation gear in their planes and the Martlets had them removed.

Pilots did not necessarily have the shoulder harnesses seen today. In the early days of the war, many planes only had a simple two-point seatbelt. Shoulder harnesses were added as pilots kept smashing their foreheads against the gun sight during ditching or crash landing. Harnesses were kept loose as required to operate the gun or bomb sight and any plotting board used.

Japanese fighter pilots, both army and navy, had a habit of shooting enemy aircrew hanging in a parachute. The main defense against this was to not pull the rip cord until at fairly low altitude. Having landed in water, it was usually best not to inflate the life jacket or life raft until after the fight was over.

## Search and Rescue

All pilots and aircrew wore lifejackets. USN and RN used inflatable ones commonly nicknamed Mae Wests. Inflation was with a $CO_2$ cartridge or manually. Dye markers were often included; releasing the dye into water would create a brightly colored patch on the ocean, usually fluorescent yellow-green (using the Cy3 cyanine dye). The patch would last for half an hour and was the most effective way to get spotted from the air. A small bobbing head in the ocean is very hard to spot from even a short distance. Dye markers are still in use today. IJN used bulkier lifejackets made of kapok, a vegetable material related to cotton that is very buoyant and resistant to water but also flammable. These did not have to be inflated. IJN life jackets were khaki or dark green while USN and RN were yellow, or more exactly, a yellowish khaki.

Most planes were equipped with a liferaft for the crew, usually accessed through a hatch on the outside, to be pulled out and inflated after ditching. This liferaft had various survival equipment within it, like a flare gun, some emergency rations, and a small amount of water (but no towel). Later in the war, a small one-man liferaft was often included with each parachute so that a liferaft was available after bailing out as well as after having ditched.

Both the USN and the RN put great emphasis on recovering lost pilots. Records were kept of where comrades had bailed out or ditched and this was communicated to the search and rescue resources available. Primary tools of rescue were flying boats, floatplanes, submarines, and destroyers.

Japanese pilots saw all this and were quite envious of how much effort the Americans put into rescuing downed airmen. They were in a different situation as it was felt that the resources required were better employed elsewhere. This was probably correct from a strictly military point of view. Many planes did not have life rafts and if they had, rescue was still unlikely. The tendency of Japanese pilots to crash themselves into enemy ships, instead of hoping for a rescue, then becomes understandable. Pilots were simply expected to make whatever sacrifice was required of them, whether they liked it or not.

## Capture

IJN aircrew abhorred being captured, preferring to kill themselves instead, often by crashing into enemy ships. If they somehow survived to be captured, they were deemed to have failed in a most dishonorable way. Having nothing left to lose, they would now often acquiesce to their captor's demands and quite readily so. To facilitate this psychological defection, the few that were captured were kept isolated from each other until interrogations were completed.

Captured USN aircrew were routinely tortured and executed by the Japanese. It was accepted that they would not withstand torture. While in a combat zone, they were told as little as possible.

## Airborne Navigation

Navigation was by dead reckoning (DR) using a magnetic compass, air-speed indicator, and a watch. This basic DR was refined with estimates for wind drift, starting with the wind that was observed at the carrier. Careful observation was also made of weather patterns and possible changes in wind direction and strength. Wind drift could be gauged from the direction and length of waves but flying above the clouds the waves could not be observed. Accurate navigation depended also on being a good meteorologist. Weather forecasts of the day were often unreliable and of little help.

The DR plot was accurate to within about 5–10 percent. With a combat radius of 250 miles we then have an uncertainty of up to 20–50 miles. During a mission lasting 4 hours, the fleet would have typically moved around 50–100 miles, so before the flight, pilots were briefed on expected movements by the carrier (which implied limits on the freedom of movement of the carrier until the planes had been recovered). Longer strike ranges were avoided, not only for fuel and endurance reasons but also for navigational reasons.

Portable plotting boards (sometimes called the "chartboard") were used by the navigators of all navies. The board typically contained navigational

VT-13 pilots on USS *Franklin* with their plotting boards getting ready for a mission, October 24, 1944. The plotting boards are plugged into the instrument panel like a kitchen drawer. Note dye markers carried on life jackets.

charts with notes on positions, times, and headings written in pencil. USN pilots used a special type of plotting board that integrated the circular slide rule functionality, similar to the well-known Dalton E-6B flight computer, streamlining much of the plotting work. The board also had diagrams to help with assessing wind speed from wave length. The board was stored either as a drawer on the main instrument panel in front of the pilot or tucked away by the side of the seat. RN navigators used a common plotting board coupled with a separate Mk III Navigational Computor, later upgraded to the Mk IV version which was very similar to the E-6B. The E-6B was invented in the late 1930s by USN Lt. Philip Dalton, later killed while serving as an instructor pilot in another one of those all too common training accidents.

The compass was normally of the fluxgate type with a basic card compass as backup. The fluxgate sensor was placed in a magnetically quiet part of the aircraft, that is away from the engine and electrical equipment (aluminum is not magnetic). Repeaters were placed on the instrument panel, both for pilot and navigator. Neither type of compass works during combat maneuvers—the aircraft had to be flying level. Gyroscopes are not affected by maneuvers but, as it drifted, it needed periodic manual alignment with the compass. The most sophisticated solution was a gyroscope with automatic alignment to a fluxgate compass. True gyro compasses were not used on aircraft, being much too heavy and expensive. They were used extensively on ships, however. They use the earth's rotation and not its magnetic field and are therefore not affected by the presence of large masses of steel.

It was the responsibility of the pilot to fly the exact compass course that he was supposed to. This required concentration. The further away from the carrier, the more the pilot felt the pressure to be accurate in his flying.

Navigation by sextant and chronograph was possible but required a dedicated navigator. The sextant was of the bubble type with an artificial horizon. Fix accuracy was rather poor at about 10–20 miles. Obviously a clear sky was needed but then so did combat operations. Ships with their better sextants, stable decks and true horizons usually navigated with an accuracy of 2–5 miles. Taking the height of the sun using a sextant will only yield a line, not a position. As the sun moves across the sky, a second line can be obtained that can then be compared with the first by transposing it with DR. Getting a true position fix is therefore something that is only possible for flights lasting longer than a few hours and depended on good DR. At night, the stars can be used, each providing a line of position and true fixes can be obtained directly.

Navigators of Japanese naval aviation used the Bygrave tubular slide rule for sight reduction. The Bygrave was invented in 1920 by RAF Captain L. G.

Bygrave. A modified version of the original Bygrave was used by the German U-boats. It solved the mathematical equations directly but was replaced by books with printed sight reduction tables, a faster and easier solution, when these became available before and during the war.

Navigation could be done by the pilot if needed, but was usually better and more accurately done by a dedicated navigator. The pilot could be busy not only with basic flying but also with keeping position within the formation. As it could be difficult for a single-seat fighter pilot to also do navigation, he tended to just tag along with the bombers, at least early in the war.

The RN frequently operated in low-visibility conditions and, before electronic navigation aids had been developed, tended to operate two-seat fighters for this reason, for example the Fulmar. Despite the cost in performance, being able to reliably find one's way back to the carrier after a mission was seen as essential.

The following is a rather vivid description of life as an observer/navigator on board a Swordfish torpedo bomber with the added complexity of having an open cockpit (from the book *Achtung! Swordfish!* by Stanley Brand):

> It was indeed a miracle that an observer could concentrate on the difficult task of keeping track of our whereabouts with a chart and chart board balanced on his knee, without a table for his instruments, needing pencils, ruler, rubber, dividers, compasses, records of deviations, variations, courses and times flown, wind speeds and direction and a calculator for drift and distance flown. Gloved hands and sometimes numb fingers made it difficult to hold these awkward things and if they were dropped Sod's Law decreed that they would rest just out of reach, with movement restricted in the confines of the cockpit and by the many layers of clumsy protective clothing. There was a limit on the number of bits of string which could be used to restrain individual items of equipment such as rubber, ruler, pencil and protractor without creating a spider's web when in use.

Val and Judy dive bombers had two crew, pilot and navigator/radio operator/rear gunner. Kate and Jill torpedo bombers had a three-man crew of pilot, navigator/bombardier/observer and radio operator/gunner.

Zero pilots did only basic navigation, some courses and times jotted down on a kneeboard. This was just a backup solution, and they depended on bombers to bring them back to the carrier. A pair of Kate torpedo bombers was sometimes dedicated to act as guides or pathfinders for the whole formation but most importantly for the fighters. Bombers also had the capability to drop blobs of white dye into the ocean, a series of which would form a line telling the fighter pilots the direction of the carriers. If a Zero pilot, at the end of the combat, found himself without a bomber or anything else to guide him home, then he was lost, usually fatally. The lack of navigation facilities in the Zero also had implications for fighter direction. Telling the pilot where the target was meant little to him as he did not have a plot. Telling him where to go also meant little as he did not have the means to navigate there.

Dauntless and Helldiver dive bombers both had two crew, pilot and radio operator/rear gunner. At Coral Sea and at Midway, Devastators flew most missions with a two-man crew, pilot and radio operator/rear gunner. The Devastator actually had a third crewman in the middle position but his main purpose was to man the Norden bomb sight which was not used with torpedoes. Avengers had a three-man crew consisting of pilot, radioman/radar operator/bombardier/ventral gunner, and rear turret gunner (cooped up in a small powered turret he was unable to do much else). USN practice was to always have the pilot do the navigation, even on bombers, but then they used that special plotting board mentioned previously that simplified things for them. USN fighter pilots are known to pay attention to their dead reckoning even while dogfighting, jotting down courses and times on a knee pad and then plotting them once out of the fight.

The Dauntless and Devastator both had duplicate sets of controls which at least in principle enabled the pilot to leave the flying to his crew for a while as he tended to his navigation or if incapacitated. In the case of the Devastator, when flying without the bombardier, those controls were not manned. Neither the Avenger nor the Helldiver had duplicate controls.

Autopilots became common on USN carrier aircraft toward the end of the war (autopilots were common on large bombers even at the outbreak of war; it was part of the bomb sight). These were true autopilots based on gyros and kept the aircraft on a constant heading, roll, and attitude. A similar effect could be achieved by a combination of proper trimming of the aircraft and maybe some kind of lockon stick movement. With both his hands now free, at least for a moment, it was easier for the pilot to keep his plot updated.

Once the pilot or navigator had found his way back to the general area of where the carrier was supposed to be, it could generally be spotted. Toward the end of the war, US task forces were so big that, spread out over 20–25 miles of ocean, they were easier to find. By then it had become a chore to find the right carrier to land on, there were so many to choose from. If the task force was obscured by clouds or low visibility, a homing beacon was used. If the navigator still could not find the carrier, this was often fatal. The problem was especially serious for long-range patrol planes. Some never found their way back to the base and disappeared forever. The reason why it was called "dead reckoning" was that if you reckon wrong, you are dead, or so went the joke. In many cases it was not a joke. If you wanted to survive the next mission, you had to be a good navigator, especially in bad weather and despite the inevitable equipment failures. The sea can be very cold and unforgiving.

## Homing Beacons

These were used to allow planes to find their way back to the carrier. Both RN and USN developed very similar systems in the early 1930s and both were operational before the war. But this does not necessarily mean that aircrew had had the time and training needed to develop much faith in it. Particularly during the early years of the war, it was regarded as an unreliable and generally weird contraption.

The carrier had a large antenna high up the superstructure that transmitted a continuous signal with different letters broadcast in different directions as the beam rotated. Letters were top secret and changed daily. Using letters in this way meant that aircraft got directional information just by listening to which letter they received. The frequency used was in the high VHF band (246MHz) and range was limited to 30–35 miles. Being essentially a line-of-sight system, the longer ranges required the aircraft not to be at low altitude (as in "under the radar" or "below the horizon"). On the USN version, the transmitter on the carrier was called "YE" and the receiver on board the aircraft was called "ZB."

The IJN never developed a homing beacon system along these lines; their doctrine focused on strict adherence to radio silence. They did have common RDF transmitters on their carriers but these worked on the long-range MF and HF bands and were kept switched off if the enemy could be listening. These transmitters did not transmit directional information and the receivers on board the aircraft had to manually rotate an antenna to find the direction of the transmitter. These receivers could be used to find the direction of any suitable transmitter, however, as was done using the KGU AM radio station in Honolulu on the approach to the Pearl Harbor attack. Without homing beacons, the IJN lost more planes due to navigational errors, particularly as they searched and attacked out to a relatively long range. Some of the range advantage the Japanese had was lost to the need of having some fuel in reserve in case they had difficulty finding the carriers.

The RN and USN homing beacon systems could in principle be used by the enemy to home in on the carriers during a battle. The very high frequency and the limited range were the main guards against that. The homing beacon might also be turned completely off if required for reasons of radio silence. The rotating beam also made it awkward to use for direction finding. In practice this did not matter much as both navies made heavy use of radar anyway, as well as radio communications for fighter direction, both of which were easier to detect.

## Carrier Pigeons

### Use on Carriers

Homing pigeons were used greatly during World War I, as they had been for thousands of years. Standard practice was to have a loft of pigeons somewhere in the rear of the fighting. One of the pigeons was then brought up to the front and when the need arose was used to send a message back to headquarters.

The success rate for returning pigeons was typically in the region of 95–98 percent. Amazingly, pigeons also have an ability to find their way back to their loft even after it has moved while they have been away. This ability was important if they were to operate from a mobile base like a ship.

The general use of pigeons was carried over to early seaplane tenders and carriers. The first true American carrier, the *Langley*, had a loft at the stern. Early drawings of the *Lexington* and *Saratoga* conversions also included lofts at the stern but these were not included in the final design. The intended use of pigeons on board a carrier was for one of them to be carried inside an aircraft and then released to report back to the carrier, perhaps a sighting report or that the plane had been forced down and the crew needed rescuing.

Releasing the pigeon involved tossing it out of an aircraft moving at something like 150mph. This was undoubtedly character forming for the pigeon. Various container contraptions were used to make the transition easier for the birds but they seemed to be quite robust and it took quite a lot before their wings were ripped off by the slipstream. Altitude did not seem affect them either. They appeared quite unfazed while sitting inside an unpressurized plane at 30,000 feet without oxygen. When tossed out, they immediately went to a low altitude and then went about their business as usual.

Early attempts on the *Langley* worked fine but one day when all the pigeons were released at the same time, they decided to forget about the carrier and flew back to the carrier's homeport instead. The mutinous pigeons were never brought back to the *Langley*.

The basic principle of releasing pigeons from downed aircraft remained, however. For certain bombing missions over Germany in World War II, all bombers carried two pigeons. On occasions when the bomber had ditched and the radio was inoperable, released pigeons initiated the search-and-rescue operation that in some cases saved the crew. This could in principle have been done by carrier-borne aircraft as well but does not appear to have been used by anybody. The Japanese never paid much attention to search and rescue and the British and Americans let their pigeon capability lapse between the wars. Neither the RN nor the USN restarted it. The Germans retained their pigeons between the wars, but then they never operated carriers.

Most armed forces stopped using pigeons in the 1950s as radios became reliable and commonly used. Pigeons are still used in asymmetrical warfare where the technologically superior enemy can be assumed to either jam or intercept radio communications.

## Training

Pigeon performance and homing ability can be greatly enhanced by training. Not all pigeons are born the same. With proper breeding and training, flying speeds of about 60mph and an endurance of 700 miles or more can be achieved. Homing ability also needs training. Some pigeons are initially so horribly bad at navigation that they have difficulty even finding their way out of the loft. Pigeons also do not like flying over water and require some training to be comfortable doing it. Lack of such training might be the reason behind the *Langley* debacle.

Performance can be improved by other means, such as letting the pigeon go hungry. A particularly evil trick was to show a male pigeon his favorite female in the company of another male before the mission. Both of these tricks tended to make the pigeon fly faster back to the loft.

## Countermeasures

The extensive use of pigeons to pass important messages called for countermeasures. The most obvious was rifle fire but that only worked at close range and then only barely (this has been tested by the author). Shotguns have a much better chance of bringing down a bird. It turns out that what hunters consider to be the optimum shotgun pellets weigh about 1/3000th of a pigeon, about the same weight ratio as a 40mm shell to a single-engine aircraft. Rifle fire against pigeons is suboptimal in the same way as heavy AA is suboptimal against single-engine aircraft: the projectiles in the air are simply too few and the additional weight cannot make up for lack of numbers.

A more effective method was to use Peregrine falcons. These were favored by the Germans who used them to stop the British from using pigeons dropped over occupied Europe to carry messages from the Resistance back to London.

Peregrine falcons are not much faster than pigeons in level flight. They hunt by patrolling an area at some altitude and then swooping down at great speed, overtaking and surprising the target pigeon. A Peregrine falcon has an eyesight about ten times better than a human and can spot a pigeon about a mile away. They dive in at six o'clock of the pigeon, with the final approach slightly below the pigeon to exploit its blind spot, and then quickly climb up with full flaps to reduce speed, grasping it with the inch-long claws of their landing gear. Some pigeons had a counter to this: at the last moment they would simply stop flying and drop like a stone, forcing an overshoot. Some pigeons repeatedly managed to come home with obvious claw injuries, presumably after tangling with these German-trained Peregrine falcons (known in colloquial Latin as *Falco peregrinus messerschmitti*).

The British, knowing the dangers posed by Peregrine falcons, had their own wild falcons culled. This had the unintended effect of making it easier for German spies to get messages out using their own pigeons. The British soon restocked their Peregrine falcons but did so with some that had been trained not to kill and eat the pigeon but to catch it and then bring it back to the falconer. This provided some information on the German design of the metal container carrying the message. These were then copied and put on British pigeons who were then secretly dropped over known pigeon lofts deep inside Germany. The British pigeons, realizing that they were too far from home to return, would then join their German colleagues, effectively acting as undercover spies. The Germans would then drop these British pigeons to German spies in England who would stuff them full with top secret messages which would then be brought to British lofts. This was of course a very clandestine activity and was handled by British Military Intelligence, Section 14, also known as MI-14, later merged with MI-6.

### *Pigeon-Guided Missiles*

Some of the homing ability of pigeons seems to depend on a highly developed sense of image recognition. In an experiment on animal cognition, pigeons were trained to distinguish between paintings done in the cubist style and paintings done in the impressionist style (interestingly, the cubist painting could be turned upside down and the pigeon would still recognize it as a cubist painting; an impressionist painting turned upside down would no longer be recognized as such).

During the war, it was obvious that guided missiles were needed to hit moving and well-defended targets like ships. The problem was the guidance system, including how to make it resistant to jamming. This is where the image-recognition capabilities of pigeons proved useful. Pigeons were successfully trained to peck at an image of a warship and where the pigeons pecked was then used to control the flight surfaces of the missile. Since pigeons might or might not display proper military attitude and discipline, three pigeons were used and their outputs combined to provide reliable guidance. This was all then integrated into the USN Bat glide bomb discussed earlier. At the end nothing came of it. The Bat bomb went on to use radar guidance instead. Radar guidance was bad at target selection and easily jammed, so it is quite possible that well-trained pigeons would have performed better. The main reason why pigeon guidance was not used seems to have been that people just refused to take it seriously.

## Radar Control

While within range of friendly radar, a radar operator can tell you where you are. Strike ranges are typically much longer than radar range so this is most commonly used with aircraft patrolling near the fleet, for example on anti-submarine and CAP duties. The big problem here is of course to tell one radar blip from the other; with many blips on the screen the operator will have a hard time to help anyone with any navigation. This could be circumvented by flying a certain pattern so that the radar operator could distinguish one particular plane—somewhat awkward but quite doable if the radar plot people were not too busy.

## Radio Navigation

This was used by both aircraft and ships to find their position. There are several ways of doing this. The most common way is to have land-based radio stations transmitting some kind of signal that aircraft and ships can listen to.

One of the earliest and perhaps best known was LORAN. It was declared operational in early 1943 and by late 1943 most of the North Atlantic was covered, followed by expansion across the Pacific. Range was 700–1,400 miles with an accuracy of 1–2 percent of the distance to the station, down to an accuracy of about a mile. This accuracy was not very good; much better accuracy was obtained by the later LORAN-C upgrade.

The first operational LORAN receiver was the AN/APN-4 weighing 71lbs. In 1945 it was followed with the lighter and more compact AN/APN-9 which still weighed 40lbs. Both models required a dedicated navigator and special charts to operate. These receivers were mounted primarily on patrol planes and on heavy bombers like the B-29.

The British Decca system was similar to LORAN but had much better accuracy, from a few meters up to a mile at the edge of coverage. The range was less, about 200–400 miles. Decca was first used by minesweepers during the Normandy landings.

These systems told the receiver where it was in relation to the ground stations but did not tell carrier-borne aircraft where they were in relation to the carrier, which to them was more important. They were rarely mounted on carrier-borne aircraft due to space and weight restrictions.

## Radio Communication

The mainstay of radio communications at the time was HF radio. These generally have long range, up to several hundred miles, but are affected by atmospheric conditions and can be quite unreliable, messages being garbled and/or effective range much less (or much more) than nominal.

HF radio was used for voice or Morse code. Using HF for voice communication was convenient and quick but was not secure and had shorter range. Using Morse code, the radio had a longer range and was more secure but also required more work and patience to operate, tending to require a dedicated radio operator even though pilots of all navies were trained to use Morse code.

Radios were typically installed behind the pilot, keeping them away from the ignition interference of the engine and with a short cable run to the antenna normally mounted just behind the cockpit. If the plane had radio operator, he would be sitting behind the pilot facing the radio.

In 1943, USN planes were equipped with VHF radios operating at 100–155MHz. Operating at higher frequencies they had shorter range, basically line of sight. VHF radios were much less affected by atmospherics and thus more reliable in combat. The sound quality was much better. At higher frequencies it was also easier to fit in more frequencies. VHF radios, as used by the USN, were voice only. They were intended for quick messages and the relatively short range provided a measure of security against eavesdropping.

These VHF radios had four channels, that is four complete transmitters/receivers, each operating on a pre-set frequency. A switch was then used to select which transceiver was connected to the headset. The pilot/radio operator could then very easily switch between these four frequencies and quite possibly also listen to more than one frequency at a time. The radio traffic needed to run a battle was in this way divided up into four separate channels, or "networks," which reduced traffic congestion.

In principle it was possible to have the same kind of set-up on the HF band, that is having four separate transmitters/receivers, but that appears to not have been implemented. If the traffic congestion could be solved in some other way, for example by being disciplined, then a single channel could be enough. It was also possible for an HF radio to be adjustable in frequency, allowing the radio operator to change channel though not listening to more than one channel at a time. Using HF radios, the RN performed effective fighter direction in 1942.

USN ships used TBS ("Talk Between Ships") radio operating at 60–80MHz for tactical communication within a formation. Fairly low power at 40 watts and basically line-of-sight, the range was limited to about 10+ miles. The short range solved problems with operational security, and communication could be in voice and without using codes. The German navy had a similar system operating higher up in the VHF band. The Japanese and British also had similar systems for communications between ships. None of these were used for communication with aircraft. During the war, it turned out that these systems were not quite as secure as first thought. The phenomenon of "ducting" meant that under certain atmospheric conditions, these signals could be picked up at considerably longer distances.

Radio communications were listened to by the enemy. All kinds of information was gleaned from this, like the number of planes in the air from the number of distinct call signs used. Both sides also loved to engage in all sorts of trickery to confuse and delay the radio traffic of the enemy, the more devious and insidious the better. Classics included transmitting false messages, false replies, and retransmitting altered messages or the same message on a different frequency. Sometimes false or simply rude messages were transmitted to goad the enemy into revealing something that was not intended to be known. Coded traffic was easy to impersonate but if somebody spoke the language well enough, voice messages were also impersonated. If deception was not enough, then there was always plain old jamming, particularly against the all-important sighting reports. The main countermeasures against this type of warfare were strict adherence to procedures, tight discipline, and generally alert and well-trained radio operators.

## Radios

### IJN

The Zero carried the Type 96 Air Mk 1 Radio Telephone. This set had problems with interference from the engine ignition plus static interference caused by improper grounding of fuselage, coupled with a general lack of technical understanding among ground crews as well as pilots. They just did not know—another consequence of Japan's meager industrial base. The Bushido spirit is all well and good, but being able to distinguish a grounding strip from a bowl of rice is also helpful. Considered unreliable, the set was sometimes removed to save weight. When these radios worked as advertised they had a range of about 50 miles, not very great but fairly decent for a fighter. From the middle of the war the unit was replaced by the Type 3 Air Mk 1 Radio Telephone which had an output power of 15 watts and a range of about 50 nautical miles.

The dive bombers carried the Type 96 Air Mk 1 Wireless Telegraph which had an output of 40 watts and an effective range of over 500 nautical miles.

The torpedo bombers had the Type 96 Air Mk 3 Wireless Telegraph which had an output of 50 watts and an effective range of over 800 nautical miles. It was later replaced by the Type 2 Air Mk 3 Wireless Telegraph that had an output power of

80 watts and a range of 1,500 nautical miles. Torpedo planes were also equipped with the Type 1 Air Mk 3 In-unit Radio Telephone.

IJN aircraft used only HF radios. No homing beacon was used.

## USN

Early in the war, the standard HF set was the ATA/ARA series. This was succeeded by the very similar AN/ARC-5 set having an output power of 25 watts.

The VHF transceiver used by both fighters and bombers was at first a unit that was used with the AN/ARC-5, a four-channel VHF unit with an output power of 8 watts. Later a 10-channel VHF unit was used, the AN/ARC-1.

Bombers also had a second more powerful HF set, the AN/ART-13 transmitter, with an output power of 100 watts combined with an ARB receiver.

The receiver used for the homing beacon was the AN/ARR-2 and was used together with the AN/ARC-5.

The above should be seen as a rough indication only, a listing of only the most common equipment used. USN radios and nomenclature is an extremely complex topic and largely beyond the scope of this book.

## RN

The TR9D was an early HF radio that was the mainstay during the battle of Britain, used by both Hurricanes and Spitfires and then carried over to the Fleet Air Arm. Frequency was set by ground personnel before the mission. Power output was low and range was limited to 5 miles between aircraft and about 30 miles to ground stations.

The TR9D was soon replaced by the TR1196 HF Radio. Frequencies were set by ground personnel before a mission. Four frequencies could be pre-selected. The range was 30 miles between aircraft and 50 miles to ground stations.

The R1082/T1083 set was introduced in the 1930s and used by bombers early in the war. Frequencies were set before take off. The R1116/T1115 set was very similar and used by carrier-borne aircraft such as the Swordfish. T1154/R1155 was a more modern set used extensively by bombers during the war. These sets were powerful with an output power in the range of 30–80 watts and had a range in the order of several hundred miles.

The R1110 receiver was used for the homing beacon operating at the VHF band.

### The Frequency Plan

There was always a frequency plan, a prior agreement as to which frequencies should be used for which purpose. This was adhered to during a battle. Frequencies could of course be changed but, as anyone with military experience will testify, doing so will cause contact to be lost with about 10 percent of the units. So frequencies were only unwillingly changed.

It would still be nice to be able to change frequency in order to escape jamming and/or eavesdropping. Alternate frequencies could be specified in the frequency plan but, then again, any jammer could follow suit to the new frequency, if only with a delay before the new frequency was found. In practice it was usually best to keep things simple and to just stick with the original frequency plan.

Often it was not possible to change the frequency, as it was pre-set by a technician before the mission. This was typical of pilots; they did not have time to fiddle with a dial anyway. Radio operators had sets that were more flexible; they also took care of the coded traffic.

## Frequency Hopping

Radio communications were critical and easily listened to and jammed. This was a problem recognized by everybody. Using Morse and secret codes offered some protection but only went so far. An obvious solution was to shift to another frequency. The problem here was that this had to be agreed upon, which meant that there typically had to be some traffic to arrange the agreement, which in many cases would violate radio silence.

A solution would be to have a pre-determined pattern of rapid hops between different frequencies. The receiver would follow the same pre-determined pattern and the enemy, not knowing the pattern, would be unable to follow the hops in frequencies and the message would get through. Such a system was indeed developed in 1941 by none other than Hollywood actress Hedy Lamarr in cooperation with composer George Antheil. Their invention worked in a manner similar to piano rolls and the patent was granted in 1942. The first practical system used electronics instead of mechanics and was not deployed until the 1960s. Today this technology is very common and is the basis for secure communications as well as well-known applications like Bluetooth, WiFi, and cell phones. In 2014, both Lamarr and Antheil were posthumously inducted into the National Inventors Hall of Fame.

Frequency hopping is but one of the techniques now used to spread out a radio signal over a wide band of frequencies using some kind of secret code. Another approach is known as 'direct sequence' and is used in, for example, GPS units. Spread-spectrum techniques make the signal secure and resistant to jamming. Spreading the signal out so much that it disappears below the noise floor of that frequency band, the signal can also be made invisible. Without knowledge of the pattern or code used, the enemy is unaware that there is even a communication going on. The availability of communications links that are both secure and resistant to jamming is why drones are now so widely used in combat, why the pilot no longer has to be present in the plane. However, there are radio links that are secure and there are radio links that are broadband, but there are some very hard limits on how secure a broadband radio link can be. Manned aircraft remain a more robust solution against a more capable foe.

# CHAPTER 2

# Flight Operations

## Flight and Hangar Decks

USN carriers had a single hangar deck. They also used deck parks. Unless away on a mission, there were always planes parked on the flight deck, either forward while landing or aft while launching. With the exception of the Dauntless and early Wildcats, all planes had folding wings since parking space was at a premium.

The *Lexington* and *Saratoga* did not have large side openings but *Ranger* and all later carriers did. These openings provided ventilation that made it

USS *Yorktown* stopped and burning at the battle of Midway. The flight deck is a lightly built structure on top of the main hull. The openings in the sides of the hangar deck are clearly visible and with only one hangar deck, these openings are well above the waterline.

possible to warm up engines while in the hangar. As the single hangar deck was well above the waterline, seaworthiness was not affected by the openings. Aircrafts were arranged facing forward, themselves acting as fans blowing air through the hangar. The *Independence* class of light carriers had relatively small side openings but by partially lowering both elevators, the buildup of carbon monoxide was kept to within safe levels. During warm-up, the hangar was closed off from the rest of the ship. The time to warm-up a Hellcat, Avenger, or Corsair was about 15–20 minutes. In practice this does not seem to have mattered much, as a strike was typically arranged on deck, well in advance of launch time, with engines off and then warmed up a suitable time before launch. Warming up a large number of engines in the hangar and then bringing them up on the elevators does not seem to have been common. It was done on occasion, though, for example to speed up the launch of a second deck-load strike. Warming up a small number of planes seems to have been more common, for example to launch a CAP rotation flight without blocking the flight deck for the length of the warm-up time. Refueling and rearming was done both on the flight deck and inside the hangar.

Hellcats, Helldivers, and Avengers having their engines warmed up before launch onboard USS *Intrepid* in 1944.

Most IJN and RN carriers had two hangar decks (the first three *Illustrious* class carriers had only one). Hangars were enclosed because the lower hangar deck was close to the waterline. For the same reason, deck-edge elevators were impractical as they could not reach the lower hangar in a seaworthy manner. For example, with the *Taiho*, with its armored flight deck, the lower hangar deck was almost at the waterline. Most IJN carriers were built like the US carriers, with no armor on the flight deck, while the later RN carriers had armored flight decks.

IJN and RN doctrine was that all planes should be stored below at all times, which meant that fewer planes were carried. Most RN planes had folding wings while most IJN planes did not and Japanese hangars had to be comparatively large. With folding wings, RN elevators could be kept small while those on IJN carriers had to be larger.

As the war progressed, however, having planes parked on the flight deck allowed both navies to operate more aircraft. British carriers were modified during construction or during wartime refits, the round-downs fore and aft were reduced to increase the available deck space. During the war, British carriers were also fitted with up to half a dozen outriggers on the flight deck (where the tails of the planes were outboard of the ship on a pylon). Planes could be parked on these without obstructing flight operations and without having folding wings (for example, Sea Hurricanes or early Seafires).

Engine warm-up could not be done while in the hangar, only while up on flight deck. In 1944 the RN introduced engine oil heaters that enabled most of the warm-up to be done in the hangar and without the engines running. The RN was not alone, the IJN also using engine oil heaters on the I-400 class of aircraft-carrying submarines, borrowing the idea from the Germans who planned to use them on the Graf Zeppelin.

IJN doctrine was to rearm and refuel on the hangar deck, but facilities were available to do it on the flight deck if required. Dive bombers were rearmed up on the flight deck. RN doctrine was to rearm and refuel mainly on the flight deck, the thinking being to avoid having combustible materials below where fires and explosions would cause more damage. This reflects RN emphasis on survivability of the ship at the expense of the tempo of operations. Same usage as the Americans but for a different reason.

All navies had crash barriers available on the flight deck. Deck parks meant that they also had to be used at all times. Using crash barriers meant that a plane that failed to catch an arresting wire would always end up in the barriers, which meant that the accident rate was higher. Hitting the crash barriers could result in anything from a bent propeller to a completely destroyed plane but the pilot was rarely seriously injured. As pilots are fond of saying, any landing you can walk away from is a perfectly acceptable landing.

## Ship and Wind Speed

With the obviously very limited length of the carrier flight deck, taking off required a wind over the deck. The carrier would steam into the wind, adding the wind generated by the carrier travelling at a good speed, to produce a good wind over the deck.

The faster the carrier the better. With a calm sea and a slow carrier, flight operations might be affected. When launching a deck-load strike, the first planes to take off might not have enough length of flight deck available to do a standard rolling take off and might have to use the catapult instead. Alternatively, it might have a reduced fuel or bomb load. Torpedo planes in particular could have problems taking off from a short flight deck in low wind conditions.

Landing was also made easier by a good wind over the deck but was less sensitive to the wind as arresting wires were used anyway.

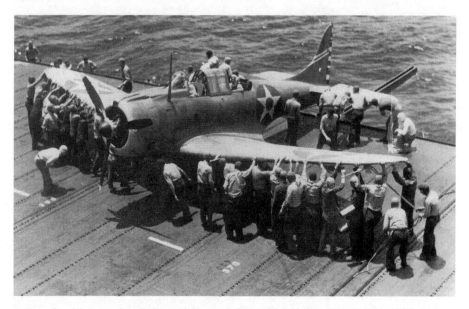

A Dauntless being manhandled onto an outrigger on USS *Enterprise*. The Dauntless did not have folding wings so this was one way of storing them. Outriggers interfered with the angles of fire of the AA guns and were not used on the *Essex* class. Having dive bombers with folding wings was seen as a better solution.

Building up maximum speed of the carrier took some time. Carriers of the day used oil-fired boilers to build up steam pressure to drive the (geared) turbines. Starting from completely cold boilers, it would take hours for a ship to get going. Steaming at normal cruising speed, it could take many minutes to get close to maximum speed—actually reaching that maximum would take still more. This was not usually a problem, as flight operations were planned well in advance.

## Cycle Times

USN landing cycle time was about one plane every 20–50 seconds. The lower number was achieved toward the end of the war with a well-trained crew but could be much longer with less training or in adverse landing conditions. Average cycle time was also heavily affected by landing accidents.

With planes parked forward at all times, crash barriers had to be used when landing. As each plane was disengaged from the arresting wire, the crash

USS *Hancock* in late 1944 appearing to be ready to launch some CAP. Nice view of the deck edge elevator in the down position. The deck edge elevator was a successful design feature and became the norm for all future carriers. For seaworthiness, this design requires the hangar deck to be at least 24–26 feet above the waterline. The deck edge elevator must not be placed too close to the bow.

barriers were lowered and the plane rolled forward to be parked, folding its wings as it did so, and the crash barriers were then raised again.

IJN and RN landing cycle times were generally slower, as each plane had to be struck down before the next was landed. By waiting until the elevator had cycled back up before landing the next plane, each landing took 2 minutes or more. The Japanese used crash barriers, as they did not always strike every plane down immediately, but they retained some flexibility there and could at times use a deck park as a buffer. The RN started the war without crash barriers but gradually added them to all carriers, both to speed up landings and to allow deck parks. With a crash barrier, both IJN and RN could make landings at the same intervals as the USN.

On the *Yorktown* and *Essex* classes the elevator cycle time was 45 seconds (13 up, 10 moving plane on, 12 down, 10 moving plane off) while the elevators on *Lexington* and *Saratoga* were slower. IJN and RN carriers had similar cycle times, only marginally slower when servicing the lower of two hangars. The elevators on the armored carriers of the RN were faster at about 30 seconds but then these carriers only had two of them, wishing to preserve the integrity of the armored flight deck. *Ark Royal*, *Akagi*, and *Kaga* had elevators with two deck levels that only moved one level, requiring two full cycles to move a plane from the lower hangar to the flight deck. The aft elevator of the *Akagi* could actually move two levels, in the fully raised position, and the upper level of the elevator was up in the air above the flight deck. Depending on relative sizes and of the weight-carrying capacity of the elevator, it was sometimes possible to load more than one plane on an elevator.

The time to launch a prepared deck strike was quite short, around 10–20 seconds per plane. It was necessary to allow the turbulence created by the previous plane to die down. At 30 knots of wind speed over the deck it took about 20 seconds for the wind to travel the length of a typical flight deck. Once clear of the carrier, a newly launched plane would often veer away slightly to starboard so that the turbulence would not disturb the next launch. The reason for going to starboard was that with the island on the starboard side, carriers liked to have the wind in slightly from port to keep the turbulence created by the island away from the ship.

On a runway on land, take offs can be sped up by doing formation take offs but there is not room for that on a carrier. Launching was much less prone to accidents than landings and thus on the average faster and more predictable. The most common cause of problems during launch was the engine. If so, that plane was quickly pushed aside and launching resumed.

In a deck strike, the fighters were typically positioned to be launched first as they needed the shortest runway to get airborne. Then came the dive bombers and in the rear the torpedo bombers, which, loaded with heavy torpedoes, needed the longest runway.

Large fleet carriers had the speed and deck space required for planes to get airborne without the need for a catapult. At times the first planes in a deck-load strike did not have enough deck space to take off and in those circumstances a catapult was used. The cycle time of a catapult was 45–60 seconds which slowed down operations compared to unassisted launches. Catapults were useful for launching planes without having the entire task force change course into the wind. As the war progressed, catapult launches became more common even on fleet carriers. By the end of the war, close to half of the launches were made using catapults. Almost all of these launches were of bombers, while fighter pilots tended to prefer unassisted take offs. Smaller and slower carriers had to use catapults for almost all launches. With much fewer planes to handle, the longer launch cycles were not a problem.

In 1943, the surviving prewar carriers *Enterprise* and *Saratoga* had their catapults upgraded to the same type as used on the *Essex* class, in order to meet the requirements of the heavier types that were coming into use, particularly the Avenger. Sideways catapults in the hangar were removed to save weight.

Ford BNO-40 flight-deck tractors used to tow an Avenger and some Hellcats. Without these tractors it would take a dozen or more men to handle each aircraft.

Japanese carriers did not have catapults. This was initially not a serious problem, as all Japanese planes were lightly built and had very good low-speed characteristics. As the war went on and faster and heavier aircraft came into use, such as the Judy and Jill, it then became more difficult to operate all planes in low wind conditions. The faster carriers had less problems but the smaller and slower carriers had real problems in launching torpedo planes in calm conditions. As an alternative solution, rocket-assisted take-off gear was tried. This consisted of two cordite rockets attached to each side of the fuselage. They burned for three seconds and generated 700kg of thrust each. This solution, however, was never used operationally.

## Flight Deck Tractors

Flight-deck crews on US carriers suddenly found they had a problem when the Avenger appeared right after Midway. This behemoth of a carrier plane weighed 8 tons or more fully loaded. Previous planes had weighed at most about 4 tons. The new plane was really too heavy to manhandle, for example when re-spotting the flight deck. The later Helldiver and Hellcat types were almost as heavy, as was the Corsair. The solution was a tractor. Initially, the Willy's Jeep was used together with the Clarktor 6 Tractors already in use on USAAF airfields. In 1943, the Ford BNO-40 tractor came into widespread service. These tractors were used on all types of carrier, including light carriers and the smaller escort carriers, as they all operated Avengers if not Hellcats (escort carriers often used Wildcats).

RN carriers inherited these tractors when they started to use the same planes as the Americans but also used their own Light Flight Deck Tractor, a tiny design adapted from an industrial tow vehicle. Japanese planes were generally lightly built and never reached much beyond 4 tons in weight and tractors were not necessary.

## Launching and Recovering Deck-Load Strikes

IJN doctrine was that carriers operated in pairs, launching coordinated strikes, with each carrier contributing about half its planes to the strike, retaining a possibility for a second strike. A common strike setup consisted of half the fighters of each carrier, the dive bombers from one carrier, and the torpedo bombers from the other carrier.

USN practice in 1942, if not doctrine, was that each carrier launched independent strikes and that each squadron, once launched, proceeded to target directly and independent of other squadrons. Again, not all planes could be launched in one strike; exactly how many were sent off varied but was typically somewhat more than half. There was no strike coordination at all, not even between squadrons from the same carrier. Each squadron attacked separately and the whole squadron attacked the same target. The focus was on carriers being able to launch as big a strike as possible and to do it quickly. With the relatively short range of the planes used, less time aloft was available for coordinating a strike. The slow cruising speed of the Devastator also made strike coordination difficult.

In 1944, strike coordination had developed vastly but was still primarily between squadrons from the same carrier. A carrier would send a strike of fighters, dive bombers, and torpedo bombers. The dive bombers would initiate the attack followed by fighters strafing the target to suppress AA fire, and while strafing was going on, the vulnerable but deadly torpedo bombers would attack. Coordination between strike groups from different carriers was still marginal. If they happened to arrive over a target at the same time, one air group would simply wait until the other air group had finished.

A deck-load strike consisted of about half the planes, typically about 30–40. Usually one strike would sit on the flight deck with a second ready in the hangar. In 1944 the *Essex* class carriers often carried so many planes that they had to divide their air group into three strikes.

As the planes of a formation were launched, they would climb into a holding pattern at some predetermined altitude. Once in the pattern, planes would cut the corners of the pattern to arrive at their assigned position in the formation.

Preparing a strike for launch took a minimum of half an hour but more realistically up to an hour. Once aloft, the strike would return in something like 4–5 hours. Time to rearm and refuel a strike depended on many factors, such as whether a bomb or torpedo was to be fitted or how much preparation had been made (which in turn depended on planning).

RN doctrine was less oriented toward large strikes, acting more as a part of the surface fleet in the way it scouted, defended, and attacked. Hence, the emphasis on continuous operations, on keeping the flight deck free, and not worrying too much about the tempo of deck operations.

## Landing on a Carrier

### Landing Patterns

The landing pattern has three functions. It acts as a queue for arriving squadrons, it splits up squadron formations into individual planes, and it sets up each plane for the final approach to land.

Arriving squadrons first enter a holding pattern away from the carrier. The size, shape, location, and altitude of this pattern can vary. This holding pattern can hold more than one squadron flying in squadron formation. On command, one squadron then proceeds to an oval over the carrier at an altitude of about 500–1,000 feet. While in this oval, the squadron splits up into divisions of 3–6 planes each. The desired separation is achieved by extending or cutting the corners of the oval. On further command, one of these divisions descend into a lower oval, at an altitude of 100–300 feet, where it splits up into individual planes. In the ovals, planes fly the upwind leg close by to starboard of the carrier. While passing close to the carrier, people on the carrier can check that the arresting hook has been properly extended. The downwind leg is flown about 800–1200 yards to port of the carrier. The length of the oval is such that it can hold 3–6 planes at 20-second intervals. Final approach is a downwind leg, with the pilot lowering the landing gear and flaps, followed by a descending 180° turn to the left to come up aft of the carrier and on a suitable glide slope.

Holding patterns are typically left-handed patterns with left turns. This has to do with the final approach being a left turn. This is different from holding patterns used at civilian airports which are typically right-handed. Civilian airports also use simple vertical stacking of planes: the lowest plane lands and everybody else then drops one level, as there is no need to handle formations of planes.

These landing patterns have implications for carrier formations. It is generally easier and safer if the ovals of different carriers do not interfere with each other. This leads to a minimum separation between the carriers determined by the size of ovals. This is the reason why the *Kaga* and *Akagi*, as well as *Hiryu* and *Soryu*, operated as pairs with the island at opposite sides of the ships. Now the ovals can be at opposite sides of the ships enabling them to steam closer together without the traffic patterns conflicting with each other. Interesting patterns but ultimately dropped in favor of simpler and more robust solutions. Pilots objected to having to handle both left-handed and right-handed patterns. Left-handed landings are easier for most pilots as left turns are more natural for right-handed persons using a center stick (using a civilian type yoke it matters less). With a left turn used for the final approach, the island should then be on the starboard side as the turbulence it creates will now interfere less with the final approach.

## Landing a "Taildragger"

Almost all planes of World War II, including all carrier-based planes, were "tail-draggers." They had the main landing gear forward and then a small wheel to the rear of the plane. The reason for having tailwheels was that this was a more robust configuration on the uneven grass fields of the day. Another reason was that, before retracting landing gears, a small tailwheel offered less wind resistance than a necessarily large nose wheel (with the main landing gear being roughly the same in both cases).

Taildraggers have their center of gravity aft of the main landing gear, making the plane fundamentally unstable on landing. A small deviation in the path forward will tend to be exacerbated as the mass of the plane will pull the plane around, either left or right, in what is known as a "ground loop." On a carrier deck, there is little room for ground loops. For the same reason, a taildragger tends to bounce on deck. As the main landing gear hits the deck, the center of gravity tends to lower the tail, increasing the angle of attack and hence lift, causing the plane to go airborne again. Having the tail wheel hit the deck before the main landing gear reverses the effect and is dangerous as done too much it will cause the main landing gear to slam down hard on deck.

On a carrier, the normal landing is the "three-point landing." A slight improvement is with the tail wheel hitting the deck slightly before the main landing gear. This is the landing with the shortest roll. The drawback of this style of landing is that it is vulnerable to a cross wind. On the other hand, one of the few advantages that carrier pilots had was that they normally did not have to deal with a cross wind, the carrier steaming straight into the wind for most flight operations.

A plane with a nose wheel instead of a tailwheel is said to have "tricycle" landing gear. Tricycles are easier to land as the center of gravity is forward of the main landing gear; the plane is fundamentally stable as a small deviation from the path forward will tend to correct itself. Once hard surface runways became standard, so did tricycle landing gear. Beyond being more stable, tricycles also have much better forward visibility while taxiing. The first carrier-based aircraft to use tricycle landing gear was the postwar F7F Tigercat. Almost all modern planes are tricycles. Modern pilots respect those that fly and land taildraggers, as it takes skill to handle a taildragger. The prevalence of taildraggers was one more reason for the high accident rate of World War II pilots, particularly in training.

The pilot has to judge the turn in to the final approach, as well as the descent, to end up on the correct glide slope. Having done that, he will then adjust ("ride") the throttle to reach stall as the tail hook engages one of the arresting wires.

There were several arresting wires the plane could catch but pilots usually took pride in catching the wire they had aimed for, usually the second. A good landing catches the wire in the middle as it stretches across the deck, that is close to the centerline of the flight deck. Catching the wire to the left or right of the middle results in an effective landing but the plane will be whipped around a bit as the wire stretches out before the plane has come to a complete stop.

A plane that landed without catching a wire could attempt to brake to a stop but that could be tricky without doing a ground loop or standing the plane on its nose, possibly flipping over and/or ending up over the side. Neither catching a wire nor braking, the plane would end up in the barriers set up to protect planes parked forward. The plane would be damaged—at a minimum the propeller would have to be replaced and the engine checked—but the pilot would most often be able to walk away.

A good strong wind over the flight deck makes everything easier, as the plane's speed relative to the carrier is reduced. The carrier was usually steered so that the wind over the flight deck came in slightly from port. This had the effect of reducing the effects of turbulence caused by the island and from the prop wash of the plane that had just landed. With the wind too much from the side, however, a ground loop or worse became more likely.

## LSO and Batsman

To assist the pilot in landing, the USN developed the use of an experienced pilot standing on the deck of the carrier, waving paddles to tell the pilot how he was doing and what corrections he needed to make. In the USN he was called the LSO (Landing Signals Officer); in the RN he was called the "batsman." There were usually two on board each carrier so that they could take turns.

Different LSOs had different styles in how they used their bodies and paddles to convey their instructions—some were more intense and some were more discreet. The pilot had to know the language of the LSO, and trust was obviously essential for teamwork.

More experienced pilots did not need much assistance and would tend to ignore the LSO. Each pilot developed his own habits in how tight he did the final turn and how to set up the approach. The LSO's order to the pilot, of either to cut his engine and land or to wave him off, telling him to go around, must at all times be obeyed, however. The pilot could ignore a wave-off but he had better have an extremely good reason for it.

If waved off by the LSO, power had to be applied but this had to be done with care. Applying power too quickly, the torque of the engine will make the plane roll. This known as "torque roll." Flying at low speeds, such as while landing, the airflow over the control surfaces might not be enough to counteract this roll, making it uncontrollable. The plane could easily end up over the side and upside down in the water. The direction of the roll depended on which way the propeller rotated and it was better if the roll was away from the island rather than into it. Most propellers rotated clockwise, as seen by the pilot, which indeed resulted in a torque roll to the left and away from an island on the starboard side. Applying power gently, when desperately trying to avoid a crash, is easier said than done. Things can go very wrong very quickly.

Postwar, after the mirror landing aid had been introduced, the LSO remained but he was now more of a supervisor. He was still needed for the occasional wave-off when the deck was fouled.

Japanese carriers did not use a man with paddles. They used a system of red and green lamps to indicate the glide slope, arranged much like iron sights on a rifle. The pilot could see if he was above or below as well as to the left or right of the intended glide slope. The lamps had mirrors that directed the light in the direction of the landing planes, and the angle of the glide slope could be adjusted for different types of aircraft. This was a simple and robust system but the pilot also got less in the way of support. A nervous pilot with poor technique would certainly welcome the assistance of a good LSO/batsman. There was still a need to tell pilots when to land or not, for example if the flight deck was fouled or if the hook or landing gear was not down. This was done by a signalman aft on the port side waving a flag, under the command of a man on the bridge.

## Complications

No two landings were the same. From the viewpoint of the pilot, every landing was a new challenge. A runway on land is stationary and the scenery around it is relatively constant. At sea, conditions are constantly changing. The wind and waves have their own rhythms and patterns, the surface of the ocean reflecting changes in light as the day slowly passes.

This adds interest but also complications. The first is ship motion. Steaming into the waves, the ship will usually have a pitching motion. This means that the flight deck will continuously move up and down and judging the correct glide slope becomes that much more difficult. Aiming for an arresting wire further up the deck was one way to avoid some of the pitching problems. Rolling motion was easier to deal with but only up to a point: as the rolling motion increased the pilot also had to deal with significant sideways motion. As always, the only solution was training and more training.

The second major complication was landing at night. In this situation the sense of depth and distance is weakened. The human brain also has a tendency alter how the surroundings are perceived. The natural solution was to have special landing lights on the deck and on the paddles of the LSO. This certainly helped the pilot but it was still a difficult and dangerous operation. A landing plane would display landing lights but it was still difficult for the LSO to gauge its speed —he had to estimate it by the sound of the engine (on the assumption that speed and engine sound were correlated, which might or might not be true). Again, the only solution was training and then more training to make everybody accustomed to night operations.

Finally, returning from combat, the plane is often damaged in some way and/or the pilot may have been injured, adding to the difficulties. As an example, returning from the late-night attack on the Japanese carriers at Philippine Sea, a Helldiver pilot was both wounded himself and had one wing badly hit. The plane was now unbalanced. To keep going in a straight line, he had to compensate with his controls. With all the drag that this created, the engine had to be at full power to keep the plane flying. Not seeing anything, only hearing the engine screaming at full power, the LSO assumed he was going too fast and waved him off just as the wounded Helldiver came crashing down onto the flight deck.

Life as a carrier pilot was challenging and the consequences of an error were often harsh and unforgiving. Pilots tended not to discuss much beyond the immediate future. There was little point—life was too uncertain. Tomorrow might never come. This often turned out to be true. To the carrier itself this was not a major issue: plenty of spare planes and pilots were carried.

## Maintaining Patrols

In the 1942 battles, both USN and IJN used all available decks in a task force in the same manner, that is for both strikes and CAP. Launching and recovering CAP usually required that a flight deck was relatively empty. Preparing, launching, and recovering a strike meant a suspension of CAP operations for something like half an hour or more.

With deck-load strikes, it was a big advantage to have more than one deck available. This way a deck-load strike could be ready to go from one deck while the other handled CAP. Once the strike was launched, that deck could take over CAP servicing while the other carrier readied a follow-up strike. To have one carrier designated solely for defensive CAP was proposed and extensively debated within the USN after the Eastern Solomons battle. One advantage would be that this carrier would control all CAP at all times, with no shifting of responsibilities such as fighter direction. In this scenario, other carriers would handle only strike aircraft, including the fighters needed as escorts for the strike.

In 1944 USN doctrine had evolved into the idea of groups of three or four carriers operating together. The smaller *Independence* class carriers were used as "duty carriers" tasked with providing continuous CAP and ASW patrols while the larger *Essex* class carriers were freed up to concentrate on deck-load strikes.

In principle, CAP could still be serviced with a strike up on the flight deck. The strike would be spotted forward while landing CAP, then re-spotted aft to enable the CAP to take off, while the CAP planes moved through the hangar (possible even if a second strike was in the hangar, with a bit of preparation) or somehow allowed to pass between the planes parked on the flight deck.

The endurance of a CAP fighter depends not only on fuel carried but also on ammunition. The lightly built Zero carried very limited amounts of 20mm ammunition. In actual combat, it needed to land and rearm quite frequently. The early Wildcat had similar limitations in ammunition carried. In both cases, pilot training and marksmanship also had an important role.

## Launching Strikes vs. Maintaining Patrols

Launching strikes and maintaining patrols are two very different types of flight operation which has some subtle and not so subtle effects on the relative numbers during a battle.

When a carrier attacks, about half the fighters will be sent with the strike and half will be retained for defensive CAP. With limited space on the flight deck from which to range a strike, it is usually sent as two waves, about an hour apart, arriving separately over the target.

If a carrier elects to be in a purely defensive mode, it can have all its fighters in the air and on CAP. Eventually some will have to land and refuel but most of the time will be spent on station. The bombers are assumed to be out of the way, either inside the hangar or sent off to orbit away from the carrier.

This means that when a wave arrives over the target, defending fighters will outnumber attacking fighters about 4:1, while still assuming equal numbers on both sides. Indeed, defending fighters might well outnumber the total number of attacking planes in each individual wave, with possibly disastrous results for the attacker.

With the limited size of flight decks, it is much harder to mass a strike together than it is to keep a large number of fighters on CAP. An aircraft carrier is better at maintaining patrols than at launching strikes. In that sense, a carrier is better at defending than attacking.

The attacker does not know if he will be counterattacked. If he is not, then he has wasted half his fighters. The defender has the advantage that he knows he is going to be attacked. If he is not attacked, then nothing has happened and his defense has been successful. This is another fundamental problem for the attacker. The attacker can gamble on no counterattack taking place and including all his fighters in the strike but that also exacerbates the flight deck space problem and he might have to split his attack into three separate waves.

The high value placed by US carrier designers on being able to warm up engines in the hangar then becomes understandable if it might enable all planes to be launched as one large strike. This advantage was not realized in 1942, as the planes used did not have the range to loiter until everybody had been launched. In 1944 they might have had that range but by then the US carriers were mainly operating in a defensive mode.

In 1942, it was very dangerous to go purely defensive despite the advantages. Fighter direction was unreliable and a group of bombers might well get through. This is what happened at Midway. With repeated American attacks the Japanese found themselves on the defensive. The strikes arrived piecemeal, however, and each wave was successfully dealt with by the available CAP. That is until the dive bombers arrived, surprising and overwhelming the defenses.

In 1944, with radar and efficient fighter direction, going purely defensive was a much safer and ultimately effective alternative. This is what happened at Philippine Sea. The Japanese strikes arrived as several waves, with each one not only intercepted well before reaching their targets but with a strength much smaller than the number of fighters available on CAP. Very few attackers got through.

## Night Operations

There are nights and there are nights. Not all nights are dark and stormy. Some nights are quite pleasant with a nice bright moon up. In many cases it is possible to conduct operations using the available light.

Nautical twilight is a term used to describe the light that is available when the sun is under the horizon but still provides light. As the sun drops further and further below the horizon, this remaining light gradually disappears. The general rule is that there is some light available until the sun is 12° below the horizon. This definition is quite arbitrary but it gives a rough measure of how long the sun provides some usable light.

How long nautical twilight lasts varies with latitude. Most of the carrier battles in the Pacific were fought quite close to the equator, so nautical twilight lasted somewhat less than an hour before/after sunrise/sundown. At the latitude of the northern polar circle, about 66°N, the sun never goes below the horizon in summer. Up at latitude 56°N, about the middle of the North Sea, in the summer there will be at least some nautical twilight throughout the whole night.

The often heard saying that "it is darkest just before the dawn" is just silly. It might be *coldest* just before dawn but the darkest time is when the sun is as much below the horizon as it is going to get, that is in the middle of the night.

Light at night can be highly asymmetrical. Looking down-moon all you see is blackness but looking toward the moon everything is brightly silhouetted against it. If no moon is available, similar conditions can be created with flares.

Flying at night is a lot about training, about habituation, and about getting used to make do with whatever light and cues were available, in combination with learning to rely on the instruments. The more experienced the pilot the better he will be at flying safely and efficiently in conditions with marginal or very little light. With enough practice it is possible to fly with very little light, when your mind understands that there is vision beyond sight.

Before the war, all USN pilots trained for night landings. Practice was mandatory but usually conducted in less than complete darkness—for example, with a setting sun or in moonlight—meaning that this was more like a low-light operation than a true night operation. Starting in 1944, some USN carriers operated a small number of dedicated night fighters using highly trained pilots.

Taking off is relatively straightforward. The position on the deck is known and all you have to do is a normal take off. If needed, there will be some lights along the deck to act as guides. Pre-dawn take offs were standard for search missions. Once airborne and in complete darkness, everything depended on flying by instruments. Flying in formation is possible, mainly using the red-hot exhausts as references. The challenge was to assume the formation and to distinguish the identities of the other planes in the formation. Flight paths were carefully planned and, together with timed take offs, forming up was reasonably reliable.

Landing at night was the really difficult part. Finding the carrier was the first problem, but this was assumed to have been done by DR navigation or by homing aids. Once found there would be some kind of lights along the deck. The Landing Signals Officer (LSO) would also be there to guide the pilot in his landing, as in normal daylight landings. The LSO would now be wearing some kind of lighting so he could be seen, and his paddles would also have some kind of light on them. The plane would also have the position lights turned on so that the LSO could see where it was, and the sound of the engine would help the LSO gauge the speed of the plane. Landing at night was easier in a slow plane as everything happened slower. This was a factor in the successful use of Swordfish biplanes in the night attack against the Italian battleships at Taranto. Finally, as can be imagined, night landings on a carrier required extensive training to be reasonably safe. Before the Taranto attack, the pilots involved trained intensively for two months.

At night, planes are relatively safe from both AA and CAP. This makes night attacks especially suitable for torpedo bombers, as they now have a chance to get close to the target. Flying low, they both avoid radar and can see the target silhouetted against the sky, perhaps augmented by flares. Dive bombers did not have the same advantages; they were themselves silhouetted against the sky and had trouble picking out a target against the dark surface of the sea.

The raid on Taranto is a classic example of torpedo bombers attacking at night, but this was against ships in a harbor. The Japanese used specially trained Betty land-based bombers to do night-time torpedo attacks against ships at sea. These were the same squadrons that had sunk the *Repulse* and *Prince of Wales*. Their first major night-time success was in January 1943 at the battle of Rennell Island when the cruiser *Chicago* was sunk. In February 1944, the carrier *Intrepid* was hit by a torpedo in another such attack. Radar was useful for locating the target but for actual targeting, it was limited by its minimum range (given by pulse length and receiver recovery time). The target had to be acquired visually before a bomb or a torpedo could be dropped with any degree of accuracy. Against U-boats the answer was the Leigh light. Against ships, flares were deployed on one side of the formation and the attackers then came in from the other side. Ships were then silhouetted, not against the flares themselves but against their reflections on the sea surface. It was generally very difficult to detect aircraft attacking in this way, and were very difficult to spot, depending on clouds and other conditions.

During the Indian Ocean incursion by Nagumo in April 1942, RN Admiral Somerville planned a night attack on the Japanese carriers, using Albacore torpedo bombers equipped with ASV radar. Searching Albacores found Nagumo late in the afternoon of the 5th but were shot down before an accurate sighting report could be made. Further searches during the night did not manage to make contact again and nothing came of it.

An interesting possibility is if the Marine Corps bombers stationed at Henderson Field had been trained in attacking ships at night. In principle this would have given the Americans control of the waters around Guadalcanal at night as well as during the day. The Americans did use Catalina flying boats for night attacks on Japanese shipping, including using torpedoes, becoming known as the "Black Cats." The slow and cumbersome Catalinas were unsuited for daylight attacks but as with the Swordfish, their slow speed made them well suited for night operations. These Catalinas had radar altimeters and could fly safely at very low altitude. If jumped by a Japanese night fighter, they would descend to just above the sea. Lacking a radar altimeter, the fighter could not fly as low and would lose the Catalina against the dark sea, unable to silhouette it against the sky.

Against an enemy aircraft, a night intercept would start with the fighter directors vectoring a fighter to within radar range of the target aircraft. Radar was then used to approach the target until it could be seen, usually by the spotting engine exhausts that glowed dark red. The target was then identified as an enemy aircraft, usually by going slightly below the target to silhouette it against the sky or by the arrangement of the exhausts. Once the target was identified as the enemy, the attacker then maneuvered into position and opened fire. If the target had a tail gunner who had spotted the attacker, this was very dangerous for the attacker.

Later radar sets, usually some high-resolution centimetric device, could provide a two-dimensional map-like image of the surroundings. This made it useful not only for targeting but also for navigation around land masses and for finding and targeting shipping. The AN/APS-6 mentioned earlier is an example of such a device. Range was a few thousand yards against other aircraft but could be several tens of miles against large ships and land masses.

## Effects of Weather

The optimum wind speed over the flight deck was in the range of 30–50 knots for monoplanes; biplanes preferred a lower range. A good wind over the deck is usually needed for flight operations, particularly for launching torpedo bombers. At 50 knots the wind has the strength of a storm, standing up is difficult and aircraft can be tossed around. In calm weather, the speed of the carrier provided the wind. In windier conditions, the carrier slowed down to keep the wind over the flight deck to within a suitable range. There is a limit to how much a carrier can slow down and still have positive steering. At over-the-water wind speeds of 30–35 knots and above, flight operations start to become unsafe and will at least have to proceed slower and with more care.

The wind is not necessarily stable or predictable. It can be quite gusty and these gusts often come from a somewhat different direction than the base wind. Gusts could and did cause problems while in the critical stage of a landing or a take off.

Flight operations require steaming into the wind. They are difficult enough, as they are without a significant cross wind over the deck for the pilots to deal with. Steaming into the wind, the carrier will normally also steam into the dominant waves. It is not unusual, however, for waves to come from more than one direction. The dominant waves can also come from a different direction than the current wind. Waves generated by nearby weather systems can travel long distances and might also be of considerable size, affecting even the biggest carrier.

This means that the carrier will often have both a pitching and rolling motion; the ship can be doing what is known as corkscrewing. This naturally causes problems for flight operations and can make them quite dangerous. One cure was to move the intended point of touchdown forward where pitching motion was less. Another remedy was to try to time landings or take offs such that the deck was more or less where it ought to be. This often meant waiting for the right moment or going around and trying again, which of course had the effect of slowing down operations.

Visibility is also major consideration, both in terms of flight operations and in terms of the risk of the carrier colliding with the escorts. As has been pointed out before, carriers are big ships that take time to change course, and that latency can be very dangerous. Later in the war, radar was a big help in station keeping but the basic problem was very much still there. The carrier often had to turn into the wind for flight operations and the escorts had to be attentive and ready for it, which might not be as easy as it sounds given the latency involved in moving the rudder.

Weather can be quite local. The carrier might experience rain and wind while it is sunny not far away. Radio silence could prevent this from being communicated to the carrier.

As a result of these complications, carrier operations are quite dependent on weather. This is often masked by the fact that most, if not all, carrier battles were conducted in areas with relatively benign weather. It should also be kept in mind when declaring the battleship to have been made obsolete by the carrier. In fine weather, yes, but perhaps not always and everywhere.

Wind also affected task force movements. With the carrier forced to steam into the wind at regular intervals, the task force moved with it. This meant that a task force had trouble moving downwind when doing flight operations. Moving upwind was easy, as no course change was needed for flight operations but downwind could be effectively impossible. Any significant move downwind would have to be done at night.

In really bad weather, even if flight operations had ceased, the planes must still be parked somewhere. If using deck parks, the carrier would have to weather the storm with planes on deck. This was done by having them huddled together in the lee of the island, protecting each other from the wind and away from the salt spray coming over the bow, securely tied down and with canopies covered. The planes would obviously have been much more protected in the hangar but there was simply not enough space for everything down there. Exactly how many planes can be stored in the hangar depends to a degree on the effort made but the more planes that are hanging from the overhead girders and/or are in various stages of disassembly, the more cramped the hangar is going to be and the more time it will take to get both the hangar and the planes back in operation.

RN carriers had to deal with the conditions of the North Atlantic. This is one of the reasons for having enclosed hangars and for the philosophy of keeping all planes in the hangar. It was also the reason for the "hurricane bow" typical of RN carriers. During a typhoon in August 1945, the carriers *Wasp* and *Randolph* both suffered significant damage. When Admiral Halsey contacted the *Indefatigable* to inquire about any typhoon damage, the bridge cheekily replied "What typhoon?"

## The Ubiquitous Plane Guard Destroyer

During flight operations, all navies had a destroyer or two stationed aft of the carrier. Its task was to pick airmen that had ditched while trying to land or take off. Given the accident rate of the time, a destroyer was devoted to do just that. Floatplanes could have been used but it was simply easier and faster to use a destroyer. When flight operations were no longer in progress, the destroyer could return to its normal position in the screen.

The memoirs of carrier pilots tend to read like a long list of accidents, often ending up in the sea and sometimes fatal. With enough practice, the plane guard destroyer could pick up a downed airman without coming to a complete stop. They got the practice.

## Speed and Endurance of Escorts

Flight operations usually means that the carrier changes course into the wind and starts building up speed. The task force as a whole is probably not traveling in the same direction that the carrier needs to go for flight operations, which raises the question of how this situation is handled.

Usually, the escorts turn with the carrier and follow into the wind. Flight operations may take some time. If the escorts did not follow the carrier, the carrier might be well over the horizon before flight operations had been completed. This is obviously not good. Escorts are supposed to do what escorts do—escort the carrier.

On the other hand, this means that the escorts are forced to do a lot of high-speed steaming back and forth that does not really take them anywhere. Particularly for destroyers, this is a problem as their endurance is quite limited. Keeping the destroyers refueled was a constant headache for any task force commander. Any battleship in the formation might also be too slow to keep up with the carrier and would have to struggle to regain its place in the formation after the high-speed run. For these reasons, the whole task force might not follow the carrier into the wind; part of it might keep going in the overall direction that the task force is supposed to be going. As can be understood, there is a tension here between the security of the formation and practical considerations like the speed and endurance of the escorts. That tradeoff was ultimately up to the commander of the task force.

## Operation of Flying Boats and Floatplanes

Flying boats can land on water. In principle, they can use the open ocean as the flight deck, relying on a tender or even a submarine for refueling. In practice, they have problems with the long swells typical of deep water. They were limited to taking off with only moderate loads when operating in medium swells and not taking off at all in heavy swells. Swells are notoriously difficult to predict, so the USN eventually gave up on using the open ocean as a base. A flying boat can handle a bit of a choppy sea though, so as long as there was some kind of sheltered water available, they could operate in most weather conditions. The sheltered water was provided by a port, an island, or the lagoon of an atoll.

Ship-borne floatplanes were also affected by swells. USN doctrine limited floatplane operations to a smooth sea and a maximum wind of 22 knots with some latitude given to allow for local conditions. Planes were launched by a hydraulic catapult. The launch was a rather violent event but reasonably independent of the state of the wind and the sea. Landing was the difficult part, with the plane bouncing on the waves and crashing being the major danger. Floatplanes were less stable than flying boats, as it was easy to trip on the floats. Landing on the hull itself was more forgiving. The Supermarine Walrus biplane used by the RN may have looked outmoded but was actually an eminently practical plane that remained in service throughout the war. With its very low landing speed it could land on a carrier, despite not having an arrestor hook, making it very useful indeed.

Before the floatplane landed, the parent ship slowed down and did a maneuver that created a relatively sheltered area to the lee of the ship. The plane landed in that area and then taxied up to the ship. The observer/rear gunner excited the cockpit, grabbed the hook of the crane and connected it to the plane which could then be hoisted aboard. Successfully hooking up the plane could be quite problematic with the plane bobbing about and the hook swinging from the end of the crane. Most nations used some type of a mat towed by the parent ship that the floatplane taxied on. It was then much more stable and secure, making it easier for the crew to hook up to the crane.

# CHAPTER 3

# Aircraft Carried

## USN

The main fighter at the beginning of the war was the Wildcat. It was rugged, it could take a lot of punishment and still return to the carrier. It was well suited for attritional warfare, but was also relatively heavy and underpowered and could not turn with the Zero. Pilots therefore had to rely on tactics like boom-and-zoom and the Thach Weave. If the pilot succeeded in employing these tactics, then the Wildcat was hard to kill.

The Devastator was quite modern for its time but by 1942 it was underpowered. Its slow speed was quite a hindrance as it could not keep pace with the dive bombers or fighters in a strike. Operating without coordination with the dive bombers and unescorted by fighters, it suffered badly against any enemy fighters encountered.

The Avenger made quite an impression when it first appeared on the carriers. It was huge, looking like a three-room apartment dressed up as a pregnant turkey and was of course promptly dubbed as such. To reduce drag, the torpedo was carried inside the plane, hence the bulky appearance. With the torpedo inside, it was good at dummy torpedo runs, something that was put to good use in the action off Samar. The Avenger had big wings, the largest span of all carrier-based aircraft at the time, but at least they folded compactly. The plane soon proved itself. The powerful radial engine pulled it along at a good pace, it was strongly built, and it could carry a lot of ordnance or other gear. There was excellent room in the cockpit which made it suitable for all kinds of electronics like communication radios and various radars of more or less bulky types.

The Dauntless was popular with pilots. It was reasonably fast and quite maneuverable with good flight characteristics. At a pinch it could double as an interceptor against slower enemy torpedo bombers. The wings did not fold, which meant that it took up more room than really desirable, particularly important since US carriers often carried a large number of these planes. With good speed and range it was extensively used for scouting.

The later Helldiver was much more powerful, could carry a bigger bomb further, and had folding wings. It had a troubled development and a poor reputation, however, being known as "The Beast." One reason was simply poor quality control by Curtiss. Another problem was the way Curtiss had interpreted the requirement that two planes should be able to fit on an elevator. This had them design a plane that was really too short for its size and this then caused problems with handling, only partly solved by the huge vertical stabilizer. The Avenger had the same requirement but Grumman handled it better. Once the problems were sorted out the Helldiver proved it could do the job and do it well. It was also used for scouting.

The Hellcat had a much more powerful engine than the Wildcat. It started development as an update to the Wildcat but ended up being a completely new plane. Faster than the Zero, it climbed just as well but could still not turn with the Zero at low speeds. A rugged build made it a forgiving plane to fight with and well suited to attritional warfare. It had excellent range, its wings folded compactly, and it became the mainstay of the fast carriers in 1944–45. It never had a bubble canopy, however, like the P-47 or P-51 had during the war. The manufacturer did not tinker with the design, and only two versions ever existed. It was designed in a short time, then built in large numbers with excellent quality control. Just what was needed at the time.

The Corsair was the prima donna of carrier fighters. It was very advanced aerodynamically but also temperamental. The design took a long time to sort out. It was originally intended as the replacement for the Wildcat but with the delays in development, combined with the difficulties of operating it from a carrier, the Hellcat got the opportunity to take over that role.

The Bearcat is everybody's favorite fighter. It had the same engine as the Hellcat but optimized differently, with barely enough aluminum for the pilot to hang on to, sacrificing range and armament. It was built to be as small and light as possible and had a fantastic climb rate. It was still not as agile as the Zero at low speeds due to its higher wing loading. It had a bubble canopy for excellent visibility and probably the best piston engine fighter of World War II despite being carrier-based with folding wings and a heavy-duty undercarriage. The Bearcat arrived just too late to see any combat against the Japanese.

The US Navy was interested in the P-51 Mustang. The newly invented laminar-flow type of wing provided very long range, very useful for a carrier fighter. A naval prototype was built and tested. It was found that the plane had a rather high stall speed as well as a rather sudden and vicious stall, very dangerous while landing. Coupled with generally marginal control at low speeds, this necessitated a relatively high landing speed that was close to what the arrestor gear could handle. The laminar-flow wing certainly had low drag but paid for it with poor low speed characteristics. The P-51 was never adopted for carrier use.

The number of planes operated increased as the war went on. At Coral Sea the F4F-3 Wildcat did not have folding wings and one squadron of about 18 planes was carried on each carrier. At Midway, the F4F-4 with folding wings had been introduced and each carrier had about 27 on board, as at Eastern Solomons, while at Santa Cruz about 36 F4F-4 were carried. During the 1944 battles about 40–45 Hellcat fighters were carried, and in 1945 this had risen further to about 72 fighters (Hellcat and/or Corsair) in response to the threat of the kamikazes.

In all battles of 1942 and 1944, about 36 dive bombers and 14 torpedo bombers were carried. The Dauntless never had folding wings but was a relatively small design. Both the Avenger and the Helldiver had folding wings. It was the folding wings of the Helldiver that allowed more fighters to be carried in 1944 without removing any bombers. In 1945 about 15 Helldivers and 15 Avengers were carried. These low numbers were offset by the fact that fighters, both the Hellcat and Corsair, were now used extensively in a ground-support role. By this time the IJN was largely gone and there was little need for a dedicated anti-ship capability. The smaller *Independence* class carriers carried mostly fighters, about 21–26 Hellcats plus 8–9 Avengers, as they were used mainly for CAP and ASW duties.

On an *Essex* class carrier, using deck parks, the flight deck had room for about 22 rows of five planes each. On the hangar deck, there was room for about 13 rows of four planes each. In total, there was room for about 174 planes. This is with everybody jammed in with wings folded and with no room to move, much less operate. A more realistic capacity would be 60 on the flight deck and 40–50 in the hangar. In the raids on the Japanese home islands in July 1945, the *Bennington* carried 37 Corsairs, 37 Hellcats, 15 Helldivers, and 15 Avengers for a total of 105 planes which was close to the maximum an *Essex* carried during the war. By this time there was less need for deck-load strikes and it was mostly a question of keeping a large number of fighters on station doing ground support and/or CAP.

The numbers given in most sources for the aircraft-carrying capacities of US carriers typically include planes carried as spares. The number of aircraft actually operated at any one time was usually lower. Spares were carried hanging from the roof of the hangar in a disassembled state. With only a single hangar, the floor space was limited and the height of the hangar was used instead.

## IJN

The Zero was very lightly built with a generous wing area and it soon became famous for its agility. It could not take much punishment, however, lacking self-sealing fuel tanks and armor for the pilot. It was the ideal tool for a very well-trained pilot who could use it effectively and who did not get into trouble. As the war went on and as pilot quality deteriorated, its fragility made it an unforgiving plane to fly and losses mounted. Limited ammunition was a problem, particularly facing the more rugged US aircraft. Speed was reasonably good, climbing very good, and range excellent. Initially the wings did not fold but small folding wing tips were introduced on later versions, mainly to improve clearance on the elevators.

The Val dive bomber was also relatively lightly built. With a generous wing area, it had excellent maneuverability, no folding wings, no self-sealing fuel tanks, and no pilot armor. Its major weakness was that it was a bit slow, the fixed undercarriage not helping. It was due to be replaced in late 1942 by the faster Judy but this type had problems in development so the Val had to soldier on well into 1944. The Judy was a big improvement in speed but still did not have folding wings.

The Kate was relatively fast for a torpedo bomber and thus well suited for the coordinated strikes the Japanese did so well. It had a combination of speed and range and was extensively used for search missions. Like all Japanese planes it was lightly built, but as with all torpedo bombers, losses were heavy. The lack of self-sealing fuel tanks and pilot armor did not help. An improved Kate, the Jill, appeared late in the war but was only a marginal improvement on the same design. Both had folding wings.

Japanese aircraft were optimized for aggressive warfare and a short war, and focused on the performance and range of their aircraft. They did not want to pay the penalty associated with folding wings unless they absolutely had to. Most IJN carriers had two hangar decks, allowing for more room. The IJN can be criticized for poor pilot protection and an inadequate pilot training and replacement program, but it should be recognized that that would only be relevant in a war they could not win anyway.

At Coral Sea and at Midway, about 18 Zeros, 18 Vals and 18 Kates were carried on each carrier. At Eastern Solomons this had been raised to 27 fighters with 27 Vals and 18 Kates on each fleet carrier. At Santa Cruz it was

Zero fighters ready for launch onboard IJN carrier *Zuikaku* the day before the Coral Sea battle. Note the awnings to protect from the hot equatorial sun, and the deck crew resting underneath the wings. The planes are most likely ready for launch on relatively short notice, once the awnings have been removed and the engines warmed up.

back to 20 fighters with about 22 Vals and 22 Kates on each fleet carrier. At Philippine Sea in 1944 it had again risen to 26–27 fighters with about 23 Judys and 17 Jills/Kates on each of the three fleet carriers. After the Philippine Sea battle, the IJN carrier force had effectively ceased to exist. There was never again a question of operating air groups in any real sense. Spares were carried disassembled and stowed in the corners of the hangars in the space left over, as the non-folding wings meant that the hangars were not very tightly packed.

## RN

British carriers operated much more in the traditional role of scouting and raiding and usually did so in cooperation with battleships. The European theater was much more crowded and complex, with poor visibility and land often not far away. These conditions differed from the vast distances of the Pacific where a task force of several carriers, loaded with deck load strikes, could successfully dominate and defeat land-based opposition.

The Fleet Air Arm operated many different planes, most of which were not very competitive for various reasons. On the other hand, in many ways they did not have to be. The British did not attempt to dominate land-based fighters, as it simply was not very realistic given the geostrategic realities. The Fulmar and the Swordfish are good examples. The Fulmar was a two-seat fighter and as such was reasonably well designed but could never compete with modern land-based single-seat fighters in a dogfight. Having a back-seater was useful for fighter direction, and having good forward-firing firepower made it good at breaking up attacking formations. The Swordfish was an antiquated biplane torpedo bomber but was still quite successful as long as it did not have to face modern fighters. Left to carry on its job like ASW patrol, it was an eminently practical plane in many ways. Both the Fulmar and Swordfish had folding wings.

The Albacore was essentially a Swordfish with an enclosed cockpit. It had some advantages over the Swordfish but many of the same limitations and none of the quaintness. The Barracuda was a combined dive and torpedo bomber, a monoplane with a relatively powerful engine but still underpowered for its size and weight. It had problematic diving characteristics but handled well on a carrier. Both the Albacore and the Barracuda had folding wings.

For more mainstream tasks, the Fleet Air Arm tried to make do by recycling successful land-based planes. This led to the adoption of the Sea Hurricane and the Seafire. The Sea Hurricane had short range, was not as fast as modern fighters, and its air inlet on the underside made ditching dangerous. The Seafire had rather average performance once the tail hook and associated strengthening had been added. As with the Sea Hurricane, the Seafire had short range and the air inlets meant that ditching was often fatal. The plane was quite difficult to land with less than adequate wind over the flight deck. It had a nasty habit of "floating" on landing which often led to the plane ending up in the barriers. During operations in support of the Salerno landings, wind was very light and the carriers steamed slowly to stay close to the beaches. In these conditions, about 10 percent of the landings resulted in a crash of some sort and after a few days like this, the carriers simply ran out of Seafires. A folding wing version of the Sea Hurricane was designed but never built. Later versions of the Seafire had folding wings.

The French had ordered 40 US Wildcats, and after the fall of France these were given to the Fleet Air Arm instead. They were christened Martlets and proved very practical and popular.

Toward the end of the war and for operations in the Pacific, more USN planes were adopted. Hellcats and Corsairs were used as well as Avengers. Barracudas were retained for ground support.

One of very few multi-carrier operations by the RN during World War II was Operation *Pedestal*. This was a critical Malta convoy that was heavily

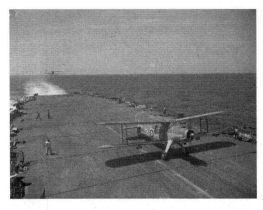

Albacore torpedo bombers landing on HMS *Formidable*. The Albacore that has just landed needs to get past the barricade which has to be raised before the next arrives at the barricade if it misses the arrestor wires. There is not much margin of error here. Good tempo of landing operations was not just a question of a well-trained deck crew but also of pilots well trained on how to fly the landing pattern.

attacked by German and Italian land-based aircraft. The aircraft carried were as follows:

| | |
|---|---|
| *Eagle* | 16 Sea Hurricanes |
| *Victorious* | 6 Sea Hurricanes, 16 Fulmars, 12 Albacores |
| *Indomitable* | 24 Sea Hurricanes, 10 Martlets, 16 Albacores |

Over the three carriers, this adds up to 72 fighters and 28 torpedo bombers, a largely defensive force which was probably very correct for the overall mission of defending a convoy. The torpedo bombers were kept to deal with any Italian surface forces.

A true dive bomber was never developed. The early-war Blackburn Skua was a two-seat combination fighter and dive bomber but was not very successful, at least not as a fighter facing modern German counterparts. Not developing dive bombers made sense as neither the Italians nor Germans operated carriers; hence there were no unarmored flight decks for dive bombers to feast upon. The main targets were the enemy battleships, and against those, torpedo bombers were more effective. The hunt for the *Bismarck* is a prime example—an attack by dive bombers would not have slowed the ship down the way a torpedo hit did.

From March 1944 onwards, the RN successfully tested carrier operations with the de Havilland Mosquito. Compared to the largest carrier-borne plane of the time—the Avenger—the Mosquito had the same wing span but was twice as heavy. Landing had to be at a very slow speed or the arrestor wires could break. This was achieved by a combination of powerful engines and four-bladed propellers—the landing Mosquito would "hang on the props" during final approach. An early variant was a standard Mosquito that had been equipped with arrestor hooks and strengthened landing gear but no folding wings. These were intended to be used against ships in port, with each plane carrying two Highball bouncing bombs designed by Barnes Wallis. The concept was basically a carrier-borne version of the Dam Busters raid. The squadron was operational but no attack was ever carried out for various reasons. Another variant, less exotic in nature, had folding wings and could carry a torpedo but was not ready before the war ended. A postwar version of the Mosquito, the Sea Hornet, had folding wings and saw service on carriers for several years.

Late in the war, the US practice of deck parks had been adopted and air groups were larger. In the attacks on the Japanese home islands, the brand new *Implacable* carried 48 Seafires, 12 Fireflies, and 21 Avengers. Its sister *Indefatigable* carried 40 Seafires, 12 Fireflies, and 21 Avengers. At around 80 planes each, this is very comparable to what US carriers had during the war.

The numbers for the aircraft-carrying capacities of RN carriers are usually based on the number of planes that can be stowed in the hangar and reflects well the actual number operated. The use of deck parks later in the war significantly increased the number of aircraft actually operated above that number. Disassembled spare aircraft were carried inside the hangar with parts hanging from the ceiling. With relatively low headroom, these parts tended to interfere with stowage of aircraft.

# CHAPTER 4

# Finding the Enemy

## Radio Intelligence

Before a battle, radio intelligence is used to try figure out what the enemy is up to, what forces are involved, and anything else that might matter. It is not really connected to carrier operations as such but since it is an important factor in the set-up of the battle, it is still a worthy topic.

The most common form of radio intelligence is traffic analysis. This does not involve cracking codes, but involves looking for features or properties that might reveal something.

Call signs are a brief series of letters and/or numbers that denote what station is transmitting and who the message is for. Some are permanent and some live only a short time. If you know what call signs a carrier uses, then you can deduce a lot about what is going on with that carrier. The characteristics of a station of a particular radio operator, for example, his keying habits, can be used to track call signs as they are changed. Frequencies are usually in the HF band. Some frequencies are usually reserved for some use or user. If you know who uses what frequencies for what, then that can also tell you something about the enemy. Likewise with schedules, there tend to be patterns to who sends what messages at what time. Message length can also provide some clues; long messages are usually more important. A certain station may service several units and if you can figure out the system used, then that will tell you what composition of forces use that station. Finally, just ordinary chatter in plain text by a careless radio operator can sometimes reveal important bits of information, such as if something big is about to happen or if he is bored or hungry or whatever. By putting all these little signs together it is often possible to make educated guesses about what is going on.

Everybody is of course aware that the enemy is listening in this way, but radio communication is a necessity. There are many ways to make traffic analysis more difficult, such as constantly changing call signs, frequencies, etc. Dummy stations can be used as well as stations that pretend to be some other station. It is game between how good one side is at keeping leaks to a minimum, spoofing the listener, and how good the listening team is in piecing the signs together.

Cryptanalysis is the art of actually reading the content of the enemy's messages, that is cracking the codes used, not just observing the flow. Code breaking is aided by traffic analysis, and traffic analysis is aided by code breaking, so good teamwork is important.

Codes come in many forms and some require more time, work, and equipment to use than others. There is often a trade-off between operational expediency and security. Navies use many different types of codes; some are low-level codes that are easy to use but also easier to crack. Higher-level codes are more secure but require more time, people, and equipment to use.

Sometimes a code can be completely cracked but most of the time, only parts of the code can be understood. Everybody cracked at least some of the codes of the enemy. Security is hard, and there are so many ways it can fail against a persistent, smart, and resourceful attacker.

The ultimate example of code cracking, within the context of carrier operations, is of course the battle of Midway. American code crackers were able to predict well in advance the time and position of the Japanese attack down to a few minutes and miles. In the absence of this, the enemy has to be located using regular methods.

The direction of a transmitter can be found with the proper receiving equipment. With two such directional receivers, typically land-based, the position of the transmitter can be triangulated to a precision of typically 50–100 miles using realistic distances between the transmitter and the receivers.

The British HF/DF (High Frequency/Direction Finder or 'huff-duff') equipment was a ship-borne directional receiver that provided the bearing from the escort to any transmitting U-boat. If the U-boat was reasonably close, the bearing was obtained from the ground wave and was thus accurate. It was only a bearing, not the position, but it was still very useful, as all the escort had to do was to race down that bearing and would then often find a surfaced U-boat. At longer distances the propagation of an HF signal is affected by atmospherics and bearings are less accurate.

## Radar Warning Receivers

In a typical carrier battle, both sides are desperately searching for the carriers of the enemy. Finding the enemy without him finding you and then being able to get in that unanswered first strike was the holy grail of every carrier captain. Since a carrier task force will normally operate air search radars to detect any incoming strike, it then becomes very tempting to try to use those transmissions to find the enemy carriers.

Radar transmissions can indeed be detected by a suitable receiver. Since the radar transmission only has to go one way to reach the radar warning receiver, the radar can usually be detected at much longer ranges than it can itself see targets. Mounted on a search plane at altitude, a receiver can detect radar transmissions at upwards of 200 miles. Mounted on a ship, detection range will be limited to the ship's horizon distance.

There are some caveats, however. The first is that a radar warning receiver will only provide the bearing to the radar transmitter and not the range. A series of bearings could possibly yield the range but this is usually hard to arrange during combat conditions. It is basically a given that no information will be provided about the altitude of the radar transmitter, if airborne.

A deeper problem is that it is only the existence of a radar transmitter that is detected. No information is given about the size and composition of the enemy task force. It might be a large force; it might be a lone radar picket destroyer. Some information can be gleaned from the type of radar being detected, such as a radar mounted on a large ship or an airborne radar. If it is an airborne radar, then the detection means even less, as the aircraft can be almost anywhere in relation to the fleet.

A subtler reason, for a carrier task force, is that the visual scouting already done using search planes provides the same information and more.

Then we have the question of practicality and cost-effectiveness. On a small carrier-based search plane there is not much room for electronic suites. Any radar warning receiver will have to be seen as useful and important enough to motivate the weight, effort, and training. Both sides were slow in equipping their search planes with radar warning receivers. In 1943 the USN put some effort into doing characterization of enemy land-based radar using patrol bombers like the Catalina (carrying an ARC-1 receiver) but it was only in early 1945 that the first Avenger went into operation equipped with a radar transmission receiver (most likely one of the AN/APR series).

Surface search radar mounted on enemy patrol aircraft can well be detected from ships. Radar warning receivers were used extensively by German U-boats. The first receiver was the Metox operating at a wavelength of 1.5m. The later Naxos worked on the 10cm band. The Japanese received the design details of the Metox receivers from the Germans and built about 2,000 units, equipping most of their ships with them but by that time the USN had largely shifted

Hellcat with AN/APS-6 radar in a pylon on the starboard wing. This is the night fighter variant of the Hellcat, and the radar was intended for night interceptions but was useful against ships as well, having a range of 20–30 miles against large surface targets.

to newer radar (ASB, ASG, ASD etc.) that worked on shorter wavelengths, and the receivers were not of much use.

## Radar

If the scout plane was equipped with radar, it could detect ships at a very long range, depending on radar model and size and number of ships. A basic drawback of radar scouting is that the type of ship is not shown. The number and sizes of the blips might enable the scout to count the number of ships but even that required a radar with good resolution and coming reasonably close. There was never any hope of distinguishing a carrier from any other large echo. Having been found, however, the enemy fleet could then be visually identified and attacked at dawn.

The range of early airborne sets were not much better than the visual sighting range, so the radar was mainly useful in cases of bad visibility or at night. The radar used by the scout can of course be detected by ships mounting warning receivers but those will not yield much beyond what the air search radar already knows (as long as the radar is switched on).

Long-range patrol planes like the Catalina had radar fitted already in June 1942 with the first model being the ASV Mk II. Smaller US carrier-borne planes like the Avenger had surface search radar fitted in late 1942 but the set used was bulky and only some were fitted. By 1944 even fighters could have a set and some were mounted on Hellcat night fighters.

Japanese patrol planes were fitted with radar in late 1943. Japanese carrier-borne planes like the Kate or Jill were never fitted with surface search radar to any real extent. The number of available sets available was very small, and by the time they were available in late 1944, the Japanese carriers had ceased to be a relevant platform anyway.

## Visual Scouting

Scout planes typically searched in fan-shaped pattern but the full azimuth circle was not necessarily searched, depending on the tactical situation. Each fan would typically cover 15° of arc but could be denser if a more careful search was deemed necessary. Doing a dense and wide search had a cost associated with it in that it diverted planes from other duties, for example strikes. Searches could also be out to different ranges depending on how extensive the search needed to be.

While the search planes were in the air, the ship that had launched them would normally move. The fan usually ended at a place different from the starting point. Beyond the outbound leg, the dogleg and the inbound leg, there was often a short fourth leg to catch up with the carrier. Search planes were told of the expected movements of the ship they were launched from, as well as a backup flying pattern in case the ship was not found.

Sunrise occurs earlier at a high altitude but not enough to have much of an impact on search operations. The horizon distance at 12,000 feet is 134 miles and the sun covers this distance in only about 5–10 minutes, traveling at 900 knots at the equator.

A flying height of around 10,000–12,000 feet typically gave the best cruising speed and range. Lower altitudes meant thicker air and slower speed and/or higher fuel consumption. Above 12,000 feet the pilot needed to use oxygen. Flying height depended heavily on the cloud layers of the day and could be much lower. An altitude of 1,000 feet still gives a horizon distance of 40 miles or more. Flying at a lower altitude had the advantage that it was easier to see the prevailing wave patter, and thus to estimate wind drift and navigate accurately. Flying low, it was also more likely that the observed wind at wave-top level was the same as the wind the plane was flying in as wind speed and direction usually varies with altitude, sometimes dramatically so. Visibility varied greatly but could in optimal conditions be up to 25–30 miles, thus covering a 50–60-mile wide swath of ocean.

At Coral Sea and Midway the USN searched out to 250 miles by using a pair of Dauntless dive bombers for each 10° or 15° of azimuth angle. Cruising speed was about 150 knots and a search mission took about 4–5 hours to complete. The Dauntless was later replaced with Helldivers which were then each complemented by a Hellcat for protection. Later in the war search was done out to about 350 miles. Later still, Hellcats only were used for scouting but still often flying in pairs. USN doctrine was to do searches in pairs when enemy air opposition could be expected, otherwise single planes were used.

At Coral Sea and Midway the Japanese searched out to 300 miles using a mix of floatplanes (from cruisers *Tone* and *Chikuma*) and carrier-based planes. Cruise speed was about 120 knots for Jake floatplanes and about 150 for Val dive bombers and Kate torpedo planes, taking about 5–6 hours to complete a search mission. Later in the war, scouting was done out to 500–550 miles. Also later in the war, from 1944 on, a two-stage search process was often used where a batch of search planes was launched well before dawn in order to be out at long range at sunrise, then a second batch of search planes was launched to be at medium range at sunrise.

A scout plane should ideally be fast. The higher the speed, the more surface of the ocean could be covered in a given amount of time. High speed was also helpful in not getting shot down once in contact. Toward the end of the war, mainly fighters were used.

Floatplanes are not really suited to scouting. Being rather slow they are both inefficient at searching and easy to catch and shoot down. The Japanese used Jake floatplanes extensively as scouts, catapulted from cruisers and battleships. The Americans did not use their Kingfisher floatplanes as a replacement for carrier-based scouting, but used them as observers for shore bombardment and for search-and-rescue missions. Neither of these two tasks were of much relevance for the Japanese.

The large flying boats had very long range, but being large and expensive there were also relatively few of them available. Long range does not mean that a large area can be searched quickly, only that the area searched can be a long way from the base. Area searched depends on speed, and flying boats were typically not very fast. They were flexible in their basing, however, and with their excellent range they could be deployed to scout areas far away from the carriers. They also had the advantage in that they could carry bulky radar gear which enabled them to search in poor visibility and at night.

If anything substantial was found, the scout was in a very dangerous position. As a scout approached a carrier task force, it was often picked up on radar. It was then a race for defending CAP to shoot down the intruder before the fleet had been spotted and a sighting report sent. This is why USN scouted in pairs, despite it diverting more planes from strike operations. The USN did not worry about losses so much us making certain that the sighting report was sent successfully.

Getting in closer for an identification of the ships was even more dangerous; hanging around and tracking the formation was almost suicidal. The best way to avoid being shot down was to head for any nearby cloud. Darting in and out of clouds was the only viable strategy to get close and/or to track the fleet for any length of time. Lacking suitable clouds, the only hope was to try to outrun the fighters. Floatplanes were very vulnerable and were routinely shot down, while a faster long-range flying boat had a better chance of survival. It was understood that scouts were essentially disposable, especially floatplanes. As the joke went, "enemy fleet found, notify next of kin …."

Japanese scouts sometimes used a different method to ensure that the sighting report got through. They continuously sent out a short Morse code message. When they were shot down, the transmission would stop. Back at the base, the position of where they were shot down could be deduced from the time when the transmission stopped. Slightly morbid but necessary given the realities of scouting. This method did not provide any information of what was found but then again, depending on where it was shot down, it could be deduced that it was most likely by a carrier-based plane which of course meant that there was a carrier in the area.

Autopilots made it easier for fighters to act as scouts; the lone pilot could now do the navigation as well as handling the transmission of coded messages. Being faster, a fighter was also both more efficient at searching and less vulnerable to being shot down.

When scouting, the first thing seen of a formation are the wakes, not the ships themselves. A stationary ship, without a wake, is harder to spot. A scout plane can visually spot ships at much longer ranges (about 25–30 miles) than a ship can visually spot the plane (about 5 miles).

From a distance it is very difficult to see what types of ships there are in the formation. For that, a much closer look was needed. In many cases it was a race to get close enough to make an accurate report before getting shot down and killed. Judging the relative size of the wake, a rough estimate of the speed can be made, even at a distance. Ship recognition was never very reliable, despite intensive training on the subject, and it is easy to understand why.

Scout planes were sent on long missions lasting several hours. Quite a lot could and did happen during that period. Due to radio silence, the scouts were often not aware of what had happened and could be in for quite a surprise when they had found their way back to the carrier.

# Radar

## Fundamentals

Radar works by emitting a beam of a signal in a certain direction. If the signal hits something it bounces. Some of that signal will be bounced back in the direction of the radar receiver and can then be detected by it.

Not much of the original signal will bounce and find its way back to the receiver but if the power output is high enough to begin with, that bounced signal will still be detectable.

The first rule of radar design is therefore that you need to have a very powerful transmitter. Furthermore, if the signal sent out is a pulse and not a continuous signal, then the bounce received will also be in the form of a pulse. This is important, as the delay between the outgoing pulse and the bounce is proportional to the distance to the target. The essence of radar is then to transmit a short pulse of very high power and then to listen for the (weak) bounces.

How easy it is to generate a pulse of high power depends on the wavelength. Generally speaking, for reasons that we do not need to go into here, the shorter the wavelength the more difficult it is to generate a high power signal. The multi-cavity magnetron was the breakthrough device that enabled much higher power levels at shorter wavelengths than was possible with other methods.

The cavity magnetron had been known since 1921. Multi-cavity magnetrons were first built by Russian scientists in 1936–37 with results published in 1940. British scientists (i.e. Randall and Boot) had a very good multi-cavity magnetron design by late 1939 and passed the design on to the Americans. The Germans did not work on cavity magnetrons.

Japan did some very advanced work and had multi-cavity magnetron designs that were just as good as the British ones. The Japanese were quite good at radar technology in general but just did not have the industrial base to make much use of it. As an example, the Yagi antenna is named after the Japanese scientist Hidetsugu Yagi whose assistant Shintaro Uda invented this type of antenna in the 1930s.

Working within the limitations on how much power the pulse can have, there are other ways to have a decent return signal for the receiver to work with. One way is to send out more pulses, to have a higher pulse repetition rate (PRF). If the pulses come with less time between them there is less time for the pulse echo to return before the next pulse happens and the range is reduced. Another way to make life easier for the receiver is to have longer pulses but that will then affect resolution in range.

## Beams

The beam transmitted can be of different shapes. It can be wide or narrow. Generally speaking, a narrow beam will provide better precision in what direction the echo comes from and hence the direction of the target.

However, for each direction the radar is pointed, you have to wait for any possible echo. With a narrow beam, each direction only covers a small sector. If searching for targets, scanning a certain sector will take longer. There is then a trade-off between precision and the time it takes to search a sector.

The shape of the beam can also be different in horizontal plane and in the vertical plane. For example, when looking for a surface target such as a ship, we are very interested in direction in the horizontal plane but we know beforehand where it is going to be in the vertical plane (on the surface) so there is no need for precision in the vertical plane. The beam will be narrow in the horizontal plane but wide in the vertical plane.

It is customary to have two radars for air search, one with a wide beam that can quickly scan a large volume of airspace and then an additional radar with a narrow beam to inspect targets with a higher resolution.

## Antennas

The shape of the antenna determines the shape of the beam. There are fundamental physical limitations on how much an antenna can shape the beam, and this has a major impact on all radar design. To produce a narrow beam, the antenna must be much bigger that the wavelength of the signal. For a given wavelength, the bigger the antenna the narrower the beam. For a given size of antenna, the shorter wavelength the narrower the beam.

On a ship or an aircraft, the size of the antenna is often limited by weight and size. Hence the constant drive toward shorter wavelength and hence the importance of the magnetron.

Large antennas necessitated by long wavelengths were often built as a kind of wire-frame structure to save weight. This was possible, as an electromagnetic wave does not really notice structures that are much smaller than the wavelength. With a wavelength in the order of meters, designers had ample opportunity to lighten the antenna.

A surface search radar does not care much about altitude information, as it knows that the targets it is interested in are at sea level but the horizontal resolution is very important. That antenna should then be wide and flat. The SG antenna is typical.

A radar for fighter direction needs to be good in both the horizontal and the vertical plane. It also needs to have a high resolution to resolve individual aircraft or groups of aircraft. The antenna needs to be much greater than the wavelength in both the horizontal and vertical. Such a radar uses a short wavelength and most likely a parabolic dish antenna. Being high resolution and mounted on a moving ship, the antenna needs to be gyro stabilized. The SM radar used by the USN is typical, together with the SP, the smaller and lighter version of SM that was fitted on some ships. For the RN, the Type 277 is typical of this type of radar.

### Long vs. Short Wavelengths

Shorter wavelengths enable higher resolution and smaller antennas, but that is not the whole story. Longer wavelengths have their advantages. For one, radar range is usually longer with a longer wavelength—the signal has "longer legs." Another property of longer wavelengths is that they tend to follow the curvature of the earth, allowing us to see somewhat beyond the horizon. Shorter wavelengths are more line-of-sight and nothing beyond that.

Longer wavelengths are therefore well suited for long-range applications. One such is air warning. These were the first operational radar sets and operated at a wavelength of a few meters. This meant by necessity that the antennas had to be very large and hence were limited to major warships. With a long wavelength, generating sufficient output power was quite feasible before the invention of the magnetron. This is the type of radar that is important from a carrier-operations point of view.

In the RN the long wavelength sets in use were the Type 279 and 281 sets (7.5m and 3.5m wavelength respectively). In the USN it was the CXAM and SK radar sets (both using a wavelength of 1.5m).

The IJN was late in producing an air-warning radar. Their first operational set was the Type 21 (also known as Type 2 Mk 2 Model 1 or "21-Go"). This set operated at 1.5m and was first used in the summer of 1942. The later and much more common Type 13 (also known as Type 3 Mk 1 Model 3 or "13-Go") operated at 2m and first became operational in March 1943.

### Airborne Radar

An airborne installation immediately imposes severe limitations on the available space and weight. The size of the antenna is very limited and must cause as little drag as possible. Weight and power are other problems which limit available output power and thus range.

Long-range patrol aircraft were the first to get surface search radar. These were often used for searching for U-boats. Torpedo bombers were the next to get surface search radar. These bombers were often three-man planes with enough room to fit a reasonably compact radar installation.

Fighters had very little space and the radars fitted here were usually short-range sets intended for interception of other aircraft, not long-range search. Single-seat fighters also had only very limited room available on the instrument panel, so the display had to be very small and the controls had to be simple.

## *RN Airborne Radar*

The ASV Mk II was the first airborne radar (ASV = Airborne Anti-Surface Vessel). Developed by the British, it operated at 1.7m and consisted on two Yagi (or "fishbone") antennas, one under each wing, one used for transmission and the other for receiving. The antennas were fixed forward. Useful against submarine and surface targets with a range of up to 35–50 miles against a large ship, ASV Mk II sets were installed from 1940 on Swordfish torpedo bombers and larger patrol planes. They were used to detect the *Bismarck*.

The ASV Mk III operated at 10cm and were in service from 1943 and installed on Swordfish and Barracuda aircraft, among others.

## *USN Airborne Radar*

In the Pacific, ASV Mk II sets were mounted on large patrol planes from June 1942 onwards. They were refined into the later ASE set in which the two antennas were combined into one, reducing drag.

Next was the ASB series of radars, the last of the non-magnetron sets. This set operated at 60cm and had two Yagi antennas, one under each wing, with both acting as transceivers. Antennas could me moved to the side ±90°. About 26,000 units were built with production starting in late 1942. This was the most common of the airborne radar sets used in World War II. Mounted on patrol planes and carrier-borne bombers like the Dauntless, Helldiver, and Avenger, their range against ships was up to 35–50 miles but resolution was not as good as the later 10cm and 3cm sets.

The first magnetron-based set was the ASG (later renamed AN/APS-2) operating at 10cm. It was fairly bulky and was installed on large patrol planes and bombers. It had a range of up to 60 miles against ships. About 5,000 were built with production beginning in October 1942.

The next set, the ASD (later renamed AN/APS-3) operated at 3cm. The shorter wavelength enabled a three-fold reduction in antenna size. A parabolic reflector-type antenna was now housed in the nose or in an under-wing fairing beneath the plane's wing. Mounted on medium patrol planes and on the Avenger, it could detect ships up to 40 miles away. About 6,000 sets were produced from June 1943 onwards.

The ASH set (later renamed AN/APS-4) was a smaller and lighter version of the -3 intended to be a general-purpose radar to be mounted on almost any type of aircraft, including fighters and torpedo bombers. It had the same range as the -3, up to 40 miles against ships, and entered production in October 1943.

The AN/APS-6 was the same as the -4 but with a simplified display suitable for interception duties by single-seat night fighters. About 2,000 were produced with operational use starting in mid-1944.

The AN/APS-20 was a 10cm set based on the AN/APS-2 that had been made to fit into a carrier-borne aircraft like the Avenger (heavily modified). It did not come into production until after the war had ended.

Before February 1943, the army and navy used different designations for their radar sets. The same set could be named differently by the two services. To reduce confusion, the AN (Army-Navy) nomenclature was introduced and the ASx series of names (AS = Air Search) was replaced by the AN/APS-x series.

## IJN Airborne Radar

Type H6 (also known as Type 3 Mk 6 Model 4) operated at 2m and was used on twin-engine bombers and on large flying boats. About 2,000 were built, becoming operational in August 1942. It employed a single Yagi antenna for both transmit and receive, and was mainly used for air search with a range of 60 miles against a formation of planes, and about 40 miles against single aircraft. Its range against ships was unknown and so may not have been used much in that role.

Type N6 operated at 1.2m and could be fitted on single-engine carrier-borne aircraft like a torpedo bomber. It used a single Yagi antenna and was mainly used for air search with a range of 40 miles. It became operational in October 1944 but only 20 were built and use never went beyond the experimental.

## Displays

The first display was the A-scope. This was a very basic display showing the raw return signal. It had signal strength on one axis and range on the other. The antenna was often hand-rotated through 360° and when something was found, the operator would stay there and examine the size and range of the echo. This type of display was very good for seeing the size of the echo and to measure range accurately but did not give an intuitive feeling for the overall situation.

Airborne radar had their own displays. The B-scope was used for airborne search and the C-scope for airborne targeting, showing range and elevation versus azimuth respectively.

The display most commonly associated with radar is the Plan Position Indicator (PPI). It gives a map-like presentation which is very easy to understand.

## Radar Warning Receivers

It is relatively easy to build a detector for signals of a certain wavelength. If the enemy uses a radar, the receiver will provide warning of this. Depending on the receiver, the direction of the enemy will be provided. The range will not be given, at least not directly. An experienced operator might be able to guess the approximate range to the enemy radar.

Using receivers of similar sensitivity, the distance at which that receiver detects the radar signal will be much greater than the range at which the radar will detect the bounced echo. The receiver will outrange the radar.

The Germans developed a series of radar detectors for their U-boats. The first was the Metox, which was used to detect transmissions with wavelengths of 1.3–2.6m. The antenna was a simple dipole which in principle did not provide any bearing to the transmitter. The receiver was very sensitive and yielded long detection ranges. The high sensitivity was a bit of problem as it gave many false warnings. It became operational in August 1942.

The later Naxos detected wavelengths of 8–12cm. The first practical version had a parabolic reflector antenna that was rotated by hand, providing some directional information. The receiver was not very sensitive and the detection range was only about 3 miles but this still gave the U-boat a warning time of about a minute, which was usually enough to do a crash dive. It became operational in December 1943.

After the Naxos came the Tunis which could detect transmissions on the 3cm band. A horn antenna was used. The antenna was rotated by hand and could provide directional information. It entered German service in May 1944.

## Radio Silence vs. Active Radar

The big disadvantage with radar is that it gives away your position. Listen to the right frequency and it is the equivalent of a giant lighthouse, broadcasting its position to everyone in the area that cares to listen. Generally speaking, against an alert and well-equipped enemy, you want to use radar as little as possible.

The Americans made heavy use of radar but got away with it because the Japanese did not have the equipment to intercept and track American radar transmissions. Since the Japanese used radio/radar silence as one of their main guiding principles, nothing much came of this. Thus the Americans were unhindered in their use of radar and made much use of it, making it a much bigger advantage than it really should have been had they faced a more sophisticated enemy. If the Japanese search aircraft had been fitted with radar warning receivers, this would have forced the Americans to be much more restrictive in using radar for fear of giving their position away. As soon they had been spotted, all radars would obviously be switched on but that requires knowledge of having been spotted.

With the appearance of AEW, the value of radar warning receivers decreased. The bearing was now not toward someone in the task force but toward a small plane buzzing around somewhere which could be anywhere in relation to the fleet. Correspondingly, the effectiveness of fighter direction was much increased as the range of the radar increased and as it became impossible to sneak in under the radar. AEW is essential for carrier operations. Effective AEW requires several planes, preferably as large as possible to have room for as large an antenna as possible, which then imposes a minimum size on the carrier.

# CHAPTER 5

# Detecting Incoming Strikes

## Using Pickets

A screen of radar-equipped destroyers could be placed somewhere where enemy aircraft were expected to pass, providing more time for fighter direction to put them where they were needed. As the distance to the fleet increases, more and more pickets are required to cover the perimeter. The number increases with the square of the distance gained. Another strategy is to place the pickets off the coast of where the enemy airfields are, if known, picking them up on radar as they take off.

An advantage with pickets is that they provide good height estimation of an incoming strike. Height estimation depends on range, and since the picket is closer to the strike as it passes through the picket line, height data will be accurate relatively far out from the main fleet, a major advantage for a successful interception of the strike.

These pickets are highly vulnerable, however, being alone in the path of the attacker and with marginal CAP (remember, the pickets are there to assist CAP, not the other way around). They can make themselves less vulnerable by steaming and maneuvering at high speed but that requires constant refueling and does not work so well against kamikazes.

IJN sometimes used an advance force to scout, to act as picket and to soak up strikes. Here "advance force" should probably at least partly be read as a euphemism for "live bait." Note that this broke with USN doctrine of keeping a force together. Japanese doctrine was much more open to advance or diversionary forces.

## Using Radar

For a radar at sea level the horizon distance against a target at 10,000 feet is 122 miles, to which can be added 12 miles for an assumed height of 100 feet for the ship-borne antenna.

Type 281 was the standard RN air-search radar from 1940 onwards. It had a range of 70–120 miles against groups of planes, depending on height.

Detection ranges for the USN CXAM and later SK models were 50–100 miles depending on height of target. At Coral Sea, an incoming Japanese attack was detected at 70 miles.

The Japanese Type 21 had a range of 50 miles. First installed on the carrier *Shokaku* in September 1942, it probably saved the ship at Santa Cruz as it gave the crew enough warning time to purge aviation gas pipes before an incoming attack of dive bombers scored a hit on the ship (and actually hit its aviation gas piping).

Air-warning radar could detect single planes, not just large formations, albeit perhaps not at maximum range, and was thus useful in detecting enemy search planes snooping around. These snoopers can then be attacked and shot down. Keeping snoopers timid and at a distance will make their reports less accurate. Attacking a snooper might give away the presence of a nearby carrier force, however, if the snooper is too far away for it to detect the force, so leaving the snooper alone might be the smartest move. Since radar detection range is much greater than the visual detection range of a snooper, it might be possible for the formation to have enough time to move out of the path of the snooper, but then sneaking away with a large formation might not be that easy. You might also bump into the next search plane in the fan search pattern (if not detected on radar).

A detection range of 70 miles gives a warning time of 20–30 minutes before an attack reaches target. With combat ranges of up to 250 miles, the detection is a large chunk of that. If the fleets are close enough, you can actually see the targets appearing on radar as they take off.

Air-warning sets are big and heavy. Since they must be carried high up on the superstructure, only the largest ships carried them. Carriers obviously had priority but battleships and cruisers also had them. Destroyers had smaller and shorter range sets installed, for example, the SC instead of the SK used on the big ships of the USN.

It was possible to mount radar sets on carrier-borne aircraft, but given size and weight restrictions these had short range against enemy aircraft, in the order of a few thousand yards, and were mainly useful for intercepting bombers at night. The short range meant that these fighters had to be directed toward the incoming bomber by the fighter direction team using some ship-borne radar (preferably with height estimation).

True airborne air-search radar (AEW) requires a large rotating antenna, the bigger the better. The first real attempt in this direction was the USN mounting an AN/APS-20 S-band (10cm) radar in a large belly radome on an Avenger or a B-17 (designated TBM-3W and PB-1W respectively). It could detect incoming low-flying formations at 100+ miles (at 12,000 feet the distance to the horizon is 135 miles, at the service ceiling of 28,500 feet it is 200 miles). There was now full control of everything up to 200 miles away, including at the surface level, which was very impressive. It represented nothing less than a revolution in both carrier warfare and in naval warfare in general. However, it should be noted that these AEW systems were essentially *warning* systems, and usually provided no information on target height, and for fighter direction purposes would ideally be combined with a height-finding radar, particularly for night-time intercepts.

The Avenger only acted as a radar platform and there was no attempt to do any fighter direction from within it. The radar screen picture was sent by radio link to the CIC on the carrier. The CIC also had a link back to control the radar and thus to what was shown. These radio links worked at the 300MHz band and had a range of about 45 miles. Installed on a B-17, there was room for more operators and it could now act as flying command center. Neither variant was used operationally before the end of the war but both were planned to be used for the invasion of Japan, providing the fleet with early warning against kamikazes.

In these early AEW systems the radar antenna was installed in a radome in the belly of the aircraft looking downwards. This was fairly obvious given that the intention was to catch low-flying targets. Somewhat counter-intuitively, this turned out to be bad practice since it led to a massive return from the sea immediately below which tended to blank out the useful signal. Mounting the radome on top of the fuselage, with the aircraft itself acting as a screen against the sea return, turned out to be a better solution. There was also more room on top of the aircraft. By the time this was realized it was too late to change the basic design. Both the Avenger and the B-17 variants went into operation with belly-mounted radomes. A later B-17 variant had the radome on top. Most modern AEW systems have the radome on top and are actually blind to targets close to and below them. The minimum distance against surface targets can be a few tens of miles.

Heavily modified Avenger with AN/APS-20 search radar mounted.

## Detecting Strikes Visually

If nothing else worked, it was back to the Mk 1 Eyeball. Using the naked eye and standing on a ship, a relatively small carrier-borne aircraft may be spotted about 5 miles out under good conditions. The maximum resolution of the human eye is about 0.1 milliradians and at 5 miles this corresponds to resolving objects about 3 feet across. Persons with an eyesight approaching this, or well trained in spotting techniques, have been reported to be able to spot aircraft at much longer ranges. Binoculars could increase spotting range but at a price in area scanned per unit of time, and were usually best used to identify a target that had already been spotted. Looking out from inside an aircraft, typical detection range of other single-engine aircraft was about 3 miles. Aircrew tended to miss targets that were below and above their own altitude—eyes tended to scan against the horizon. Larger formations were easier to spot visually but detection range was not much greater than for single planes. At optical wavelengths, it was still many small targets. One moment nothing was there, the next moment dozens of tiny dots appeared. This is different from radar, where detecting a large formation is easier than detecting a single plane. The beam of a typical World War II air-warning radar was wide enough to cover the whole formation, and the returns from many small targets would add up to appear as one large return and a large formation could be detected at something like a 30–50 percent longer range compared to a single aircraft.

# CHAPTER 6

# Aerial Attacks

## Wave Tactics

This is the most common tactic. Attacks are most effective when done in groups that can temporarily overload AA defense by sheer numbers. One large well-coordinated attack, ideally several types of attacks simultaneously, is usually best.

Deck-load attacks were the norm for all navies—both the IJN and USN put great emphasis on them.

## Trickle Tactics

Trickling involves coming in with a small number of planes and surprising the defender. The point of using trickling against a carrier is to catch it with refueled and rearmed planes on deck, on the flight deck, or on the hangar deck.

The attacker does not know when the defender will be vulnerable but if attacks are coming during an extended period of time, sooner or later one of them is likely to catch a carrier off guard. When caught in such a way, it is often enough with a single bomb to initiate uncontrollable fires that then wrecks the ship.

One can argue that the US attacks on the Japanese carriers at Midway amounted to trickle tactics. The incessant attacks on the US carriers at Santa Cruz led to a situation where the US carriers were unable to conduct flight operations for an extended period and many planes then had to ditch as they ran out of fuel before they could land.

Later in the war, the carriers *Princeton*, *Franklin*, and *Bunker Hill* were all struck by bombs from lone planes that started massive fires. *Princeton* was sunk and *Franklin* narrowly avoided sinking but was effectively a total loss.

## Approach and Range

Cruising speed was about 120–150 knots for most of the bombers involved, with the exception of the Devastator which was comparatively slow at 100–110 knots. The Swordfish biplane was even slower, cruising along at a leisurely 80–100 knots. All cruising speeds are somewhat arbitrary; if needed the pilot can go faster or slower. Cruising altitude was typically 6,000–12,000 feet.

In 1942 the Japanese would attack out to about 250–300 miles, in 1944 out to about 300–400 miles. The USN would attack out to about 200 miles in 1942, extended to 250 miles in 1944. The RN would attack out to 250–270 miles with the Swordfish, slightly further with the Albacore.

Range numbers are always tricky as they can be tweaked quite a bit. Any carrier aircraft has a maximum weight with which it can successfully take off from a carrier. For a given type of aircraft, that weight depends on how much wind there is over the flight deck on that day and on how long the available take-off run is for that plane, as well as what safety margin for the take off is considered necessary, which might in turn depend on the type and importance of the mission.

That weight can then be used to carry a combination of fuel or ordnance, assuming that suitable drop tanks are available. The fuel carried can then be used for different purposes, such as forming up a formation, waiting for other planes in the strike, getting to the target area, searching for targets, avoiding defending CAP, organizing attack coordination over the target and finally as a safety margin against unknowns such as unfavorable winds, navigation mistakes, and time spent waiting in the landing pattern. These factors are all negotiable and maximum distance to target is only one of them.


## High-Level Bombing

Prewar, level bombing by multi-engine bombers was seen as a major threat to warships. Flying at high altitude, the bombers were immune from automatic AA, and AP bombs had time to build up the speed needed to penetrate deck armor. It was accepted that a fairly low percentage of bombs would hit but this was compensated for by simply dropping more bombs from bigger planes. US Army Air Corps general Billy Mitchell went so far as to claim that heavy bombers had made navies obsolete. Countering this threat is why all navies put considerable resources into developing the heavy AA guns and fire-control systems needed for targeting high-altitude level bombers.

Bombing accuracy depends on precise estimates of aircraft height, speed, and direction as well as wind speed and direction all the way down to the surface. There should also be no clouds obscuring the target. Flying had to be very precise, as the slightest roll or pitch of the aircraft would throw off the aim. Any turbulence would obviously cause difficulties here. For these reasons, a gyro-stabilized bombsight was often used. The Norden bombsight was originally developed for the USN for the task of hitting warships. It was first installed on Devastators and later on B-17 Flying Fortresses with the latter originally developed for long-range coastal defense and strikes against shipping (with strategic bombing a secondary consideration).

Against ships, level bombing was usually done at an altitude of 10,000–20,000 feet. The bombs take 30–40 seconds to fall and while doing so travel a horizontal distance of 2,000–5,000 yards. During that time of fall the target ship can travel about 500 yards and turn 45–90°.

Assuming that target size is 260×30 yards and that bombs will fall randomly within an area of 1,000×1,000 yards, then only about 0.7 percent of bombs will hit anything. In practice it was not even that good: ships will see the bombers making their bombing run and will simply go somewhere else. Also, bombing is not always as accurate as in the assumption above: bombs could well miss by miles under combat conditions. To be effective, high-level bombing must be against stationary targets, at a relatively low level, with good visibility and undisturbed by AA and CAP. Accuracy also depended heavily on training. The level bombing done at Pearl Harbor was done from 10,000 feet by Kate torpedo bombers carrying AP bombs and was quite successful, but then the pilots had trained extensively before the mission.

The Tallboys used against *Tirpitz* were released at 12,000–16,000 feet, weighed 22,000lbs, took about 30 seconds to fall and hit with an average error of 300–500 yards. Three out of the 16 bombs released hit the ship during the final attack. This accuracy was achieved under good conditions as the *Tirpitz* was stationary and visibility was good, AA was relatively light and the crews were highly experienced. The Tallboys were equipped with tail fins that made them spin as they fell. This made them significantly more accurate than standard bombs, comparable to how a bullet fired from a rifled barrel is more accurate than one fired from a smoothbore (or pitches that have the ball spinning are more consistent and predictable than the non-spinning "knuckleballs," to use baseball terminology). Being very heavy and well streamlined, the Tallboys reached about 120 percent of the speed of sound while standard bombs released at high altitude reach about 80–90 percent of the speed of sound.

The Japanese carrier *Hiryu* evading sticks of bombs dropped by B-17 high-level bombers at the battle of Midway. Note the lack of escorts—IJN carriers operated in a very loose formation while under attack. Being free to maneuver was seen as more important than the additional AA. Note also how the wake of the ship is much more visible from the air than the ship itself and how a dark color on the flight deck makes it stand out less against the sea.

## Torpedo Bombers

The main advantage of torpedoes is that they sink ships of all types, reliably and well. Once sunk, a ship tends to stay sunk (except those sunk inside a harbor). A ship that has been hit by bombs tends to make it back to port and eventually back to battle. Few ships that sank did so without the help of torpedoes.

During the approach to the target area, the flying height of a torpedo bomber varied but 5,000–7,000 feet was typical. The altitude was needed to find the target and to get an overview of the target area to set up the attack. As the bombers approached, a shallow dive was started about 7,000–8,000 yards out. A slower torpedo bomber like the Swordfish did a steeper dive to get up to speed. The speed gained in the dive was used to get in position and to be a difficult target to intercept for defending fighters as well as to reduce the time exposed to AA.

Torpedo bombers were generally able to attack in spite of cloud cover and generally bad weather. The flying height of the approach might have to be adjusted due to any cloud layers present but as long as the visibility was reasonable the attack would proceed. Wind had no effect on a torpedo once it was running, at least not in the same way as it affected the fall of a bomb or the dive of a dive bomber. Large waves might be problematic, however. The impact of dropping the torpedo into a large wave might throw the torpedo off course or ruin the run completely.

The attacking torpedo bombers will be able to see the target formation well before the attack commences. The targets will also spot the incoming attack several thousand yards out. The targets will try to evade the incoming torpedoes, normally by turning away and only presenting the stern as a target. The target will also be able to see both the launch and track of the torpedo. Attacking a target like a battleship or a carrier maneuvering at full speed, the torpedo will be only somewhat faster than the ship. The target will be able to move some distance as well as turn in any direction in order to evade the approaching torpedo. One can imagine the stress level of the captain while doing this.

To catch such a slippery target, the attacking torpedo planes need to set up a coordinated approach, with attacks coming in from several directions at the same time. This is called an "anvil" attack. Avoiding one attack element, the ship will present itself as a good target to the other attack element. These elements must attack at more or less the same time, otherwise the target will be able to evade each attack in turn. Ideally, each element should also attack in a tight formation to overload defenses. Looser formations, or attacks in streams of planes, allows for more margin in timing but are also easier to shoot down. As can be understood, a torpedo attack requires considerable training and courage to successfully execute.

Attacking as several elements, with each element consisting of enough planes so that not all can be easily shot down, means that there is a minimum number of bombers needed for an attack to have a realistic chance of success. This minimum number was something like ten planes. Any additional planes will have good chances of scoring a hit. Against non-maneuvering targets, fewer torpedo bombers are needed for a reasonable probability of one or more hits.

The torpedo drop itself was essentially at wave-top level and at slow to medium air speed. The lower and slower, the better the odds for a flawless and accurate torpedo run. Think of the torpedo as a delicate flower to be carefully planted. The torpedo then ran straight ahead as dropped. Typical release distance for a torpedo was about 1,000 yards. Getting in close to the target was critical but had to be weighed against odds of survival.

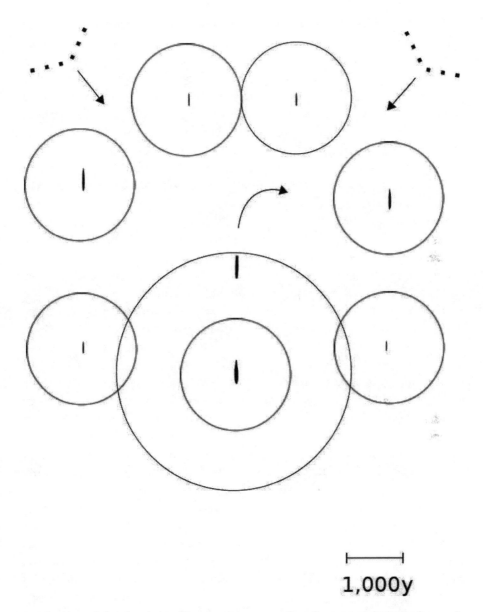

1,000y

Attacking torpedo bombers have split up into two or more formations approaching simultaneously from different directions, in what is known as an 'anvil' attack. The target can attempt to escape one of the formations but in doing so, will present itself as a good target to the other formation. The defending formation consists of a carrier at the center and a screen of cruisers and destroyers plus a battleship astern of the carrier to provide additional AA support. Torpedo bombers had to pass through this screen to launch torpedoes. Circles indicate approximate effective range of 20 and 40 mm fire at 1000 yards and 2000 yards respectively. To scale.

Aerial torpedoes have to be relatively light for a single-engine aircraft to be able to lift it off a short flight deck. The warhead is often smaller and range is shorter. Aerial torpedoes can be seen when they are dropped and the ship will try to evade them, making long-range drops ineffective anyway. Most navies opted for fast torpedoes with short range, typically 40 knots and 2,500 yards. The USN opted for slower and longer-range torpedoes, 33 knots and 6,300 yards. These torpedoes were unreliable early in the war, not becoming reliable until 1943. The Japanese did *not* use the famous Long Lance torpedo for aerial attacks, but used conventional torpedoes. The huge and long-range Long Lance weighed 2.7 tons and although prototypes for airborne use existed, nothing came of it.

Late in the war, the USN dropped modified torpedoes from a release altitude of up to 2,400 feet as well as at faster speeds, both to evade AA. The torpedo traveled about 1,000 yards in the air, taking about 7 seconds. Typical release distance was now 2,000 yards, with part of that distance now traveled in the air. The time to reach the target was roughly the same.

The most common error made by pilots was releasing at too great a distance from the target. This was not entirely due to the very reasonable survival instinct—range estimation was non-trivial. Another common mistake was not to allow for enough lead or to misjudge target speed.

Torpedo bombers are relatively easy to shoot down as they come in low and slow. That low level was easy to reach and left little room for escape. They also had to pass close to the escorts on their attack run. The standard anvil attack could be difficult to set up in the face of AA and CAP. Torpedo-bomber pilots needed to be very brave indeed. They suffered heavy losses throughout the war, the same in all navies. On the other hand, few pilots had to execute more than one attack as the intended targets were so rare.

The loss of all those Devastators at Midway was not necessarily the fault of the Devastator being obsolete; it was a reasonably competitive bomber compared to what other navies were using. There was also nothing wrong with it at Coral Sea and did the job very well against the light carrier *Shoho*. The problem at Midway was the way the attack was set up, coming in alone and without fighter cover against a well-organized defense. It was never a case of a "brave sacrifice" in an "obsolete plane,"—the problem was the complete lack of coordination with other attack elements. The slow cruising speed of the Devastator did not help with strike coordination. The subsequent withdrawal of the Devastator from front-line duty was planned long beforehand and when the more modern Avengers were used in the same way, the result was the same.

Because of the heavy losses, torpedo bombers were most cost-effective against ships that had reduced AA capabilities, lacked escorts, or were less able to take evasive action. The best use of torpedo bombers was against ships that had been crippled, in harbor or against shipping.

Torpedo bombers could be equipped with depth charges, bombs, or rockets instead of torpedoes but then so could fighters and dive bombers. Toward the end of the war, fewer torpedo bombers were carried and those that remained were used mainly for other tasks such as bombing, ASW, or AEW duty.

## Dive Bombers

The main advantage with dive bombing was accuracy. The steeper the dive the more accurate the dive bomber was. The uncertainty in estimating and compensating for the forward speed of the aircraft was much reduced. The very low release point also meant that the target had very little time for evasive maneuvers. The short exposure time and high speed made the dive bomber a very difficult target for AA.

The main disadvantage of dive bombing was that the bomber had to be small enough to survive the high-g pull-out, limiting the number and size of the bombs carried. For obvious reasons, a four-engine bomber would have problems handling and surviving the pull-out. Accuracy and small size is a very good fit for single-engine bombers operating from a carrier and targeting other ships.

Diving from high altitude, dive bombers depended on clear skies and an absence of cloud layers obstructing the view of the target. Dive bombers tended to be more successful in areas with clear weather like the Mediterranean and the Pacific, less so in Northern European waters. With a clear view of the target and sitting at an altitude of 10,000 feet, the pilot can distinguish target features about 1–2 feet across. For the pilot, a warship appears as a very large target and he has no problems identifying even relatively small details of the target ship as he prepares for the attack.

Dive bombers liked to start the attack from a relatively high altitude, up to 20,000 feet, in order to avoid AA and CAP as far as possible before the dive has started. The approach was often a slow climb to this altitude. As AA fire began, the formation could go into a shallow dive to increase speed, then slightly varying both the dive and the course to give the AA gunners a target that varied in all dimensions. The actual dive itself would depend on the tactical situation: it might start as a shallow glide at high speed to get in position or it might be a steep dive right away. The final part of the dive was at an angle of about 60–70° and this is where the aiming was done. Control was disciplined with stick and ailerons only; any rudder input was to be avoided as any skidding would throw off the aim. Steeper dives were more accurate but also more difficult to control.

Attacking was typically in single file. The commander in the lead plane selected the target and the others followed him down in a line astern. Those awaiting their turn flew a pattern that fed planes into the file at the required intervals. Some distance was maintained between the planes, a minimum of 3–4 seconds, typically 5 seconds or more, so as not to be hit by the blast of bomb of the plane in front of you. Having several dive-bomber units attacking at the same time was avoided for largely the same reasons. There was also a risk of interfering with each other's bombing runs. However, the risk of midair collision could be offset by the advantage of saturating the AA defenses and doing an anvil style of attack. Another approach was to attack in small formations, for example three bombers at a time with the middle bomber leading the way and the other two following him down as his wingmen. Keeping formation complicated the dive but allowed for more attacks to be done in a shorter time.

A dive from a cruising altitude of 12,000 feet to release altitude of 2,000 feet takes roughly 30 seconds. The time of fall of a bomb released at 2,000 feet is about 3 seconds. A ship at 30 knots travels about 50m in 3 seconds, which is not much compared to the 200–300m length of a major warship. A well-trained pilot can hit repeatedly within about 10–20m which should be compared to the 25–40m width of a major warship. This means that an attack can be made on any quarter and that a major warship is only able to do very limited evasive maneuvering while the bomb falls. On the other hand, once the dive has started, the pilot has committed himself to an aiming point and thus to where he thinks the target is going to be when it is time to release the bomb. If the target has maneuvered somewhere else, the pilot will have to adjust his dive and his accuracy will suffer.

Dive bombers were relatively certain of their aim sideways but had greater uncertainty along the flight path. For this reason, they liked setting up the attack along the length of the ship. During a steep dive the horizontal speed drops to that of the ship and for this reason the preferred approach was usually from astern. This is why most ships had their AA set up with good firing angles toward the stern (literally a cover-your-rear kind of thing). This attack profile is actually quite similar to how seagulls and terns like to set up their attacks on encroaching humans.

Attacking in a file, it was very important that the commander in the lead plane did a good job of setting up the attack run. If so, everybody else

— 12,000 feet

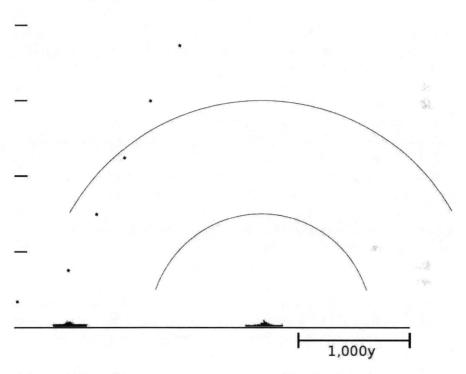

1,000y

A formation of dive bombers executing an attack on a carrier with a battleship close astern providing AA support. The dots show the approximate path and angle of the dive bombers. They would typically dive about something like 2,000 feet apart but might dive closer together or with a much greater separation. Circle arcs indicate approximate effective range of 20 and 40 mm AA fire at 1000 yards and 2000 yards respectively. To scale.

following him down would also have a good attack run. If he failed in the setup, those following him would often miss as well. With a squadron of 12 planes and a separation of 5 seconds, the attack takes 60 seconds. During that time the target ship can do significant maneuvering. Even if the lead plane did a good setup, later planes might still face an awkward attack run. The very high hit percentages scored by Vals against RN cruisers *Cornwall* and *Dorsetshire*, around 80 percent, were most likely based on the commanders succeeding with perfect setups.

In an interview, Ju-87 pilot Heinz Migeod said that the standard diving angle was 70° and standard release height was 500m (about 1,500 feet). This is for small land targets and in the absence of strong defenses. RN carrier *Indomitable*, attacked during Operation *Pedestal*, was felt to be huge and, not taking evasive action, was impossible to miss. Tanks were difficult to find and hit, too small and too nimble and usually dispersed. Better targets were bridges, buildings, and ships with the latter being the favorite target.

The Ju-87 was slow but agile. It could out-turn attacking fighters and indeed dogfight successfully. Ju-87 ace Hans-Ulrich Rudel had 25 air-to-air kills. Migeod himself was shot down while target fixated on a Hurricane. The Val and Dauntless also had similar characteristics. USN dive bomber pilot Stanley "Swede" Vejtasa shot down three Zeros while flying a Dauntless at Coral Sea.

A release height of 2,000–3,000 feet is typical against heavily defended targets but can be as low as 1,500 feet, in which case most bombs will hit a ship. The release height used, that is between 3,000 and 1,500 feet, is essentially an exercise in raw courage in the face of intense AA and ultimately in the willingness to take casualties. Minimum release height was mainly limited by the altitude needed for the pull-out and the risk of being hit by fragments from your own bomb (which could be mitigated by using an AP bomb or a delay fuze but then you have to take into account the danger posed to the plane after you). A release height of 1,000 feet could be considered the lower limit. After having used the dive brakes to bleed off most of the energy in the dive and after having done a sharp pull-out, a dive bomber was not necessarily going all that fast. They were also very low, presenting good targets for defending fighters bent on vengeance.

Dive bombers dive at about 35–45 percent of the speed of sound while the terminal velocity of a free-falling bomb is about 80–90 percent. The low release height of a dive bombing attack means that the bomb will not have had the time to reach terminal velocity, only about 50 percent of the speed of sound. This means that AP bombs might only be marginally useful and that deck armor can be quite effective against dive bombing. A bomb released higher up will have more time to get closer to terminal velocity which will provide better penetration. On the other hand, the higher release height will also mean that the bomb will be less accurate. Plunging fire from heavy naval artillery at long range typically also hit with a higher vertical velocity than did bombs from dive bombers. Modern battleships with thick deck armor were largely immune against dive bombers, although bombs and strafing from dive bombers could still be used to suppress AA for a later attack by the deadlier but more vulnerable torpedo bombers.

An HE bomb typically has an instantaneous or short delay fuse while an AP bomb has a longer delay fuse. An HE bomb is effective at wrecking a lightly built flight deck but might or might not be effective against an armored deck. A HE bomb will not penetrate the ship's vitals and will not sink it. An AP bomb will usually punch a hole in a lightly built flight and then explode deep within the vitals of the ship, possibly wrecking the propulsion plant and slowing the ship down, to be sunk by the next attack. Against an armored flight deck, the AP bomb has a much greater chance of penetrating the deck but will most likely not penetrate as deep as against an unarmored flight deck. With a smaller explosive charge, an AP bomb will be less effective at wrecking the flight deck and the flight deck will be relatively easy to repair.

Dive bombing can be done with almost any aircraft, like a fighter. The first requirement is to arrange so the bombs can clear the propeller. One way is to have bomb racks on the wings outside of the propeller disc. A centerline bomb will have to have some sort of device that throws the bomb clear of the propeller, otherwise the dive angle will be limited, typically to 40–50° depending on the weight of the bomb. Without dive brakes, the dive will have to be initiated from a relatively low altitude and at a low speed. One trick was to use the landing gear as dive brakes; this was used by both Hellcats and Corsairs. Another trick was to use the propeller pitch control to increase propeller drag but this also made the dive less stable and more difficult to control. With a faster dive, the release altitude will have to be higher up to provide enough room for the pull-out. The alternative to a high release is to do a shallower dive of 30–50° but the flatter dive was less accurate.

Fighters struggled to dive bomb well-defended targets. The flatter attack profile meant an easier target and a longer exposure to AA. Without rear gunners, the attacking formation could only defend itself against enemy fighters by evasive maneuvering and it was then easy to break up the formation.

Dive bombing was a fine art requiring specialized equipment and extensive training. After the IJN had been sunk, and with no other enemy navy to replace them as targets, dedicated dive bombers were no longer needed to the extent they had been before. Toward the end of the war, ground support had become the most common mission, and that did not necessarily mean using a dive bomber. Emphasis shifted to the more versatile fighter-bomber, for example using rockets that operated much like the guns that fighter pilots were accustomed to.

## Kamikazes

Kamikazes commonly attacked using either the high or low approach. The high approach was basically a dive-bomber attack. Any plane could be used. There was no need for a bomb sight or to throw the bomb clear of the propeller; there was also no need for dive brakes as there was no pull-out. Diving into the target at maximum speed, the speed of bomb at impact was still relatively low and armor piercing performance was not very good. The low mode involved sneaking in below radar and while still outside of automatic AA range to pull up to about 1,500 feet and then plunge through automatic AA fire using gravity to complete the attack even if the pilot was hit or the controls shot away. The best attack would be a coordinated attack by several planes with both methods being used. With poor armor penetration, kamikazes were mainly useful against unarmored targets such as US carriers, destroyers, and landing craft.

The Ohka was a manned glide bomb. It weighed 2,140kg and had a 1,200kg warhead. Released from a land-based twin-engine bomber at high altitude it then glided toward the target area. It could only glide for so long and had to be released within about 20 miles of the target. This was well within range of radar and CAP which made it a very dangerous mission for the bomber. During the final approach, rockets boosted it to about 80 percent the speed of sound which made it much more effective against armored targets as well as largely impervious to AA.

## Guided Bombs

Guided bombs are standoff weapons used to do precision attacks on heavily defended targets, typically ships and bridges. Development had started before the war with Germany and the US being the most active in the development.

The German Henschel Hs-293 was the first guided bomb to go operational which it did in mid-1943. It was essentially a glider but with a small rocket engine that powered it for 10 seconds. It could be released from any altitude. Initial versions had a flare and a radio receiver and was steered to the target by an operator with a joystick. A later version had a TV camera in the nose with the picture transmitted by radio to the operator, enabling it to attack through clouds.

The German Fritz-X was perhaps the most successful guided bomb of the war. It had cruciform-shaped flight surfaces and could do limited gliding. Guidance consisted of a flare and a radio receiver controlling the flight surfaces. It was released from high altitude by a level bomber and then steered toward the target by an operator with a joystick. Approaching the target at high speed it required a well-trained operator. The advantage was that it had good armor penetration. Operational in mid-1943, it sank or damaged several Allied warships. The primary defenses against this bomb was effective CAP plus jamming the radio link.

The US Azon bomb was similar to the Fritz-X but was actually a guidance kit strapped to a standard 1,000lb bomb. First used in mid-1944, mainly against bridges, it was guided only in the sideways direction (Azimuth Only = AzOn).

The US Bat bomb had a complete radar inside the nose and guided itself to its target, primarily ships. It was by far the most advanced guided bomb of its time, costing about $70 million to develop. It was released at 15,000–25,000 feet about 10–20 miles from the target area. It would then glide toward that area and then head for the ship with the strongest radar return, much like an actual bat would against its prey. There was no need for an operator or a radio link—the Bat guided itself to the target it had selected. This autonomous operation was also a weakness as the radar could quite easily be fooled. The Bat became operational in late 1944 and was used successfully against Japanese shipping. It was initially carried by B-24s but was quickly fitted to Corsair, Helldiver, and Avenger aircraft. What was available in 1944 could well have been available two years earlier, had the need for them been understood and had the resources been there. One can only speculate how the carrier battles would have turned out had it been available in 1942.

All of these early guided bombs were quite easy to jam. With the limited electronics of the day, once the enemy had figured out how the guidance worked, it was a reasonably simple job to build a jammer and there was really no cost-effective way around being jammed. The advent of the atomic bomb also put a damper on the development of guided bombs, as precision was now seen as less important. Guided bombs were not necessarily liked by the aircrews as they tended to be quite vulnerable during the guidance phase. For several years then, these bombs were seen as suitable only for special targets. This situation prevailed until the late 1960s with the introduction of the laser-guided Paveway series, the first truly practical guided bomb.

## Pressing Home the Attack

Pressing home an attack with more aggressiveness will probably result in more hits but will also result in higher losses. That is the very cold and matter-of-fact description of an attack, but also what all combat eventually boils down to—the fight between the skill and determination of the defenders and the skill and courage of the attackers.

Carrier planes were cheap and the pilots were few in number compared to the overall manpower required in a carrier task force. From a systems point of view, carrier planes were very much expendable while the carriers represented the core of a very large investment. A Hellcat cost in the order of $50,000 to produce, whereas an *Essex* class carrier cost about $50–75 million. A carrier is then worth about 1,000–1,500 planes. From a purely economic perspective, planes and pilots are therefore highly expendable, to the point of being considered ammunition (actually not that far from the truth—a torpedo cost something like $10,000). The cost of the pilot is more of a moral question but the cost of training was probably somewhere in the range of $5,000–10,000. The widow's pension was around $12,000. These numbers had to be kept in mind when commanders faced a decision of whether or not to launch an attack at long range with the prospect of the planes then not having enough fuel to return to the carriers.

While on this topic, it is interesting to note that the cost of military hardware in World War II was roughly $2,000 per ton. This number is a reasonably good estimate for pretty much everything from shovels to trucks to tanks to carriers. Aircraft were more expensive at about $10,000 per ton, but then aluminum cost more than steel. As Japanese planes were about half the weight of corresponding American types, it can then be assumed that their production cost was about half that of American planes, making them look even more like ammunition, which should be kept in mind when looking at kamikazes.

Beginning in 1944, the Japanese faced a very effective CAP and not many aircraft survived the gauntlet to make an attack on the fleet. Suffering heavy losses just getting to the target, as they did at Philippine Sea, it makes sense to make sure you get the hit once you finally get to the target. If that involves suicidal bravery then so be it—the overall loss rate does not change that much. The kamikaze tactic was then a very rational answer to the effectiveness of CAP as enabled by radar and fighter direction.

Of the kamikazes that reached the target area, about half were shot down by CAP. Of those that remained, about two-thirds were shot down by AA or missed while one third hit a target. It is estimated that the kamikazes were about 7–10 times more effective in terms of hits achieved per sortie and about 1.7–2 times more effective in terms of hits achieved per plane lost. Overall about 2,500 planes were expended to achieve 474 hits on various USN ships.

With the numbers above for the relative cost of aircraft and carriers, those 2,500 planes correspond to roughly one fleet carrier—a very good exchange for those 474 hits. In all, kamikazes were a most cost-effective weapon, both in economic and human terms, which is of course why they were used in spite of the moral problems involved.

The IJN approach of pressing home the attack, including the use of kamikaze tactics as its ultimate expression, was entirely correct. The USN never required that kind of commitment from its pilots, but certainly still selected them for youth, bravado, and an appetite for risk-taking as well as encouraging valor and sacrifice by rewarding it with medals. Convincing the individual to sacrifice himself for the good of the group has always been a necessary part of war.

Of course, with electronics gradually taking over the role of final guidance, the issue of how aggressively to press home an attack is replaced by that of who has the best engineers, not the most courageous and dedicated pilots.

## After the Attack

Convoys, fish schools, and flocks of birds all abide by the same basic principle, that there is safety in numbers. By grouping together there is a better chance of survival. The core mechanism is to locally overload the predator, allowing most of the prey to escape. The predators have to spread out to find their prey and once found there is too much to eat for one particular predator while the rest go hungry. To counter this, the predators will have to assemble some sort of wolf-pack using some sort of fighter direction, but if that has any sort of lag to it the attackers will have all the time they need to escape. This applies even without any kind of defense mechanism like escorts or rear gunners. When those are available, the effectiveness of convoying is further increased.

After the attack, the first priority was to find friends. Type and unit did not matter, just somebody to share the "I am a target" property with, for mutual benefit.

## Redirecting or Recalling an Attack

When a strike is sent off, it is given the position as well as course and speed of the target. The strike is also informed of where its own carriers are expected to be when returning from the strike. No radio communication is expected to take place between the strike and the carriers.

After an attack has been sent off, things might change. There might be new information about the location of target, and/or the carrier formation decides it needs to go somewhere else than originally planned at the time the strike was launched. Using radio is the obvious solution here but meant breaking radio silence. Depending on the tactical situation, this drawback had to be weighed against whatever could be achieved by using radio.

# CHAPTER 7

# Defending Against Aerial Attack

## Remaining Undetected

This mainly involves killing enemy snoopers before they detect the task force and before they have sent of the sighting report. Alternatively, it involves chasing off the snooper before he has figured out the true composition of the task force. Faulty sighting reports were perhaps the most effective defense there was in actual combat.

## Running Away

When it is known that an enemy task force is nearby and that a strike can be expected, a carrier can simply run away in some direction. A strike can take an hour or more to arrive and during that time a task force can disappear over the horizon. If a strike (or spotter) is detected on radar, it is also quite possible to simply move out of its path.

A possible complication here is any friendly aircraft that might be out on a mission. For them to find their way back to the carrier, the carrier had to provide them with its future movements. Radio would be the obvious way to signal the change but that meant breaking radio silence. It also might not work due to enemy jamming or some other problem. Japanese doctrine had the option of leaving a destroyer at the old rendezvous point that would then signal to the returning planes the direction of the carriers using a signaling lamp and Morse code. This would probably work in peacetime but in a combat scenario the destroyer might well be sunk by the strike.

Even if caught by a strike, it is still useful to run away from it as it gives CAP longer time to deal with the attacking aircraft while the attackers try to catch up and set up a coordinated attack.

## Hiding in a Squall

In the tropics there are frequent squalls, which usually appear in hot weather with not much wind. They look like small thunderstorms. They can be seen from quite far away and they move relatively slowly across the horizon. When sailing in an area with squalls you can sometimes see several at the same time and you might or might not be hit by one.

Squalls are in the order of a few miles wide and move at about 5–20 knots. Inside the squall, visibility is very limited and it is usually gusty and raining. The poor visibility and the rain makes it useful as refuge for a ship under attack. If a squall happens to be close by when a strike is approaching, just head for it. Depending on the size of the squall and how the ship moves in relation to it, a ship can hide in it for many minutes. While inside, flight operations might have to be suspended depending on conditions. AA is also affected.

## Combat Air Patrol

The main task was to break up attacking formations, not necessarily to shoot down attacking planes. Bombers usually flew in a tight formation as it provided mutual support by their rear gunners. Once the formation was broken up, isolated bombers where much easier to shoot down by both CAP and AA. Single bombers were also much less effective as attackers. Breaking up an attacking formation does not necessarily require a high-performance fighter or a nimble dogfighter. Anything that can dive through a formation with guns blazing can do the job.

Scrambled fighters need to get to altitude as fast as possible. The initial rate of climb was around 2,200 (Wildcat) or 3,000–3,500 (Zero & Hellcat) feet per minute. It took 4–6 minutes to get to 10,000 feet. The Bearcat, successor to the Wildcat and Hellcat, was probably the fastest climber of the war. With an initial climb rate of 6,000–6,500 feet per minute, it could climb to 10,000 feet in 2 minutes with a record of 91 seconds, which stood unbroken well into the jet age.

Early in the war, CAP was stationed above the fleet. If there was a definite direction from which the enemy was expected to attack, CAP could be stationed something like 25 miles in that direction.

CAP stationed close to the ships was layered—a lower layer to defend against torpedo bombers and a higher layer at 15,000–18,000 feet to defend against dive bombers. Dive bombers liked to come in as high as possible to make interception difficult, ideally passing unmolested over the CAP before starting their dives.

Early USN practice was to post Dauntless scouts at low level to intercept any torpedo bombers. The intention was that the fighters should not have to leave that hard-won high altitude to go down and then to work their way back up to altitude. This practice did not work very well, as these bombers were too slow to effectively intercept. Focus then came on intercepting further out, before torpedo bombers had peeled off and started their glide to low altitude.

Time aloft was up to 2–3 hours, less for the shorter-range Wildcat. Fighters typically had 4–5 hours' endurance and could stay up longer if needed but a good reserve of fuel was maintained in case combat developed. Time to rearm and refuel CAP depends on many factors but was much less than the time aloft meaning that most fighters assigned to CAP could be kept in the air. Time spent at high altitude, above 12,000 feet, was often limited by the amount of oxygen carried for the pilot.

Dive bombers are comparatively more vulnerable to CAP on the approach to the target area than to ship AA. Once in a dive with dive brakes extended, however, it was difficult for a fighter to stay with them in the dive; a fighter would tend to overshoot and would have to do a more or less continuous barrel roll and only be able to come in for short bursts.

After the attack dives had been executed, the dive bombers were quite vulnerable. They were no longer in formation, there was no mutual support, they might be smoking and limping, and they were down low at sea level. They were also not necessarily going very fast, having limited their speed during the dive and then executed a very sharp pull-out. This is good opportunity for defending CAP fighters to score kills, albeit of the revenge variety.

Shooting down a bomber is usually a two-stage process. The first part is to stay at a distance and to pick off the rear gunner. Once he is seen to be slumped over and not moving, it is then time to move in to short range for a definite kill, wasting as little time and ammunition as possible before continuing on with the next attack. If the attacking bombers are flying in a formation and sticking to it, it is possible to come in from below with less of a danger from the tail gunner, thus shortening the process. If the formation breaks up to avoid this, then so much the better; breaking up the formation will make the attack much less effective, which is why they were ordered to hold on to the formation at more or less all costs. In essence then, losses were accepted in order to drive home the attack.

The rear gunner will of course shoot back, sometimes discouraging or hurting the attacking fighter. There was nothing to stop the rear gunner from shooting off his own tail; he simply had to make sure not to do it. One of the finer points of piloting would be to execute a sideslip to give the rear gunner a less obstructed angle while still keeping his place in the formation.

## AA Guns

Effective range against a target flying in a very straight and predictable course could be quite long, mainly limited by accuracy of fire control and of the range of the gun. This is the scenario for which heavy AA is well suited, and fire could start as soon as the attacking force appeared over the fleet.

Against a maneuvering target, effective range is much shorter, dictated mainly by the time of flight of the shell to the target. Comparing our two favorite AA guns, the 5-inch and the 40mm, the 40mm had a higher muzzle velocity but its lighter shell slowed down faster due to air resistance. The range at with the 5-inch has a significant advantage in time of flight, say a 20 percent advantage, can be calculated from external ballistics and turns out to be in the order of 3,000–5,000 yards (or 9,000–15,000 feet). Against a maneuvering target, this is a very long range and probably outside of what can be considered effective. This means that against maneuvering targets, 5-inch fire did not have a significant range advantage compared to the 40mm. Against non-maneuvering targets, 5-inch fire still had the advantage of using longer range directors, and for that reason effective range was much greater.

In practice, many targets fall somewhere between the two classifications of "straight and predictable" and "maneuvering and unpredictable" and the effective range of heavy AA will vary accordingly. Even if the plane itself could maneuver, it still had to keep its place in the formation. In the final stage of the attack, jinking by the pilot has the effect of reducing the effectiveness of AA but at the cost of making his own aiming harder. Since "effective range" really is not well defined, it also depends on circumstances such as how much ammunition is available and the value of the target being defended.

The pushover point for a dive bomber is normally beyond effective range of all AA. Heavy AA could reach them there but was not very effective against small and agile planes. The only effective defense was a high rate of fire during the final stage of the attack. The ship being attacked had it easier since it was coming straight at it and because the attackers had to come close to be sure of a hit, but the best shooting was after the bomb had been released. Volume of fire is important to discourage the attacker into an early and inaccurate release. Escorting ships had more difficult deflection shots and were further away but could still contribute to the psychological pressure on the pilots.

For the USN, 40mm fire against a dive bomber started when the target was at an altitude of 9,000–10,000 feet with the effective range being around 6,000 feet. 20mm fire started at 4,000–6,000 feet with effective range being about 3,000 feet. Kills by 20mm were often revenge killings (and thus less useful against kamikazes). The early quad 1.1-inch had similar power to a single 20mm. Japanese 25mm fire was similar to a single 20mm, effective up to about 3,000 feet.

Fire discipline was very important. Early in the war, shooting was often against targets too far away, already engaged by others, or having already released its bomb or torpedo. The problem is not so much the wasted ammunition but that the wrong target has been selected. A lookout might also be too distracted by all the spectacular fireworks around him to be of much use.

The critical period for a defender was from when the attacker was within effective range to when he dropped his ordnance. For a dive bomber this was from 6,000 feet to about 1,000–3,000 feet. Traversing an altitude of 3,000 feet takes about 10 seconds. The task then became to fire as many shells as possible during this time window and, as each plane released its bomb, to shift to the next plane in the stream as it entered its dive and the killing zone. Dive bombers usually attacked in single file with enough separation not to be hit by blast from the previous plane's bomb, which gave the defenders the opportunity to shoot at each plane as it attacked.

During these 10 seconds, a single 5-inch gun will have time to fire about three shells while a quad 40mm mount will fire about 100 shells. A single 20mm will fire up to 75 shells (a spiral magazine holds 60 shells making it natural to change magazine while shifting target) during that time but will not be within effective range for most of it. The early 1.1-inch quad mount fired about 70 shells during 10 seconds (making it roughly equivalent to a single 20mm).

USN quad 40mm Bofors mounts, with a Mk 51 director in foreground. Photo taken on USS *Lexington* (CV-16).

The Japanese 25mm could theoretically fire about 40 shells per barrel but its magazine held only 15 shells forcing at least one re-load during the 10 second interval, roughly halving the volume to 60 shells from a triple mount (making it roughly equivalent to a single 20mm).

The British pompom could fire about 16 shells per barrel from ammunition feed boxes containing 112–140 shells per barrel, firing about 128 rounds per octuple mount during a 10 second attack run. This mount had problems with stoppages, and actual shells fired were sometimes much less. The relatively low muzzle velocity meant that effective range was less than that of the 40mm.

## Psychological Factors

When a dive bomber attacks a large target like a carrier, if the pilot is well trained and left undisturbed, almost every bomb will hit. In practice only about one bomb in ten hit the target, while around one plane in five was shot down, in rough numbers and on the average. This means that by far the most important effect of AA was to make the pilot miss, not necessarily shooting him down. Actually succeeding in shooting him down, in itself, had only a minor effect on the outcome of the battle. The single most important battle within the carrier war was that of pilot courage vs. how scary the AA was.

Breaking up an attacking formation was important in itself. With the formation broken up, mutual support and coordination is lost. The courage of the peer-pressured group is lost and replaced by the fear and survival instinct of the isolated individual. The breaking up of a formation is therefore the primary task of CAP, not shooting down aircraft. Heavy AA fire is usually not enough to break up an incoming formation, by then it is too late.

Japanese pilots were brave but tended to be careless in how they completely ignored AA. It appeared that in their warrior spirit, they were fully prepared to die. This might be good prior to weapons release, but when they survived it seemed to come as a surprise to them. By not making evasive maneuvers while escaping, some were needlessly shot down (which inflated the usefulness of 20mm AA guns on US ships).

## Evasive Maneuvering

Aerial attacks develop relatively slowly. They can be seen approaching. The aircraft of the day were about 5–10 times faster than the ships they were attacking but it was very possible to try to evade an incoming attack. Evasive maneuvering was not only a very valid defense; it was in many cases the most effective means of defense. The maneuverability of a ship and the skill of the captain were perhaps as important as any other factor in the survivability of a ship. A fast and reliable way to get sunk was by not maneuvering.

Torpedo bombers had to carry that big heavy torpedo. They tended to be slow and if they were not slow to begin with, then they had to slow down for the launch of the torpedo. Once launched, the torpedo was not much faster than a ship. Standard tactic against torpedo bombers was firstly to simply run away, building up as much speed as possible; secondly, once the torpedoes had been launched, to dodge them. Sometimes easy, sometimes not, depending on how well coordinated and determined the attack was. A carrier that was nimble and a captain who was cool under extreme pressure could pay huge dividends for the survivability of the carrier, much more important than armor thickness and so on.

A standard tactic against high-level bombers was to simply do nothing until the bombardiers had lined up the target. Once they had committed themselves and the bombs had been dropped, then simply step aside. It would take a while before the bombs arrived.

Dive bombers were less sensitive to evasive maneuvering of this type as they dropped their bombs so late but still needed to control their dive all the way down. The best defensive tactic seems to have been doing tight maneuvers like full circles. Presenting a broadside view to the diving bombers also worked well. It allowed all AA guns to fire and it presented a more difficult target.

During the 30 seconds or so that the dive took from an approach height of 12,000 feet, a major warship moving at 30 knots had time to move about two boat lengths. A warship typically has a minimum turning diameter of about 3–4 boat lengths. A major warship is 200–250 yards long and has a turning diameter of about 600–1,000 yards. Actual turning diameter, for a given hull length, is influenced by factors such as hull shape as well as the placing and size of rudders and can vary considerably from design to design. The *Yamatos* were very maneuverable for their size which might have to do with the skeg being an extra rudder. The *Fletcher* class of destroyers had only one rather small rudder and had a very large turning diameter for a destroyer, approaching that of an *Iowa* class battleship (the later *Sumner* and *Gearing* classes had twin rudders).

On a major warship it takes about 15–30 seconds to turn the rudder over from straight ahead to hard over, that is to a deflection of 30–35°. On a destroyer it might take around 5 seconds. A deflection more than 30–35° did not result in sharper turn, it only slowed down the ship and put great stress on the rudder. After the rudder has been put hard over, it then takes

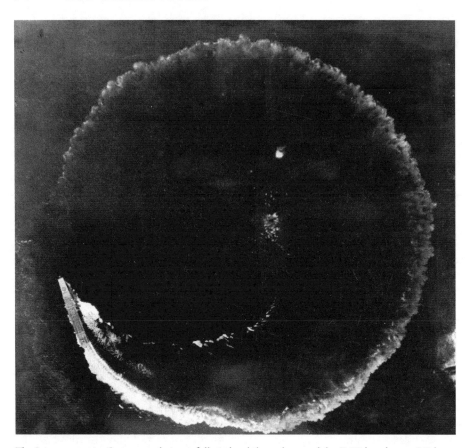

The Japanese carrier *Soryu* completing a full circle while under attack by B-17 bombers at Midway. The circle is not as tight as it could have been, probably to maintain speed. Japanese carriers almost always did full circles while under attack by level or dive bombers.

several seconds more for the turn to fully develop. Once in a turn a ship can choose to stay in that turn. Doing that avoids going in a relatively straight line while the rudder is being turned over to the other side. Staying in a hard turn might be the most difficult maneuver for the attacker to handle despite being somewhat predictable.

While in a fully developed turn, the speed of a major warship drops to about 15–20 knots. For this reason, the sharpest turns may be avoided and reserved for really critical situations like avoiding a torpedo. A smaller ship like a destroyer slows down less in a turn, having more excess horsepower at lower speeds. A destroyer will also accelerate faster out of the turn.

The latency inherent in executing a turn means that it is impossible to turn in unison with another ship by simply observing what the other ship is doing.

There has to be some sort of general command for a fleet to turn in unison. It is this latency that is the core problem why ships sometimes collide for no apparent reason. It is not enough to react to what the other ship is doing, the reaction has to be started before it is apparent what the other ship is doing—hence the need for communication between ships in close proximity.

Merchant ships do not have the large balanced rudders of a warship, only a relatively small rudder and a hull shape optimized for directional stability. This means that a carrier built from a merchant vessel will most likely be relatively poor at doing evasive maneuvers. The *Titanic* is a good example of the problems inherent in turning a large passenger liner—both the latency and the slow turn—in this case to avoid an iceberg that appeared ahead.

At low speeds a ship is usually more sluggish in a turn. Rudders need water flowing over them to have any effect, and the faster the flow the more sideways force the rudders can provide. A ship that has been slowed down is vulnerable, not just because it is slow but also because it cannot turn. When an attack was expected, speed was increased to maximum to be able to do really radical maneuvers.

Ships with steam turbines take quite a long time to work up the pressure in the boilers. It can take a good half an hour for steam pressure to build and for maximum speed to be reached. This is a danger for a carrier steaming at cruising speed, as it can be caught before it has had time to build speed. This is exactly what happened to RN carrier *Glorious* when caught and sunk by German battleships during the Norwegian campaign. Similarly, the transition from cruising speed to maximum speed needed for flight operations will take some minutes.

A carrier formation cannot just steam at full speed all day long; the escorting destroyers do not have that endurance. It had to be refueled every few days and this was a constant headache for all commanders, before and during the battles. After the battle, everybody huddled around the nearest available tanker.

Ships can come to a rapid stop by reversing the propellers. On a major warship the stopping distance, from full speed ahead, is about a mile. In a crash stop like this the rudders are kept amidships. The battleship *Wisconsin* did an experiment where the rudders, under manual control and operating independently, were both turned inwards like closing barn doors. This was done as the propellers went from flank speed ahead to flank speed astern. The result was a violent stop in less than the length of the ship. This maneuver became known as the Barn Door Stop. The rudders survived the experiment but it was never repeated. Later it was discovered that the rudders had indeed been severely stressed and had to be adjusted.

Accelerating a major warship from a crash stop, with full steam pressure available, is initially quite rapid, taking about a minute to get to half of the maximum speed. Then it takes in the order of 10 minutes to get to within a knot or two of maximum speed. Reaching absolute top speed is then a quite laborious process, taking perhaps another 10 minutes or more.

## Getting Rid of Combustibles

High-octane aviation gasoline ("avgas") is very combustible. Avgas actually has a much higher energy density than high explosives because it uses the oxygen in the air, while high explosives contain their own oxidizer. High explosives also sacrifice some energy density for a faster (=more violent) explosion. The avgas of a single fueled plane typically contains more energy than a 1 ton HE bomb. Should this avgas be allowed to leak and collect as fumes in an enclosed space, eventual ignition is likely and the resulting explosion will be massive. The first thing to do in preparation of an incoming attack is therefore to purge all fueling pipes. Removing any bombs and torpedoes lying around on the decks, usually by sending them back to the magazines, is also an obvious priority.

Then we have the question of the planes on board, particularly those that have been fueled and armed. The biggest threat is probably those stored in the hangar. Planes on the flight deck can still make a very nasty fire but there will most likely not be an avgas explosion. On an armored flight deck, should any ordnance explode from the heat of a fire, this should likely be a survivable event. On a lightly built flight deck, the consequences of such an event will be much more catastrophic. Should a fire start on the hangar deck, among fueled and armed planes, then this is a very real threat to the survival of the ship, with or without an armored flight deck. It is therefore much better to absorb an incoming strike without any planes on the decks. The question then is if it is possible to get the planes off the decks in the face of an incoming strike.

The time to move a 30-plane strike from the hangars to the flight deck is about 15 minutes using a 60 second elevator cycle time and two elevators. Time to warm up engines is about 15 minutes. Time to fly off the strike is about 10 minutes using a 20 second interval.

These numbers should be compared to the 15–30 minutes warning time that an air search radar will likely provide, having a range of 50–80 miles. It should be possible to have a strike ready to go with engines idling (or idling and periodically shut off). Ready to go with warmed-up engines, the deck load should be able to take off before the strike arrives over the formation, otherwise not.

The same warning times applies to CAP launched to ward off the incoming strike. As can be seen, the CAP really needs to be airborne and at altitude when the incoming strike is spotted on radar.

## Armored Decks

The final line of defense is the ship's armor, particularly if placed at the level of the flight deck. Carriers of the *Illustrious* and *Implacable* classes, as well as the *Taiho* and *Shinano*, all had flight deck armor about 3 inches thick. This armor was generally placed over the hangar only; the ends of the flight deck generally had lighter armor or no armor at all.

Armor of this thickness provided protection against standard high-explosive bombs of up to 1,000lbs as dropped from dive bombers. The qualification "as dropped from dive bombers" is important; it means that the bombs are released from a relatively low height of 1,500–3,000 feet. The bomb will not build up much speed in the fall and will not be very good at penetrating armor. Furthermore, bombs come in many different types with different properties and optimized for different tasks. Finally, the actual strength of the flight deck may vary by quality of armor and by design decisions. The impact of a bomb is a very violent event and as such simply is not very predictable. What all this means is that an armored deck can indeed withstand fairly substantial bombs but with some uncertainty as to exactly how heavy.

In this context it should perhaps be noted that carrier-based bombers tend to be quite constrained in how heavy a bomb they can carry. Carrier operations are generally conducted at long range which means carrying lots of fuel. Loaded down with both fuel and a bomb, they still have to be able to take off from the short runway of a carrier deck. We then have a very hard limit on how heavy a bomb can be carried, which improves the likelihood that the armored flight deck will successfully withstand it.

Most USN and IJN carriers did not have armored flight decks, only the hangar deck had armor. The flight deck was typically of a light construction with 3–4-inch teak wood planking laid on steel girders, offering little protection against bombs. On USN carriers the wood was laid on top of a 0.2-inch steel surface, but being quite thin the steel did not add much strength or protection; it was still the wood that carried the surface loads of the deck. For some reason the planking was always athwartship on US carriers but fore-and-aft on IJN carriers.

## Damage Control

All navies knew that their carriers were vulnerable and so put considerable thought into damage control. Without going into the details of equipment and methods, how well did they succeed?

First we have the catastrophes, where a bomb landed among parked planes loaded with fuel and ordnance. These include the four Japanese carriers sunk at Midway and the *Princeton*, *Bunker Hill*, and *Franklin* later in the war. In these cases, damage control was overwhelmed and the ship reduced to a burning wreck.

The next category consists of carriers hit with one or more bombs but without a large number of fueled and armed aircraft on board. In these cases, the carrier survived, regardless of nationality. Examples here include *Shokaku* at Coral Sea and Santa Cruz, *Yorktown* at Coral Sea, and *Enterprise* at both Eastern Solomons and Santa Cruz as well as *Zuikaku* at Philippine Sea. The only exception here is the small carrier *Hermes*, caught during Nagumo's foray into the Indian Ocean in 1942. Suffering many hits, it was sunk by dive bombers alone.

Then we have those carriers that were hit by both bombs and torpedoes. This applies to *Lexington* at Coral Sea, *Yorktown* at Midway, and *Hornet* at Santa Cruz. These hits all proved too much for damage control to handle. None of the ships sank before being abandoned; however, they were all scuttled.

In all, carriers proved to be able to survive considerable bomb damage and this applies to all navies. The main danger was uncontrollable fires, a problem that was unique to carriers. The Americans are often said to have had the best damage control. That might very well have been the case but the available statistics are not enough to confirm it.

A major part of damage control was to have the ship stripped of anything that could burn before going into battle. This required awareness and discipline. For example, if many layers of paint had been allowed to accumulate over the years, it would then burn quite nicely. Chipping away old paint down to the bare metal, before putting on a fresh layer, was a common and tedious activity for a wartime crew.

## Tactical Formations

Since automatic AA is only effective out to ranges of 1,000–2,000 yards, any escorts must be close by to be useful, particularly if they are to be at all effective against dive bombers. Defending against torpedo bombers, the escort can be further out, up to 2,000–6,000 yards. The shorter distance is only possible if the formation turns in unison (wagon-wheel style). Independent maneuvering requires a larger formation size, typically 2,000–3,000 yards.

All navies used the basic circular formation in some incarnation. Battleships and cruisers were kept in an inner circle. Destroyers were generally further out but could also be in the inner circle if there was room. Larger ships were better platforms to shoot from and were kept closer to the target.

The destroyers in the outer screen needed to be about 4,000 yards out from the inner screen to avoid getting hit by friendly fire. Yes, hits and shrapnel from other people's AA was a problem, a quite serious problem actually, but was simply seen as the cost of doing business. Shells were often designed to self-destruct at the end of about 4,000–4,500 yards of trajectory traveled.

The ship being attacked was usually responsible for about half the planes shot down; all escorts combined were responsible for the other half, often by becoming the targets themselves and then shooting the attackers down (particularly applicable to a large and tempting target like a battleship).

Task Force 38 maneuvering in a box formation off Japan in 1945.

IJN carriers operated their fleet carriers in pairs throughout the war. Initially the carriers maneuvered independently and with not many escorts around them. Later in the war maneuvering was more coordinated with more escorts close by to render AA support.

After the 1942 battles, there was an intense debate within the USN over whether to operate the carriers together or to have them separated. Eventually, with so many carriers becoming available, the issue became moot, as both strategies were used in conjunction. The carriers were separated into task forces each with a three–four carrier box consisting of a mix of fleet and light carriers. This made formations manageable as well as enabling mutual support, both AA and CAP. It also meant that all carriers must be doing flight operations, like steaming into the wind, at the same time. Radical maneuvers to evade bombs and torpedoes were allowed for individual ships as long as collisions were avoided and formation retained.

The RN mainly operated its carriers singly and with whatever escorts were available at the time. The RN had trained for coordinated multi-carrier operations before the war, but due to early attrition was never really able to put it into practice. The only major carrier battle in the European theater of war where more than one carrier was used was in Operation *Pedestal*, a Malta convoy. Against Japan, late in the war, there were several operations involving multiple carriers but by then the only opposition left were the kamikazes.

# CHAPTER 8

# Fighter Direction

## Usefulness

Fighter direction is very important for the efficient employment of fighters, particularly while defending as CAP. The defensive effectiveness of CAP can be increased several times. Without fighter direction, the fighters would have to select one of essentially two strategies. One would be to stay over the fleet, but that meant not intercepting the enemy until the enemy has gotten close to the fleet. It also ran the risk of interfering with AA gunfire. The other strategy would be to patrol in a rough circle around the fleet, but that meant that only some fraction of the fighters would be able to intercept the enemy and that most of the fighters would be out of position on the other side of the fleet.

CAP was also often stacked at several altitudes since the enemy strike could arrive at any altitude. Again, it is much more efficient if all the CAP can be at the right altitude for interception.

Efficient fighter direction does not really cost anything. The radar and radio equipment needed are already there for other purposes. It is simply a question of better usage of available resources by improved doctrine, organization, and training.

## Lag

Delay is the time it takes from when the enemy does something to when the fighters know what to do about it. Lag is critical for successful fighter direction. Excessive lag, beyond a minute or so, will make fighter direction much less effective.

Lag is commonly caused by saturation, when so much is happening so fast that the team is unable to keep up and fighter direction then becomes erratic.

It can happen anywhere in the chain—on the radar screen, or on the plot, or on the radio circuits used.

Lag can also be caused by the enemy, for example, by doing a complicated attack with attacks that split, change course or otherwise behave in a complex and unpredictable manner (whether or not they are conscious about their effects on the poor over-worked fighter direction team).

Avoiding lag depends heavily on organization and training, on having smooth and efficient teamwork.

## Informative vs. Directive Methods

The informative method tells the pilots where the enemy is. The pilot then has to figure out himself where to go. This was not easy to do as he did not have the full picture and was busy flying the plane anyway and worked better if the fighter had a dedicated navigator (like the Fulmar). This method was used by the RN in the early stages of the war and was easy to implement but ultimately not very effective.

The directive method tells the pilot what to do, which is much easier for pilot but also involves much more work for the fighter direction team, including remembering and tracking who has been told what and when. This quickly became the preferred method but put high demands on efficient work flow to avoid lag.

The directive method could and did break down if the fighter-direction team was saturated with too many objects to track. The first sign of saturation was an increase in lag and a decrease in accuracy caused by the lag. One solution to this problem was to go back to the informative method but that assumed that each aircraft had the capacity to handle the work offloaded to them. The best solution was obviously to streamline the information processing so that the team could handle the higher work load, but that was often easier said than done.

## Interception

Intercepting aircraft might well miss an incoming attack formation or the pilot might see it late and be at the wrong altitude. Visual spotting distance was in the order of a few miles, depending on visibility and cloud conditions. Nothing is automatic in a successful interception. The first Japanese attack during Eastern Solomons is a good example—a very muddled interception by the American fighters by an otherwise well-manned CAP.

Interception should not only allow the fighters to catch the bombers; it should ideally put them slightly above and ahead of the bomber formation. Below the bombers and the fighters might have trouble reaching an attack position. Too high above the bombers and the fighters might not see the bombers against the backdrop of the sea.

Once an intercept was achieved, it was then up to the fighters to go to work in a tactically coordinated and efficient way. There was considerable pilot skill involved in executing maneuvers to efficiently shoot down attacking bombers using as little time and ammunition as possible. This was continued until all the enemy bombers had been shot down, ammunition had been exhausted, or friendly AA became too dangerous.

## Radio Nets and Usage

Fighter direction was normally done by the carriers with each carrier controlling its own planes.

In a battle, all aircraft had had their radios set to use the same frequency (or "channel" or "net" or "circuit"). It was possible to listen to the traffic of the other carriers involved, including their planes. HF radios could use Morse code but during a battle, only voice was used (only scouts used Morse code but then they needed the range and the security). Again, lag is the critical issue here and there is no time to fiddle with codes.

As there was only one channel, it could easily be saturated with non-critical communications, for example, some pilot screaming that he has an enemy on his tail. During the 1942 battles, USN carriers had severe problems with saturation. Individual or small-scale attacks had been trained for but large-scale attacks caused the system to break down. Radio discipline was improved but the basic problem was still there.

In the 1944 battles all American aircraft had been equipped with VHF radios which gave an additional four channels which much reduced saturation. Different VHF channels were used for different purposes. For example, multi-carrier fighter direction coordination was done by communicating between the carriers using one of these VHF channels.

Japanese doctrine was to keep radio silence. There was no fighter direction and no tactical radio communication while in a fight—only hand signals were used. The purpose of radio silence was to surprise the enemy with an attack but with air-warning radar in use by the Americans, this did not work. The Japanese noted this and tried to change doctrine but it was the usual story of too little too late.

## Radar Usage

Fighter direction is based on radar. With an early "A-scope" type display, what the operator saw was a flat line representing range. A target would appear as a small squiggle on that line, with the position along the line representing range to target. The operator could turn the antenna manually. He would normally scan for targets. Once something was found, he would hold the antenna onto the target, only slowly moving it back and forth to keep it on the target. Holding a target meant that less or no searching was done. If possible, the operator could ask the radar operator of another ship to take over search duties. Otherwise the operator had to make a trade-off between holding a target and searching. He then verbally forwarded his findings to some sort of plot maintained by others of the team.

Later radar sets had PPI (Plan Position Indicator) displays. The point of this type of display was to have the radar itself do much of the plotting. Here the antenna rotates continuously. The radar is in the center of the display and as the antenna rotates, a map-like image is created of the blips. The PPI did away with much of the drudgery of interpreting and plotting blips. This made work easier, faster, and less error-prone.

Different radar sets had different resolutions. Bigger ships had bigger antennas, which allowed a narrower lobe with better angular resolution. Smaller ships such as destroyers had smaller antennas with wider lobes and less resolution. Good interceptions were easier to achieve using a radar with better resolution. The sets carried by major warships generally also had higher output power and thus longer range. An uncertainty in bearing means that the further out the target was, the fuzzier its positions were and the more uncertain the intercept would be.

Early air-warning sets did not have height estimation. Nevertheless, a skilled operator could use various tricks in order to get an estimate of the altitude of the target. One such was lobe switching, another was by observing at what ranges the incoming targets appeared and disappeared from the radar (as the target entered and left the lobes). The British used both Type 79 and Type 281, and since they had different lobes vertically, comparing target behavior could elicit useful height estimation, at least sometimes. The CXAM and SK radars used by the USN were more difficult to get usable height estimation from.

Fighter direction really needs a radar that has the resolution to be able to distinguish what is happening out there. That a big fuzzy lump of something is approaching might be good enough to prepare for being attacked but is not good enough for effective fighter direction. Good resolution includes accurate height information. The radar does not necessarily have to have a fantastic range, just enough to cover realistic ranges for fighter direction.

A high resolution in both bearing, distance, and altitude dictates a narrow "pencil" beam that scans not only in the horizontal plane but also in the vertical. The first such purpose-built fighter direction radar was the SM radar deployed on US carriers in late 1943 and early 1944. The RN's rough equivalent was the Type 277. A consequence of the high resolution in all planes was that the antenna had to be gyro stabilized. This made the unit quite heavy and the SM radar was mainly mounted on carriers. A consequence of having a high resolution and the associated narrow beam is that it makes the radar unsuited for search, as it will take too long to search through a given airspace. A high-resolution 3D radar will therefore normally be used in combination with a low-resolution air-warning radar that is better at rapidly searching through a large volume of airspace.

IFF (Identification Friend or Foe) was used to identify radar blips, to separate friendly blips from enemy blips. It was usually implemented as a transponder that on receipt of a query code responds with a reply code. These reply codes were then somehow associated with the blips on the radar. In its simplest form, the transponder replies with a pulse at the same frequency as the radar and then shows up on the radar display as secondary blips (with the shape of the blip given by the shape of the transponder return pulse). IFF was a hard problem and remains a hard problem to this day.

IFF was used by the USN during the 1942 battles but the technology was still in its infancy and few planes were thus equipped. By 1944 all USN aircraft had IFF transponders. No Japanese aircraft had any IFF during any of the carrier battles.

During World War II, there was normally no way of *uniquely* identifying individual blips/planes, the only information provided was that of "friendly." With the lack of a good "friendly" reply, the blip was assumed to be "enemy" and shot at with all available guns. The usual result was then that the very much 'friendly' pilot very quickly turned on his transponder (and perhaps had second thoughts on his choice of career).

## Plots and CIC

Some type of plotting board was used to keep track of the various targets. The plotting board operator received information from several sources, for example, from the radar operator and from the various radio operators.

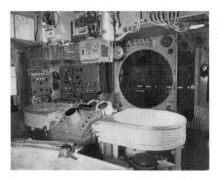

Main elements of the CIC on light carrier USS *Independence* with the vertical glass pane on the right.

A vertical glass pane, accessed from both sides, became the standard solution with additional plots for other purposes. The author has used a vertical double-sided glass pane in actual operations and it is indeed a very practical and efficient solution. There are some special skills that go with it, like writing backwards with grease pencils, but acquiring those skills is what training is for.

Around this plot, the various radar screens and radio stations were then arranged. Depending on ship type, sonar operators were also placed there. This room is what became known as the CIC or the Operations Room. It quickly evolved into a fairly large room with something like 10–20 people working in it, arranged in a very carefully thought-out layout to achieve the most efficient flow of information possible.

The key thing here is that the radar is in the same room as the plotting board. Ships had plotting boards long before the advent of radar but for the information to flow efficiently the radar has to be in the same room.

With many aircraft in the air, within range of the IFF and with their transponders turned on, the radar screen quickly becomes a jumble of received codes. It becomes hard to distinguish blips and codes. Another limitation is that at shorter range, the transponder return signal is strong enough to leak into the radar through the side-lobes or back lobes, that is, from any direction, which further complicates life for the radar operator.

## Deployment

The first primitive steps toward fighter direction was taken by the British during the Norwegian campaign. They then continued to gradually develop good methods during the Mediterranean battles. During these days the efficiency varied considerably from carrier to carrier, depending on how good the local fighter-direction team was. The first really successful use of fighter direction was during Operation *Pedestal* where the carrier *Victorious* proved to have the best team.

The USN had fighter direction from the start of the war in the Pacific. In the 1942 battles there were severe problems with saturation of the only radio channel available. By 1944 there where VHF radios with four channels and better radio discipline. Together with much improved methods and organization, fighter direction became effective, as demonstrated during the battle of Philippine Sea.

Fighter direction was sometimes done by specialized ships, for example, where land-based aircraft were involved. This type of fighter direction focused solely on combat. The practicalities of deck usage and fuel management was not done by these ships.

## Defeating Fighter Direction

The most obvious way to avoid fighter direction is to avoid being seen on radar. The classic method here is to fly low under the radar. This could in turn be countered by having destroyers stationed around the fleet acting as radar pickets. Sneaking in low became essentially impossible with the advent of airborne early warning (AEW) radar in late 1945.

Another way is to fly at night, if the mission and training allows it. Radar and fighter direction works fine at night but the intercepting fighters will have a more difficult time countering targets at night.

Perhaps the best way is to exploit weaknesses inherent in the radar and IFF systems used, to use trickle tactics instead of attacking in waves. Individual planes can be hard to distinguish on radar and hard to intercept for vectored CAP fighters. This could take the form of mixing in with the fighters but staying a bit away so as not to be spotted by them, tailing a returning strike or hopping between clouds or cloud layers or flying below or above the fighters (exploiting height finding deficiencies in the radar of the time). This is particularly useful for planes carrying guided bombs where a single large bomb can hit the target with a high probability of success and with possibly devastating effect. The drawback is that trickle tactics tend to ultimately be no more than nuisance raids.

Later in the war the Japanese had copied captured IFF transponders and sometimes managed to spoof the IFF system (there were only four frequencies). The Americans then resorted to having planes execute a predetermined maneuver to show that it was a friendly. The maneuver used changed daily.

A more brute-force approach is to attack with a large number of planes but divided up into many small groups coming in from different directions, constantly changing their heading and altitude while doing so. This presents a very challenging situation for the CIC team to handle, both in terms of resolution and in terms of numbers. The system will overload, latency will increase, intercepts will fail, and planes will get through. This was done at times during the Okinawa campaign and was quite successful in allowing attackers to get through.

## Alternatives to Fighter Direction

The above describes fighter direction using radar and radio, as practiced by the British and Americans. There was never any effective fighter direction on the Japanese carriers. They had a completely different approach, with radio silence as the foundation. They were also constrained by the fact that their fighter pilots did not maintain a plot and did not navigate. As a result, their fighters were often out of position and/or at the wrong altitude. On the other hand, as the Zero was a very good climber, it could get to where it was needed relatively quickly. What they did was to use visual signals to indicate where the fighters should go. The agreed method was to fire any big guns available in the direction of the enemy. Fighter pilots would then notice the shell splashes or air bursts and take the hint. This method only worked at short range, around the task force. No information was given about the size of the incoming strike, providing no help on target priority or on tactical dispositions.

# CHAPTER 9

# Logistics

## Fuel Oil

Below are some typical numbers for how many (metric) tons of fuel oil a warship consumes per day steaming at economical cruising speed:

Carrier     250 tons/day @ 18 knots
Battleship  250
Cruiser     140
Destroyer   50

Endurance was a problem, perhaps not so much for the big ships but the destroyers needed constant refueling. A day or two of high speed steaming to keep up with a carrier busy with flight operations would quickly deplete the fuel tanks of a destroyer. The rule of thumb was that destroyers needed to be refueled every three days. The following table lists endurance in days steaming at 18 and 28–30 knots:

|            | days @ 18 knots | days @ 28–30 knots |
|------------|-----------------|--------------------|
| Carrier    | 30              | 10                 |
| Battleship | 30              | 8                  |
| Cruiser    | 15              | 4                  |
| Destroyer  | 9               | 2                  |

The ship classes used as representative are the *Essex*, *South Dakota*, *Northampton*, and *Fletcher*, but these numbers vary relatively little from class to class. Older battleships had less efficient machinery but were also smaller and ended up using about the same at 18 knots. Numbers for other navies are very similar.

The big exception on the US side were the *Lexington* class of carriers. These ships were fuel hogs, being both large and inefficient and with an endurance about half of that of most other carriers.

The geared steam turbine machinery that was used on almost all warships were very compact and powerful but never very efficient; they could, for example, never compete with Diesel engines for efficiency. Between the wars, steam turbines developed very rapidly, with higher temperatures and pressures allowing much greater power output to be fitted within a given hull volume. The most obvious way to see this is in how battlecruisers disappeared, as all battleships could now be fast. Carriers also benefitted from compact and powerful machinery.

During a battle it was common for destroyers to snuggle up to any of the big ships and take a drink to top off the tanks, usually done at night when no flight operations were in progress. After the battle, everybody would rush to feast off the nearest available oiler. If no oiler was available, the task force would just have to retire to the nearest base. When the oiler *Neosho* was sunk during the Coral Sea battle, that meant that the entire US task force would have to retire earlier than was originally planned.

## The USN Oil Problem

When the war started, US oil production stood at about 20 million tons per month, or about two thirds of the world's oil production, a quite enviable position. The US also had a fleet of about 500 tankers. About a fifth of these were lost in 1942 but about 500 more were built during the war. At the time, there was no pipeline across the Rockies, so the war in the Pacific was kept supplied by the oil fields of California. The war in Europe was kept supplied by those of Texas, Oklahoma, and Louisiana. During the war a pipeline called Big Inch was built to transport oil to Linden, New Jersey. Venezuela and Mexico were other sources of oil but these had only a marginal role compared to the US oil fields.

Had the oil-storage facilities at Pearl Harbor been attacked on December 7, 1941, the well-known third-wave scenario, they would most likely not have been more than partly destroyed. Navy Special Fuel Oil (NSFO) is heavy, basically the same as what in the industry is known as Heavy Fuel Oil #5 with the viscosity (or "thickness") of syrup or honey. It requires heating to be easily pumped and is actually quite difficult to set on fire. A Japanese fighter pilot strafed the tanks and was surprised to see that absolutely nothing happened. The required procedure would have been to first use HE bombs to rupture the tanks and then some incendiaries to set them on fire. The smoke from burning tanks would then have obscured the remaining tanks, making complete destruction very unlikely, at least with the limited firepower available on the Japanese carriers. A raid by a thousand heavy bombers would have been a very different story.

The tank farm was mainly a strategic reserve. It was much bigger than needed if a steady supply of oil from California could be assured. This was indeed the case, as there was no shortage of civilian tankers, at least not for a priority task like keeping Pearl operational. Without the need for a strategic reserve, the tanks act merely as a buffer that enables a tanker to offload without delay and can be much more modest in size. This is what happened at the Ulithi anchorage when the fleet had moved there. Ulithi had no tank farms. No strategic reserve was held there, only a floating reserve of about 15,000 tons or more. The fleet was then kept fueled by a steady stream of 40 civilian tankers shuttling in oil from California. The same largely applies to Truk, the main Japanese naval base in the Pacific. Truk had a small tank farm but anchored tankers still had to be used for storage. Any third-wave scenario against Pearl would have had to be combined with an effective submarine blockade, or alternatively some type of strike against oil production facilities in California to pose any serious threat to the base.

Furthermore, any destroyed tanks would have been repaired and restocked within months. The tank farm capacity of 600,000 tons is certainly a very significant amount of oil but in the context of US oil production is less than one day's worth of production. The underground oil storage complex at nearby Red Hill was built to protect the oil tanks from enemy attacks so the threat was perceived as real, at least in the context of a strategic reserve and in the timeframe of a few months. Red Hill was not completed until September 1943, however, and played no role in 1941. Being underground it was also not affected by the Japanese attack.

The statement by Nimitz that had the Japanese destroyed the tank farms at Pearl on the 7th, that that would have prolonged the war by two years, is simply not correct. That statement, and similar statements by others, should be understood in the context that Red Hill was a secret and remained so long after the war. The statement sometimes attributed to Yamamoto, that it was a big mistake not to order a third strike, is most likely a canard. The real problem was not in the tank farms or in civilian tankers but in the long logistics tether so deep in the South Pacific, a scenario for which not much planning or pre-positioning had been done.

Looking at it from the perspective of a longer campaign, a task force of two carriers, a battleship, six cruisers, and a dozen destroyers consumes about 2,300 tons of fuel each day while steaming at a cruising speed of 18 knots. A USN oiler of the *Cimarron* class, like the *Neosho*, can transport up to about 16,500 tons of fuel oil, depending on loadout. It took about 18 days for a fleet oiler to make the round trip from Pearl Harbor to Noumea in New Caledonia, the main USN base in the South Pacific, a distance of about 3,000 nautical miles. At the time, the USN only had seven oilers in the Pacific, which, judging from the numbers above, clearly was not enough. Several of the old battleships sunk at Pearl Harbor were quickly raised and repaired but were still not used in the Guadalcanal campaign, at least partly due to lack of fleet oilers. It must be kept in mind that the huge fleet train created during the war did not exist in 1942. In those early days of the war the USN had shortages of pretty much everything.

## The RN Oil Problem

The RN also had a relatively minor oil problem. The US could provide what Britain and the RN needed. After the Mediterranean had been closed off and Middle Eastern oil had to transported the long way around Africa, it was simply easier and cheaper for Britain to rely on America for its oil. Middle Eastern oil was still of use for ships based in Alexandria and for the Far Eastern Fleet, however.

Almost all of the imported oil arrived at Liverpool. This was also the area where the major refineries were. As Britain was vulnerable to air attack, an underground pipeline system for the distribution of aviation fuel was built from Liverpool to the southern and eastern parts of England. The system was then connected to the PLUTO pipelines that supported the Normandy landings. The system was initially called GPSS (Government Pipelines and Storage System) and is now known as the CLH Pipeline System. It remains in use and is still a state secret.

Spain also depended on US oil, as well as on RN benevolence for overseas trade, which is why Gibraltar was left alone. If the Axis powers would have captured the Suez Canal and the oil fields of the Middle East and if perhaps they also could have managed to link up over India, it would actually have meant quite little. It would have looked great on the maps and it would have been a great photo-op but not much more than that. The real battles were fought elsewhere.

## The IJN Oil Problem

Before the war, Japan depended almost entirely on the US for oil imports. This source was cut off by Roosevelt in July 1941 in order to force Japan to evacuate China. The only remaining source of oil for Japan was then the Dutch East Indies. The Netherlands was under German occupation so this area was effectively controlled by the British.

Japan was acutely aware of the strategic vulnerability of depending on its enemies for oil. The IJN had therefore accumulated huge stocks before the war, about 6.5 million tons. This was calculated to last for about two years, which gave Japan a measure of strategic independence. As it turned out, it was not enough. The IJN alone used about 300,000 tons of oil per month in 1942 (some of which came from oil refined in Japan, some of it from the captured refineries and oil fields of the Dutch East Indies). Before the war, Japan had also built up a fleet of about 100 tankers to transport both crude oil and refined products to where they were needed but wartime consumption proved larger than expected and the shortage of transport capacity became a major bottleneck. When these tankers then began to be sunk in large numbers by US submarines, the resulting shortage of fuel oil became a severe constraint on Japan's ability to wage war.

Looking at the Midway operation, the ships involved burned about 200,000 tons per month at cruising speed with no allowance for combat. This operation alone used up all the oil (and tankers) budgeted and could not really have been sustained beyond a few weeks. The IJN had a very real logistics problem, and much of how the IJN operated during the war, what it did and did not do, can be understood from these numbers.

These numbers should be compared with US production. The IJN consumed over 12 million tons during the war, which is what the US produced in about two weeks.

## Aviation Gasoline

The Japanese carrier *Kaga* stored 154,000 gallons of avgas, *Akagi* 150,000, while *Hiryu* and *Soryu* each carried 134,000 and *Zuikaku* 150,000 gallons. The later *Unryu* class had their storage slashed to 48,000 gallons, as it was understood that a carrier or its planes was not likely to live long enough to use much more.

The US carrier *Lexington* carried 132,000 gallons while *Enterprise* had an avgas stock of 178,000 gallons. The newer *Essex* carried more, about 240,000 gallons, while the *Independence* carried 122,000 gallons.

The British carrier *Illustrious* had an avgas stock of 50,540 imperial gallons, *Indomitable* had more at 75,000, and *Implacable* carried 94,650. The relatively modest avgas capacity of RN carriers reflects not only that they were intended to operate fewer aircraft but also that they had better access to bases. It was a clear inconvenience late in the war when more and thirstier aircraft were operated.

Carrier-borne aircraft had a fuel capacity of 150–300 gallons. There was then avgas for about 10 sorties per plane before replenishment was necessary (with 5–7 sorties typical for late-war RN carriers).

## Aircraft Spares

Aircraft crew killed during the war was roughly one-third in training, one-third in operational accidents, and one-third in combat losses. The accident rate for carrier operations was 1–3 percent per mission. This number is a very rough estimate and depends on many factors. Smaller carriers had a higher accident rate, as had poorly trained pilots riding new high-powered aircraft.

The aircraft of the day did not have the precision and sophistication we are used to today. Computers did not exist; all tooling was operated by hand. Tolerances were not as tight and all calculations were done by slide rule. Much of it was done simply by trial and error. The Messerschmitt method was to design everything a bit understrength and then to reinforce the parts that broke, killing many test pilots but producing a very optimized design. Combat aircraft certainly pushed the limit of what could be achieved at the time and malfunctions were much more common than would be acceptable today. Grumman, the manufacturer of the Wildcat, Avenger, Hellcat and Bearcat planes, was famous for their quality control but there was only so much that could be done that way. The operational loss rate suffered by all types of planes reflect that.

To replace losses, spares were carried on all carriers. The number varied heavily but would typically be about a dozen. Assuming 50 sorties per day and an accident rate of 1 percent per mission, 12 spares will last 24 days. There were also spare pilots and aircrew available.

## Torpedoes and Bombs

Carriers of all navies had about 2–3 torpedoes for each torpedo bomber. The Americans almost ran out of torpedoes at Coral Sea. After the attacks on shipping at Tulagi, on the *Shoho* and on the *Shokaku* and *Zuikaku*, there was only seven torpedoes left on board *Yorktown*.

Beyond torpedoes, fleet carriers had a typical magazine capacity of about 200–400 tons of various types of bombs. A typical battleship had about

80–130 rounds per main gun, with each projectile weighing 600–1,300kg, or about three times the total destructive power of a carrier, which might be of relevance, for example, when comparing the effectiveness of ground-support missions and shore bombardment.

## Underway Replenishment

This is the US term for the transfer of supplies from one vessel to another while at sea. This can include all kinds of supplies but by far the most important was fuel oil.

The earliest and simplest method was the astern method. This involved having the two ships steaming in line astern and then for the ship ahead to lay out a hose for the ship astern to pick up and connect. This meant a fairly long and reasonably light hose which in turn limited the capacity.

The more difficult side-by-side method enabled shorter and heavier hoses which meant faster refueling. In this method a wire is connected between the

USS *Lexington* (CV-16) refuels from USS *Guadalupe* (AO-32). Side-by-side refueling took a good deal of practice.

ships which then carries the weight of the hose. In the side-by-side method, it was also possible to transfer other goods like fresh food, mail, and personnel. It was also possible to refuel two ships at the same time. The major danger was the suction effect, created by the bow waves of the ships, which tended to draw the ships toward each other. These bow waves could add up, creating very large waves in the area between the ships. For a ship with a low freeboard, like an oiler or a destroyer, steaming side by side could be a very wet experience for the crewmen handling the operation. Speed sometimes had to be reduced to minimize the bow waves but no so much that the ships started to have problems steering. At a reduced speed, a destroyer tends to roll heavily. Later in the war, equipment and techniques were developed that permitted a wider separation between the ships which then gave less problems with suction and waves, allowing for faster steaming while refueling.

Both the USN and RN used the side-by-side method; the IJN initially used only the astern method but later learned and used the side-by-side method.

Replenishment while at anchor was much simpler. In this case, there was no need for a navy oiler and trained personnel—any civilian tanker could do the job. The tanker tied up alongside, a hose was passed, and a pump was started. In the merchant marine, this was the standard way of refueling, or "bunkering" as it is called. It was typically done while tied up to a dock to load/unload cargo but might well be done while at anchor.

PART II

# Carrier Battles of World War II

CHAPTER 10

# Early Scouting and Raiding by Carriers

## Norwegian Campaign

The Germans had air superiority around southern Norway but the northern part of the country was much more contested. RN carriers did scouting, raiding and had some air cover over landings and evacuation sites. The visibility was at times limited, which hampered carrier operations.

Operation *Paul* is little known. It was a planned major attack on the Swedish port of Luleå in the Baltic. The target was the iron ore exports to Germany. The attack would have been launched from RN carriers operating around Lofoten Islands, about 300 miles from Luleå. Several different variants of this attack were scheduled for various dates in late May and early June 1940. In its largest form the attack would have used no fewer than 78 Swordfish torpedo bombers launched from the carriers *Ark Royal*, *Glorious*, and *Furious*. Heavy losses were expected as this was at the extreme range of the Swordfish even when equipped with long-range fuel tanks. Some or all of the planes would have had to continue to Russia and land there. Additional Sea Gladiators and Skuas would have been used for air cover above the carriers but did not have the range to reach Luleå. Orders for the attack had been issued to the fleet but had to be canceled by the rapidly unfolding events in France.

Had the attack been carried out it would certainly have joined the annals of naval history. It was far from traditional scouting and raiding—all fast fleet carriers now operated together in what would have been a strategic strike. This was a year before the Japanese formed the Kido Butai and long before Pearl Harbor. It would also have been a dastardly and unprovoked attack that would have lived in infamy, at least in Sweden. It is worth noting that at the time, Sweden considered Britain a friend and Germany as the enemy, while Germany considered Sweden a friend. Life as a neutral country can be complicated.

On June 8, *Glorious* was operating alone and was careless in not having any CAP over the carrier. The captain wanted to give the aircrews some rest. Despite good visibility, the carrier was surprised by German battlecruisers and sunk by gunfire before it could get its speed up and run away. Bumping into enemy surface forces was a constant worry for carriers throughout the war.

## Raid on Taranto

This was the prototypical carrier raid as envisaged before the war. Twenty Swordfish torpedo bombers were launched at night about 150 miles from Taranto, the main base of the Italian battle fleet. Twelve of these carried torpedoes and five hits were scored. The raid remains the only major carrier-based naval battle ever to take place only at night.

## The Sinking of *Bismarck*, *Prince of Wales*, and *Repulse*

The German battleship *Bismarck* had embarked on commerce raiding in the Atlantic. The RN used carriers to search, and despite variable visibility twice succeeded in locating it.

Searching out to 200 miles, a full azimuth search will cover about 130,000 square miles. A rough estimate of the area that *Bismarck* could go to would be in the order of up to a million square miles. However, much of that area would be searched by land-based aircraft and much of the rest would be considered unlikely for various reasons. This meant that a single carrier had only a marginal chance of finding the battleship but if two or more carriers were available, finding the raider became reasonably probable. The RN had both the *Ark Royal* and *Victorious* available and the *Bismarck* was indeed found. Furthermore, carrier-borne torpedo bombers managed to score a disabling hit. *Bismarck* was then caught and sunk in a surface battle.

Dive bombers would have been useless against *Bismarck*—they would have had problems diving through the clouds and their bombs would have failed to penetrate its deck armor.

The AA suite of *Bismarck* was inadequate. It had a total of 16 37mm barrels but these were semi-automatic with each shell loaded by hand. The rate of fire was only 30 rounds per minute. This is about a quarter of what the 40mm Bofors was capable of, which meant that *Bismarck* only had the equivalent of *one* quad 40mm mount (with the USN mounting around 20 of these quad mounts on a major warship). *Bismarck* also had 12 single 20mm guns but with a short range and a relatively low rate of fire these were also ineffective. It had a good complement of heavy AA but again the rate of fire was simply too low and it was unable to defend itself against even a small force of torpedo bombers. *Bismarck* also did not have any escorts or defending fighters on CAP, both of which would have been very useful against attacks by torpedo bombers.

We have the same situation a few months later with battleships *Repulse* and *Prince of Wales* targeting Japanese invasion forces and landing sites. Without air cover and with both weak AA and weak escorts, even a modern and fast battleship is quite vulnerable.

With an escorting light carrier, *Bismarck* would have been much better able to avoid search planes, do its own search, and defend against air attack. However, much of that depended on using radar and radio communications, both of which would have given its position away. A battleship used as a raider will need to have a very strong AA suite indeed and *Bismarck* did not have it.

## Raid on Kirkenes and Petsamo

This was a carrier raid in July 1941 on shipping in the harbors of Kirkenes and Petsamo, on the extreme northern tip of the Scandinavian peninsula. That far north and at that time of the year, it is light for 24 hours a day. The attacking carriers *Victorious* and *Furious* had the bad luck of being spotted by patrolling aircraft around the time of launch. The defending Germans then had ample time to get aircraft into the air and up to altitude. The somewhat clumsy Fulmars and Albacores suffered heavily against the waiting Bf 109s and Bf 110s. To add insult to injury, there was very little shipping in the harbors.

## Raid on Pearl Harbor

This is of course the biggest and by far the most famous carrier raid of the war, heavily inspired by the raid on Taranto.

The approach to Pearl Harbor is an interesting example in search methods. The approaching task force could launch it planes around 300 miles from the target. During the night, the formation could steam 200 to 300 miles. To get warning a meaningful time before launch, the carriers would have to be discovered about 600 miles out.

At 600 miles out, a picket line of ships would have to be about 1,000 miles long. Spaced 20 miles apart, this would need 50 ships. Radar was not a practical alternative in those days. The first radar on destroyers, the SC air-warning set, was beginning to be installed in late 1941 but had a range of only about

10 miles against large ships. In those early days, radar was regarded as just an unreliable gizmo and with pretty good reasons. Airborne radar was not available until June 1942. Using visual search, visibility varied considerably. It could be up to 30 miles on a clear day but could also be nil.

Long-range patrol planes can search an area far from the base but the size of the search area per plane and unit of time is not more than any other plane. The long range comes at a price in size and cost and fewer were available. Keeping continuous coverage will require a very large number of planes. Patrol planes also have the same sighting limitations as a surface ships.

Since radar was not an option at the time, sighting the formation depended on visual spotting. Riding a cold front on the approach, the Japanese raiders were quite safe from visual sighting. The attack was successful, not for lack of search but because of the impracticability of search that would have had a good chance of discovering the raiders.

The air-warning radar tasked with protecting the base was sited at Opana Point. The radar was an SCR-270, a mobile army unit with a nominal range of 150 miles. Range was shorter against targets at low altitude but since the radar site was 532 feet above sea level, range against low-flying aircraft was still good.

At 0610, the Japanese carriers started launching the attack from a position 230 miles north of Oahu. Sunrise was at 0626 local Hawaiian time (UTC -10.5). At 0702, a very large blip appeared at a range of 136 miles. The radar certainly had long range but also a low resolution and no IFF. The blip could be interpreted as anything sufficiently large. A flight of six B-17s was expected at that time and roughly from that direction. The blip was assumed to be it. The attack began about 50 minutes later.

Had there been an immediate and full-scale reaction to the blip, it would still take at least 15–20 minutes to warm up aircraft engines and then some more minutes to get to altitude, assuming pilots and planes were ready. Defending fighters would only meet the attackers as the attack was in full swing and would not have had much time to organize a defense. To mount an effective defense, the defenders should really have had 100+ fighters already in the air and available for immediate vectoring when the blip appeared on the radar. The defenders might still not be able to do much to break up the attack as they were at a disadvantage both numerically and qualitatively. It was only in 1944 that the USN had developed the high-resolution and height-finding radar and the IFF and fighter direction techniques required for effective defense against a major carrier strike, not to mention large numbers of well-trained pilots in superior fighters.

The AA guns available could not stop a determined attack. All they could do was distract the attackers, shooting down the odd plane. Even in 1944, with vastly improved AA, many attackers still got through.

On December 7, the advantage lay strongly with the attacker. A carrier raid was very difficult to defend against. Out of nowhere, a powerful strike force can approach at 150mph. There are good reasons why Taranto, Pearl Harbor, and the Doolittle Raid all succeeded, as well as many of the raids on Japanese-held islands in 1943 and 1944. The best defense was to be mobile and strike right back.

The main targets were the major warships, with the official target prioritization list actually having battleships as more important targets than carriers. Repairing a major warship takes many months, replacing them takes years. Torpedoes and AP bombs dropped from level bombers at 10,000 feet were used against battleships. No carriers were present so the dive bombers had little to do; they also had problems with having to dive through layers of clouds. Escorting fighters were used mainly for strafing aircraft on the ground, not so much for suppression of AA. Lesser targets like the oil storage and the dockyards and repair facilities could have been attacked but these targets were much harder to knock out and much easier to replace.

As the day wore on, all the main targets had been hit and as the defenses got organized, losses started to mount. With the limited daylight available at this time of year, any further strikes would have to land back at the carriers well after sunset at 1719 and there was no moon up to assist with night landings. The Japanese withdrew. The entire Western Pacific needed conquering and there was little point in dawdling.

The threat against Pearl Harbor lingered. Many planes were retained there that could otherwise have been deployed to the Solomons area.

# CHAPTER 11

# Battle of the Coral Sea

## Introduction

This was the first battle in which carriers did something beyond their prewar roles of scouting and raiding. In this battle, carriers were used to establish or deny naval supremacy. Surface forces played no significant part in determining the outcome—they never even sighted each other.

In May 1942, the Japanese sent an invasion fleet to capture Port Moresby on southern New Guinea. The intention was to thereafter complete the conquest of the Solomons, threatening to cut off Australia. The Americans wanted to stop this.

## Forces Available and Logistics

The Japanese Carrier Striking Force consisted of the carriers *Shokaku* and *Zuikaku*, two heavy cruisers, and six destroyers. Each carrier had slightly more than 18 fighters, 18 dive bombers, and 18 torpedo bombers. The invasion force was escorted by light carrier *Shoho* carrying 12 fighters and six torpedo bombers.

American Task Force 17 consisted of the carriers *Yorktown* and *Lexington*. Each went into battle with 18 fighters, 36 dive bombers, and 13 torpedo bombers. Escorts were five cruisers and seven destroyers. An additional force of three cruisers and two destroyers operated separately from the carriers.

The USN had a severe shortage of fleet oilers and could not sustain both carriers and battleships. These tankers were able to do underway replenishment and got their oil from Pearl Harbor, which in turn was kept supplied by civilian tankers. Most of the battleships sunk at Pearl Harbor were by now repaired but had to be held back due to lack of oil. The Japanese had similar problems with logistics. Indeed both sides operated at the end of their supply chains.

## Command and Control

The Japanese carriers had Rear Admiral Chuichi Hara in tactical command but Vice Admiral Takeo Takagi on cruiser *Myoko* in command of the carrier strike force. The overall operation of invading Port Moresby was commanded by Vice Admiral Shigeyoshi Inoue at Rabaul. *Shokaku* and *Zuikaku* operated together in a somewhat loose formation.

Task Force 17 was commanded by Rear Admiral Frank Fletcher on the *Yorktown*. *Yorktown* and *Lexington* steamed relatively close together with a screen surrounding both of them.

Both Japanese and American carriers could talk to the other carriers in the respective task forces using short-range radios. Once launched, radio silence generally prevented carriers from talking to their planes. The Japanese had Takagi in command on cruiser *Myoko* which did not sail with the carriers. He gave directions to strikes without revealing the position of the carriers.

American carriers had air-warning radar. Fighter direction was still in its infancy and suffered from poor radio discipline and inexperienced teams. Experimental IFF was installed on four of the Wildcat fighters. The Japanese had neither radar nor fighter direction, at least not based on radio communications; they did, however, have certain visual methods that allowed for a crude form of fighter direction.

## Visibility and Wind

On May 7, 1942, at latitude 13°S and longitude 157°E, using the UTC+11 time zone, sunrise was at 0641 and sunset at 1816. Nautical twilight began at 0553 and ended at 1904.

Moonrise was at 2339 (on the 6th) and moonset at 1237. At 0600 the moon was almost straight above, slightly more than half and waning. Late landings were not aided by moonlight but very early dawn launches could be.

The weather was dominated by a front stretching roughly east to west with clear weather south of it and scattered clouds north. Wind was a strong breeze, up to gale force, inside the front but outside of it only moderate.

## Air Operations

Fletcher knew that the Japanese intended to invade Port Moresby. His plan for the battle was to rely on the search planes based at Tulagi, Noumea, Port Moresby and northeastern Australia to spot the invasion force while he would stay out of range of Japanese search aircraft based at Rabaul. He would stay about 300–400 miles south of Guadalcanal, waiting for the enemy to reveal itself, while keeping his destroyers fueled, ready to go in when the Japanese had revealed their position.

On May 3, the Japanese occupied the recently abandoned island of Tulagi and set up a base there for flying boats doing searches.

Early on the 4th, a strike from *Yorktown* set out to attack shipping at Tulagi. The strike consisted of all operational strike aircraft, first a squadron of 12 Devastators in one deck load and then a second deck load of two squadrons with a total of 28 Dauntless dive bombers. As was the doctrine, each squadron formed up and proceeded to the target independently. The torpedo planes were slower than the dive bombers and were therefore launched first with the hope that they would all reach the target at about the same time. The Wildcats were retained for defense, six had been launched as CAP at 0631 before the strike was launched. The attackers arrived at 0815 and proceeded to attack the ships at Tulagi, sinking a small destroyer. While this attack was going on, the *Yorktown* rotated its CAP. Beginning at 0931, all strike aircraft were recovered successfully.

At 1036, *Yorktown* dispatched 14 Dauntless northwards to search that area before heading for and attacking Tulagi. About half an hour later, a second deck load strike of 13 dive bombers and 11 torpedo planes was launched against Tulagi. After this attack had been sent off, CAP was again rotated. At 1311, four Wildcats were sent to protect the bombers that were being harassed by Japanese fighters, the other fighters on deck were sent below to clear the flight deck for the returning strike. After having sunk or damaged some transports, the bombers started to return at 1319. At 1400, 21 dive bombers were launched as a third strike. The remaining strike aircraft from the second strike were then recovered and CAP rotated. The third strike arrived over Tulagi at 1500 but scored no hits against the ships still there and was recovered by about 1600. Two of the four Wildcats got lost and ditched, as did one of the Devastators. At 1628, six fighters were launched to fly dusk CAP.

At 0750 on the morning of the 5th, a Japanese long-range reconnaissance flying boat was spotted by *Yorktown*'s CXAM radar about 30 miles away. Four Wildcats scrambled, found the flying boat and shot it down. The plane never sent a report but when it did not return, the Japanese correctly deduced that it had been shot down by carrier aircraft.

At 0816 on the 5th, *Lexington* arrived to join *Yorktown* in TF 17. Together they had five cruisers and seven destroyers as escorts. The day was spent refueling.

At dawn of the 6th, Fletcher launched a search northward to a distance of 275 miles, finding nothing. Both Fletcher and Takagi spent the 6th refueling. In the afternoon, Fletcher sent out another search but again without finding anything.

At 1000 on the 6th, a reconnaissance flying boat from Tulagi spotted TF 17 and Takagi received the report at 1050. At this time, Takagi was about 350 miles north of TF 17. The report said that the carriers were heading south and that there were low clouds. This was beyond the range he could attack, and also hampered by the poor weather, Takagi did not launch a strike but detached his carriers to steam south to be in a suitable position next morning. Ironically the American carriers were steaming within range and were in an area of clear weather. Had a strike been launched it most likely would have reached and found the American carriers. At least Takagi knew where the enemy was. Fletcher knew he had been sighted but he still did not know where the Japanese carriers were. Toward the evening, Fletcher sent oiler *Neosho* and destroyer *Sims* southwards to what he believed were safer waters. A battle was about to be joined, the first time these enemies would meet in a carrier battle. Neither side knew much about the other.

At 0600 on the 7th, Takagi launched 12 Kate torpedo bombers to search to the south and southeast out to a distance of 250 miles. Deck-load strikes were prepared on both his carriers. At 0722, one of these search planes reported it had found a carrier. At 0800, a strike of 36 dive bombers, 24 torpedo bombers, and 18 fighters began launching from both carriers and by 0815 they were on their way to the target. This was done as single deck-load launches, the Japanese carriers operated fewer aircraft for their size and did not have to split up the launch into two separate deck loads. No attack aircraft now remained on the decks but 18 fighters had been withheld from the strike and were available for CAP duties.

At 0820, a floatplane from cruiser *Furutaka* found the American carriers and reported it, confirmed at 0830 by a floatplane from cruiser *Kinugasa*. The American carriers would not be attacked, however; the strike had already been sent.

What the strike found was the fleet oiler *Neosho* escorted by the destroyer *Sims*. The search report from 0722 had misidentified these two ships as the American carriers. The strike arrived at 0915 but did not attack until 1051 as the strike continued to look for the carriers they were supposed to attack. At 1051, the strike realized the error and received instructions from Takagi to attack anyway, so the dive bombers attacked and sank both ships. Radio silence was broken by this instruction but Takagi was on cruiser *Myoko*, not with the carriers. About 1530, the dive bombers had returned from the strike on *Neosho* and *Sims*, the torpedo bombers had already landed.

At 1515, a fresh search consisting of eight Kate torpedo bombers was launched from the Japanese carriers. Rueful from having made the serious error of attacking the wrong target, Takagi badly wanted to get a strike in before nightfall. At 1615, he launched a second strike consisting of 12 dive bombers and 15 torpedo bombers with orders to fly down a bearing of 277°. This was without knowledge of where the enemy carriers were, just on a hunch and assuming the search planes would find them. In the cloudy conditions the search planes missed the American carriers but they had been spotted by radar, and 11 fighters were directed to their position and took them by surprise. The formation was broken up and nine bombers were shot down. The mission was abandoned and the survivors headed back to their carriers. Night fell at 1830 and there was no moon up but Takagi had his carriers turn on their searchlights as an aid to landing. By 2200 all remaining planes had been recovered with three more being lost on their way back.

The Americans had started the 7th with the usual morning search. At 0619, *Yorktown* launched 10 Dauntless scouts to search to north and northeast out to a range of 250 miles. Unusually the search was done using single planes despite the presence of enemy forces. On the other hand, using 10 planes to search a relatively narrow sector meant a very dense search pattern was used, probably dictated by the poor visibility in the front system in the area to be searched. Furthermore, flying through clouds, the search planes were harder to spot and shoot down, reducing the need for redundancy. The weather was clear over the carriers but the search planes quickly entered into the front with thick clouds and squalls.

Beginning at 0703, *Lexington* launched a CAP consisting of four fighters and six Dauntless. Deck-load strikes were readied on both carrier flight decks, in anticipation of a sighting report.

At 0815, the Japanese invasion force was spotted by one of the planes from *Yorktown*. The force was reported as two carriers and four heavy cruisers which was quickly interpreted as the long sought after main Japanese carrier force. An attack with 53 dive bombers, 22 torpedo bombers, and 18 fighters was launched as two deck loads. *Lexington* started launching at 0926 with planes circling the carrier until all had launched, and proceeded to target as one air group departing at 0947. *Yorktown* started launching at 0944 with all the dive bombers instructed to slowly climb and circle above the carrier. Next to launch were the torpedo planes that immediately left for the target. About 15 minutes later, the eight escorting fighters took off to join the dive bombers above, departing at 1013. Being faster than the slow torpedo bombers, the fighters and dive bombers expected to arrive over the target at roughly the same time. No bombers were held back for a second strike. On the other hand, with no fueled and armed bombers on the decks, the carriers were less vulnerable. A Japanese attack was expected at any time; it was not yet understood that the Japanese had sent their main strike toward the wrong target.

At 1019, CAP was rotated and the returning search planes recovered. After the search planes had landed, it was discovered that the sighting report had been miscoded: two cruisers had been sighted, not two carriers. The strike had been sent to the wrong target! Recalling them was seen as too risky as an enemy attack was expected at any moment. At 1013, Fletcher had received a report from army bombers of the invasion force escorted by one carrier. This was only 30 miles from the position reported earlier, and at 1053 Fletcher broke radio silence and issued the correction to the strike. Between 1100 and 1130, CAP was rotated. TF 17 now kept aloft 17 fighters at medium altitude as CAP against dive bombers, and 10 Dauntless at low altitude as CAP against torpedo planes. The expected strike never materialized. Takagi had made the same blunder.

What the strike found was the small carrier *Shoho*. Attacks started at 1040 and the ship was quickly sunk by no fewer than about 13 bomb and seven torpedo hits. No other ship was damaged or sunk as the American aircrews feasted on the poor *Shoho*. Better strike coordination and target allocation would be a lesson for the future. By 1338, the planes had returned and by 1420 were refueled and rearmed. Fletcher elected not to send out a new search as it was too late for a second strike and because the weather had taken a turn for the worse, making it difficult both to find the enemy and to find the way back to the carrier. TF 17 stayed under the clouds and prepared for the next day.

Later in the day, without the close support that the *Shoho* had intended to provide, the invasion force turned back. The intention was that it would return in a few days.

What had happened during the day was that the Japanese carriers were to the east of the US carriers while both thought that the Japanese were to the north and the US to the south. The US search did not find the Japanese carriers, only the invasion force escorted by the *Shoho*. The Japanese search did not find the US carriers, only the oiler *Neosho* escorted by destroyer *Sims*. Despite all the searches going on, both land-based and carrier-based, both sides found something else. It is pretty safe to assume that the clouds and squalls contributed to all the fumbling on the 7th.

Takagi tried launching a late second strike but paid for it dearly in lost planes. Fletcher did not, and with hindsight that was probably the correct call.

As dawn approached on the 8th, Takagi had 37 fighters, 33 dive bombers, and 25 torpedo bombers operational. Fletcher had 31 fighters, 65 dive bombers, and 21 torpedo bombers.

At 0615 on the 8th, a search of seven Kate torpedo planes was launched from the Japanese carriers. The Japanese knew that the US were almost certainly to the south, so search was done only in that general direction. The search was done out to 250 miles and was assisted by floatplanes from cruisers and by land-based flying boats. At 0822, one of the carrier-based search planes sighted TF 17.

At 0615, on the American side, a search of 18 scout dive bombers was launched to conduct a 360° search out to 200 miles. Perhaps learning from the mistakes of the day before, Fletcher did not make any assumptions about the whereabouts of the enemy and invested in having a full squadron do a comprehensive search. This worked well: at 0820, the Japanese carriers were spotted and reported by one of the scouts from *Lexington*.

Both forces had now spotted the other about 210 miles away. The race was on for the first strike. No fumbling this time. Both forces headed straight for each other to shorten the return flight as both were attacking at long range. There was not much need for radar this day—both sides knew attacks were incoming and approximately at what time the guests could be expected to arrive.

At 0915, the Japanese carriers launched a strike of 33 dive bombers, 18 torpedo planes, and 18 fighters as combined deck loads from both carriers. This was all the bombers they had and half the fighters, the other fighters being retained for CAP.

At 0847, the Americans started launching and by 0915, *Yorktown* had launched 24 dive bombers, nine torpedo planes, and six fighters. At 0925, *Lexington* launched 15 dive bombers, 12 torpedo planes, and nine fighters. No bombers remained but just as did Takagi, half the fighters stayed behind to provide CAP.

*Yorktown*'s dive bombers arrived at 1032 but had to wait for the slower torpedo bombers to arrive before doing a coordinated attack. At 1057, the dive bombers commenced the attack, scoring two hits on *Shokaku* with 1,000lb bombs. All torpedoes missed. *Lexington*'s strike arrived at 1130. Two dive bombers attacked *Shokaku*, scoring a hit with a 1,000lb bomb. Two other dive bombers attacked *Zuikaku* but did not hit it. *Lexington*'s torpedo bombers all missed. Cloud cover and intermittent squalls had made attacks difficult, particularly on the *Zuikaku*.

At 1055, Lexington's CXAM radar detected an incoming strike at 78 miles out. The American carriers did not enjoy the protection from any clouds as the sky over them was clear. Only nine Wildcats were covering the force and those

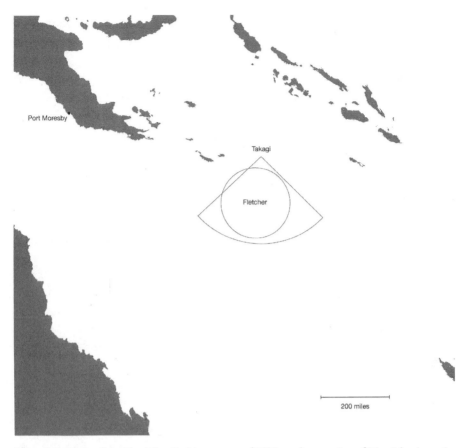

Map of the battle of the Coral Sea. Positions are as of 0700 on the morning of May 8th, about the time when the morning search was launched. The search patterns flown are shown for both sides. Nights had the effect of resetting a carrier battle. At first light the battle was resumed by both sides. The essence of a carrier battle was to remain hidden while locating the enemy and then to strike him. Preferably this should be achieved by a minimum of planes allocated to search. The narrower and longer range the search pattern could be, the better.

Fletcher positioned his carriers aggressively and then used a search pattern that was cautious and expensive. Takagi had pulled back and used a more focused search, enjoying a range advantage.

were low on fuel but nine more were immediately launched. The Dauntless used as scouts had by now returned and 12 were now used as low-level CAP against enemy torpedo bombers.

The incoming attacked was coordinated and stacked in layers. At medium altitude were the dive bombers with escorting fighters overhead. At low altitude came the torpedo bombers, also with escorting fighters above them.

Of the attacking bombers, four torpedo planes and six dive bombers were shot down by this hastily arranged CAP at the cost of five Dauntless and three Wildcats lost to escorting Zeros. Poor US fighter direction sent many of the fighters to the wrong altitude as it was difficult on radar to distinguish between friendlies and bogeys and the radio sets were being overloaded with chatter. The system had worked well in training but largely broke down in the face of a major combat.

The attack began at 1113. Of the surviving 14 torpedo bombers, 10 attacked *Lexington* and four attacked *Yorktown*. In a successful pincer attack, two hits were scored on *Lexington* but none on *Yorktown*. Of the 14 torpedo planes that made attack runs, four were shot down by AA fire.

A few minutes after the torpedo planes, the dive bombers attacked. Those from *Shokaku* attacked the *Lexington* while those from *Zuikaku* attacked *Yorktown*. *Lexington* suffered two hits from small bombs while *Yorktown* took one hit in the center of the flight deck from a 250kg semi-AP bomb. This bomb penetrated four decks and caused considerable damage but left the flight deck operational.

Both carrier forces had sent most of their planes in their respective deck-load strikes and with as much as possible of the CAP aloft; not many planes remained aboard. When the bombs struck, fires could be managed.

Between 1250 and 1430, both forces recovered their respective strikes. Japanese planes were instructed to land on the *Zuikaku* but many were lost to various operational and damage-related causes. When recovery was complete, the Japanese were now down to 24 fighters, eight dive bombers and four torpedo bombers. Spares were carried but it would take a day or two to assemble them.

*Yorktown* recovered seven fighters, 11 dive bombers, and eight torpedo planes. *Lexington* had five fighters, 12 dive bombers, and 11 torpedo planes.

Both sides had suffered heavy losses, particularly bombers. They also needed to refuel their destroyers and elected to withdraw.

At 1525, *Lexington* suffered an internal explosion due to leaking gasoline fumes. Fires spread and more explosions followed. At 1707, the order was given to abandon ship, it finally sinking at 1952 after having been scuttled by torpedoes from destroyer *Phelps*.

## Analysis

This was the first true carrier battle of the war. It showed that many errors were committed on both sides.

Both navies made extensive use of land-based search planes but with the sometimes limited visibility, they proved of little use. These planes have long range which is necessary to be useful from a land base. That range comes at the cost of being large, which means that they are few in numbers, which in turn means that at the end of their search range they depend on excellent visibility to have a reasonable chance of finding anything. Most of the useful sightings were made by carrier-based search planes and to a lesser extent by floatplanes based on surface ships. Both sides had serious problems with erroneous and/or garbled reports.

The Japanese were unable to exploit their range advantage, both in search and in attack. There was simply too much confusion and uncertainties to indulge in that kind of fine tuning of a battle.

The short range of the Wildcat was a known problem before this battle and Admiral William Halsey had already requested that they would be fitted with drop tanks. In this battle the Wildcats were able to stay with the bombers all the way to the target and to provide some protection from enemy CAP.

The USN attempt at using dive bombers as defensive fighters was not a success and was not repeated.

Neither side managed to get in an unanswered first strike. Both sides launched and attacked at about the same time. Both sides had far too few fighters and both suffered high losses among their bombers, particularly on the Japanese side. On the American side, fighter direction broke down.

Both sides had empty decks when the attacks were absorbed. No fires were started and both sides survived several bomb hits. The US 1,000lb bombs seemed to be more destructive than the Japanese 250kg semi-AP bombs, at least when it came to wrecking a flight deck. The *Lexington*, with its poor maneuverability, took two torpedo hits. Leaking avgas and inexperienced damage control was a major contributor to its loss. Both sides had one flight deck put out of action; they needed those second decks to land survivors on, plus to provide air cover for their stricken compatriot.

Both sides steamed with their two carriers relatively close to each other and sharing CAP. The Americans had more escorts with better AA but this does not seem to have mattered much—most of the planes downed were shot down by defending fighters.

During much of this battle, American dive bombers had serious problems with their bombsights and windshields fogging up as they descended from the very cold air at 17,000–19,000 feet into the moist air at lower altitudes. A squadron commander said that it reduced bombing efficiency by 75 percent which certainly must have had a significant effect on the outcome of the battle. This happened during several of the attacks but not in the attack against the *Shoho*. In that dive the air was drier and there was no problem with fogging. The immediate solution was to initiate the dive from a lower altitude, around 12,000 feet. After the battle, changes were made to route hot engine air toward the windshield and bombsight. This was not done in time for the Midway battle but conditions in the Central Pacific were more temperate than the hot and humid South Pacific and it was not a problem there. The reflector-type bombsight used in the later SBD-5 had built-in heating and was less sensitive to fogging.

CHAPTER 12

# Battle of Midway

## Introduction

By late spring 1942, the IJN had conquered almost everything they intended to. The only problem was that the American carriers had not been neutralized, not at Pearl Harbor and not later. The Japanese needed to bring them to battle to defeat them. They needed a target that would force the Americans to give battle.

Midway suited this purpose. It was close enough to Pearl Harbor to be a threat that could not be ignored. It was far enough away so that the aircraft based at Pearl would not be able to participate. Midway was at the very end of the Japanese supply chain but this difficulty was accepted, as the island was so small that only a small garrison would have to be supported.

The Japanese plan was to first invade Midway and then to deal with the inevitable counterattack. A situation would then develop with a series of battles against US carriers where the Japanese had the advantage of owning the only land base in the area. This was the same game plan that the Americans would later use at Guadalcanal by capturing Henderson Field.

The only problem with the plan was that the dastardly enemy did not go along with it. Having broken the Japanese codes, the Americans instead planned an ambush that would coincide with the strike on Midway.

## Forces Available and Logistics

Japanese carriers included *Kaga*, *Akagi*, *Soryu*, and *Hiryu* escorted by two battleships, two heavy cruisers (each with five floatplanes), one light cruiser, and 11 destroyers. Each carrier had about 18 fighters, 18 dive bombers, and 18 torpedo bombers.

American Task Force 16 included the carriers *Enterprise* and *Hornet*, six cruisers and nine destroyers. Task Force 17 consisted of the carrier *Yorktown*, two cruisers, and six destroyers. Each carrier had about 27 fighters, 36 dive bombers, and 14 torpedo bombers. The new F4F-4 model of the Wildcat had folding wings, the previous F4F-3 model used at Coral Sea had fixed wings. This permitted an increase in the number of fighters to 27, against 18 at Coral Sea. The very high losses of bombers in that battle had shown that more fighters were needed, both as bomber escorts and as CAP.

The total fuel consumption of the Japanese invasion force was about 7,000 tons per day, steaming at an economical cruising speed. They brought with them 15 oilers, each carrying about 10,000 tons of oil on average. They only had fuel for three or maybe four weeks of operations.

## Command and Control

The Japanese carriers were commanded by Vice Admiral Chuichi Nagumo on the *Akagi*. The carriers steamed in one large but somewhat loose formation. Admiral Isoroku Yamamoto on board battleship *Yamato* was in overall command of the invasion and sailed with the main body in support of the invasion fleet, not with the carriers.

US Task Force 16 was under the command of Rear Admiral Raymond Spruance, and Task Force 17 was commanded by Rear Admiral Frank Fletcher. The overall commander was Spruance on the *Enterprise*. Fletcher, actually senior to Spruance, was in tactical command of both task forces.

TF 16 and TF 17 operated separately, about 20–40 miles apart. Within TF 16, the two carriers operated together but with separate screens and a few miles apart. TF 17 had only one carrier.

Both Japanese and American carriers could talk to the other carriers in their respective task forces using short-range radios, but once the strikes were launched, radio silence prevented the carriers from talking to their planes.

American carriers had air-warning radar and basic fighter direction but radio discipline remained poor. IFF was installed on a few fighters. The Japanese had no radar, essentially no fighter direction, and no IFF.

## Visibility and Wind

On June 4, 1942, at latitude 30°N and longitude 178°W, using the UTC-11 time zone, sunrise was at 0550 and sunset at 1950. Nautical twilight began at 0450 and ended at 2050.

Moonrise was at 0021 and moonset at 1152. At 0500, the moon was at 45° above the horizon and to the southeast. It was slightly more than half and waning. The moon could possibly help with very early-morning launches but not with late night landings.

The weather was dominated by the trade winds, a light breeze coming out of the southeast.

## Air Operations

At 0430 on June 4, a Japanese strike of 36 dive bombers, 36 torpedo bombers carrying bombs, and 36 fighters was launched against Midway and began attacking at 0620. This was about half the available planes, the other half being retained for a possible second strike. The readied bombers were kept below in the hangars so the flight decks could be used for CAP rotation.

At 0430, ten search planes were launched from *Yorktown*. The Japanese carriers were detected at 0534.

At 0750, both *Enterprise* and *Hornet* launched strikes with 67 dive bombers, 29 torpedo planes, and 20 fighters. This was all the bombers and slightly fewer than half the fighters. The escorting fighters later had to return prematurely for lack of fuel and did not defend the bombers in the actual attack.

At 0800, *Yorktown* launched an attack with 17 dive bombers, 12 torpedo planes, and six fighters. This strike used most of the dive bombers that remained after the search planes were sent off but most of the fighters remained for

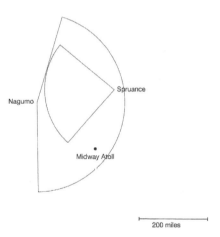

200 miles

Map of the battle of Midway. Positions are as of 0430 on the morning of June 4th, about the time when the morning search was launched. The search patterns flown are shown for both sides. Nagumo knew very little about his opponent and used a defensive pattern. Spruance knew roughly where Nagumo was and used a narrower pattern.

Devastators being spotted onboard *Enterprise* at Midway. Fourteen were sent off but only four returned. Note the ever present plane guard destroyer in the background.

CAP. The six fighters that had been sent as bomber escort also had to return prematurely for lack of fuel.

At 0740, a float plane from *Tone* sighted the American ships but made no mention of any carriers. Nagumo decided to recover his Midway strike before doing anything against the sighted ships. Recovery of the Midway strike was complete at 0917 and all aircraft were struck below. The second/reserve strike was already below, having never been launched. Now both halves of the air complements were below being readied for strikes against ships while all the flight decks were busy maintaining a defensive CAP. The Japanese carriers were now in an extremely vulnerable position. Everything hinged on the CAP being able to prevent any hits on the carriers.

The 15 torpedo bombers from *Hornet* arrived at 0925 and were promptly massacred. The 14 torpedo bombers from *Enterprise* arrived at 0930 and 10 of those were shot down. The 12 torpedo bombers from *Yorktown* arrived at 1000 and were also badly mauled. No hits were scored by any of these attacks but they did keep CAP busy and at low altitude.

The two dive-bomber squadrons from *Enterprise* arrived at 1025. Both squadrons attacked *Kaga*, scoring four or five hits. Having started his attack on *Kaga*, dive bomber pilot Rickard Best saw that *Akagi* was not being attacked. With his two wingmen he targeted *Akagi* instead, scoring one hit. That single hit was enough. Both *Kaga* and *Akagi* were soon engulfed in massive fires.

Both were later scuttled. The two dive-bomber squadrons from *Hornet* had gone off in a different direction and never found anything.

The dive-bomber squadron from *Yorktown* also happened to arrive at 1025 but from an entirely different direction. It attacked *Soryu* and scored three hits, causing massive fires. It later sank. *Hiryu* was not targeted by any of the dive bombers, only by torpedo bombers and suffered no hits.

*Hiryu* launched a counterattack at 1100 consisting of 18 dive bombers and six fighters. This strike attacked *Yorktown* at 1205 and scored three hits. Five of the attacking bombers and three of the fighters were shot down.

*Hiryu* launched a second counterattack at 1331 consisting of 10 torpedo bombers and six fighters. The vulnerable torpedo bombers had been held back for this second strike with the intention of using them to finish off the crippled *Yorktown*. *Yorktown* was attacked at 1430 and struck by two torpedoes. It was later abandoned.

*Hiryu* recovered this strike at 1540 and started preparing for a strike to launch at 1800.

At 1330, *Enterprise* launched 24 dive bombers, including 10 from *Yorktown*, against the *Hiryu*. At 1700, this strike arrived over the *Hiryu*, scoring four or five hits. For the second time this day, a Japanese carrier was caught with all planes in the hangars being armed and refueled. Again, the carrier exploded into a mass of fire and later sank.

## Analysis

Nagumo came looking for a fight and was surprised when he got it. Using superior intelligence and exquisite timing, the US carriers were able to get in an unanswered first strike. The strike also happened to catch the Japanese carriers at their most vulnerable. The battle was effectively over.

In fairness to Nagumo, it is quite uncommon that the enemy knows the exact time and place of your carrier raid. It is especially unusual and unpleasant if the enemy knows about your plans well in advance, giving him time for critical preparations. Anyone faulting Nagumo for not guarding enough against a highly unlikely threat must also accept the allocation of resources to guard against all other equally unlikely threats. The principle of "calculated risk" comes to mind.

Nagumo had an intrinsic problem in that he faced two opponents, Midway and the US carriers. Going after one meant revealing himself to the other. Nagumo could have done a sweep of the area but that could quite possibly have meant that the element of surprise would have been lost in the attack on Midway, assuming the Americans did not already know everything about his plans.

Given the actual situation, Nagumo did not maintain a thorough enough search of the surrounding seas before he busied himself with neutralizing Midway. He maintained his second strike fueled and ready to go but never used it, either against Midway or against the ships that had been found. High-level bombers posed no threat and torpedo bombers, arriving piecemeal and without escorts, was a threat he could handle. The real danger, the dive bombers, arrived and attacked when he had his strikes fully armed and fueled in the hangars, with disastrous consequences.

To avoid being hit while rearming and refueling, strikes have to be launched in sync with enemy strikes. Both sides then rearm and refuel at the same time. This is what happened at Coral Sea. As dawn broke, both sent out searches and both found and attacked each at other at more or less the same time. Nights have the effect of synchronizing everybody.

To stay in sync with any enemy carriers, Nagumo should have launched a very early search, then the strike against Midway and when the sighting report came, the second strike against those ships. In the absence of a sighting, the second strike could then be launched against Midway.

This brings us to the problem of arming planes for strikes against ships or against an island. One way around this problem is to arm all bombers against land targets and to use the torpedo bombers against Midway. Standard HE bombs used against land targets should be reasonably effective against unarmored targets like carrier decks. The relatively limited damage done by the semi-AP bomb hit on the *Yorktown* at Coral Sea should be compared to the massive damage done to the flight deck of *Shokaku* by standard HE bombs.

Staying in sync meant that Nagumo did not give the opponent any advantage—the Americans could not attack him when he was most vulnerable. On the other hand, it did not give Nagumo any advantage either. He still wanted to attack the US carriers when they were vulnerable, as happened to US carrier *Franklin* in 1944, with the same spectacular results that befell the Japanese carriers at Midway.

A better approach would therefore be to expect the ambush and to then ambush the ambushers, which is of course very easy to say in hindsight. This could have been done by the morning search and strike against Midway and then by heading west immediately after the launch of the strike. In its simplest form, the move would be pre-arranged with the Midway strike so that they would return to a position west of where they were launched. The combination of the search and the move west would have made sure that any US carrier strike would not have been able to reach them. Any US strike detected could then have been followed back to the US carriers by Nagumo's second strike, using their range advantage.

The Americans did no attempt to out-range Nagumo using the same shuttle tactics that was later used by Ozawa in the Philippine Sea battle. This would have meant flying off from the carriers, striking Nagumo, and then landing at Midway to refuel and rearm, then striking Nagumo again before landing back on the carriers. Nagumo also stayed at some distance from Midway Island, no invasion had yet been made, and there was no need get closer for ground support. If Nagumo had been tied to the beaches, shuttle tactics might have been possible. Still, any kind of outranging tactic would have been difficult to execute given the general range disadvantage of the American planes.

Also on a somewhat speculative note, the Japanese did not use a "bait" or "picket" carrier at Midway, as they did in later battles. The small carrier *Zuiho* could have been employed in this manner, acting as flank protection toward the south and east, in the general direction of Pearl Harbor. Another alternative would have been to use a surface force in that role, perhaps including the *Tone* and *Chikuma*, using their floatplanes to do searches. This force would also act as a picket line and threaten the US task force with a night surface action, as was done in later battles.

*Zuikaku* was not present for various reasons internal to the IJN. She was undamaged after Coral Sea and a full air group could have been assembled had there been a sense of urgency. On the other hand, once the invasion had been completed and the main body departed, there must be something available to guard the new possession. As it was, *Zuikaku* was used to train new pilots until sister *Shokaku* had been repaired.

The Japanese operated the carriers in one large and loose formation, providing mutual support in terms of CAP. This worked very well until CAP was out of place, then all four carriers could be attacked at the same time. It was an all-or-nothing style of defense. All flight decks were used for either CAP or strikes. There was no separation of tasks, using some for CAP and some for strikes. The Japanese liked to operate their carriers in pairs and launching coordinated strikes using a pair but at Midway there were two pairs and they need not have been used in the same way.

Mitscher was the captain of *Hornet*. He operated under Spruance, a non-aviator, flying his flag on the *Enterprise*, a few miles away. Mitscher appears to have disagreed with Spruance on where to send the strike, and the *Hornet* strike was sent off on a different vector. This did not work out very well—the *Hornet* strike never contacted anything.

After this battle, noting how the fighters did not have the range to escort the bombers all the way to the target, both Fletcher and Halsey urgently recommended that the F4F-4 Wildcats be equipped with drop tanks, a request that had been put forward before. A prototype drop tank was tested by *Yorktown* pilot Jimmy Flatley before Midway but this was not the same drop tank that was eventually adopted. The Wildcats would get their drop tanks by Santa Cruz but not in time for the upcoming Eastern Solomons battle.

US pilots were unhappy with the performance of the Wildcat. They considered it an overweight and underpowered "dog" compared to the nimble Zero. Things had got worse with the introduction of folding wings which added more weight. On the other hand, with the added weight, diving characteristics were now excellent. Things would get even worse at Santa Cruz when drop tanks had been added. However, it was at Midway that Jimmy Thach in VF-3 on *Yorktown* first demonstrated the use of the Thach Weave. This fighter tactic would do much to offset the problems the Wildcat had in a turning or climbing fight.

*Yorktown* was hit by a bomb that went through her unarmored flight deck and knocked out part of her machinery. Her speed reduced, she was very vulnerable to the torpedo attacks that eventually sank her. This means that all five carriers sunk succumbed to a sequence of events that started with a hit from a dive bomber. Had they had armored flight decks, it is quite possible that they would have all survived.

Seven fleet carriers entered this battle. After it was all over, only two remained afloat. Eggshells armed with hammers? Indeed. As the battle wound down and everybody refueled their destroyers and buried their dead, it might be worth noting what was happening elsewhere. The first of the new *Essex* class of carriers was only a few weeks away from launch, as was the first of the *Independence* class. About a dozen more carriers of these two classes were on the slipways, being built at a feverish tempo. Production of the 40mm Bofors was ramping up, and the new carriers would all be protected by large numbers of this the most effective AA weapon of the war. The Hellcat was just days away from rollout and first flight. The new carriers and the new fighter would all begin to join the fleet at Pearl Harbor less than a year after this battle.

As the *Essex* class was coming off the slipways, it was understood that the lack of an armored flight deck was a problem. Yet it would have to do. The first of the next class of carriers, what would become the *Midway* class, with armored flight decks, was still more than a year from being laid down.

Back in Japan, the *Taiho* had been laid down a year earlier but was still a year away from launch. It had an armored flight deck, something which the Japanese carriers could have used in this battle. It was the only ship of its class. More were planned but after the disaster of this battle, priority would have to go to cheaper and simpler carriers that could be built more quickly. Apart from the *Taiho*, although an excellent design, nothing much was going on.

The battle was over but in the background that huge disparity in industrial capacity was whirring away. In the preceding years, Japan had spent a good deal of its national fortune building a very impressive navy. The problem was that it was essentially a one-shot navy. Now that shot had been fired. Japan would struggle to replace its losses. It would go on to have trouble even keeping its navy fueled.

# The Commanders

## Isoroku Yamamoto

Present and badly injured at the battle of Tsushima in 1905, losing two fingers. The father of the Kido Butai, the Japanese carrier force. It is much due to Yamamoto that the Japanese were so successful in 1942, having a clear advantage over the Americans in both materiel and doctrine. He apparently never recovered from the blow at Midway and was then further ground down by the Guadalcanal campaign. He was killed in an ambush by P-38 fighters in 1943 while on an inspection tour in the Solomons. By then his hair had turned completely white.

## Chuichi Nagumo

Nagumo was skewered at Midway but was allowed to continue as commander at both Eastern Solomons and Santa Cruz, handling both battles well. In both cases he faced an opponent intent on attritional warfare which made them thankless tasks. He was stationed on Saipan when it was invaded, and as the fighting on the ground came to an end committed suicide.

## Jisaburo Ozawa

Ozawa was perhaps the most competent of the Japanese carrier commanders. He lost badly at both Philippine Sea and at Cape Engaño but through no fault of his own. Philippine Sea was handled particularly well tactically but his forces were just outclassed and Spruance played his part of the game without making mistakes. He was noted for being exceptionally tall at six feet 7 inches when the average height of Japanese men was 5 feet 4 inches (Yamamoto was 5 feet 3 inches). He was a whole foot taller than most of his men and was called "The Gargoyle." He survived the war to be interrogated by US officials who came to respect him very much. Like most Japanese after the war, he saw the conflict as a huge mistake. Wars started and then lost, decisively and badly, tend to be seen that way.

## Minoru Genda

An aviator and pioneer in using carriers together as an independent force of strategical importance, not just an adjunct to the battle line, to be used for scouting and raiding. Responsible for much of the training in preparation for the Pearl Harbor attack, he also served as staff officer under Nagumo on board *Akagi*. He fought as a fighter pilot and survived the war, becoming a politician.

## Chester W. Nimitz

Like Yamamoto, Nimitz was the able administrator and strategist. He drew up the main plans for the Pacific campaign, judiciously using his forces while cooperating with MacArthur. His emphasis on "calculated risk" as the guiding principle is of course an exemplary application of Operations Research.

## William F. Halsey

Known as "Bull" to the press, Halsey was very popular with the public at the time but his popularity has not aged well. Historians have analyzed his sometimes erratic behavior in some detail and he is now quite a controversial figure.

He can be criticized for charging everything in sight, but this fighting instinct was genuinely needed, at least in 1942. Peacetime produces many rule-followers but when the body parts start flying there is a need for ruthlessness and aggressiveness that during peacetime may not have had time and opportunity to be properly calibrated. At Leyte he made some serious mistakes but the end result was still good. Being lucky is an important part of being a good commander.

Halsey suffered from a skin condition. He should have commanded the US forces at Midway but his skin condition was so bad that Spruance substituted for him.

## Raymond A. Spruance

Played very intelligent games at both Midway and Philippine Sea. Noted for being very cool and calculated in his thinking; he made no errors.

## Miles R. Browning

Browning is a lesser known but interesting man. He served as Halsey's chief of staff, and when Spruance replaced Halsey at Midway, he inherited Browning. It was Browning who persuaded Spruance to time the strike so as to catch the Japanese while rearming and refueling planes.

A brilliant man but somewhat irascible and a heavy drinker, he was protected by Halsey but eventually there were just too many incidents and in early 1944 he was removed from command as captain of the (new) *Hornet* and exiled to Kansas, serving as an instructor in carrier tactics at Fort Leavenworth until the end of the war. He would probably have been better employed helping Halsey avoid the mistakes at Leyte. For all his skill and success at Midway, he was universally hated by the aviators for failing to assist in the rescue of downed aircrew.

### Frank Jack Fletcher

Fletcher has been harshly treated by historians. Much of his papers were lost during the war and he declined to be interviewed. Morison mostly ignored him, with subsequent historians largely following in that path. Furthermore, aviators found it useful to criticize a non-aviator like Fletcher. The Solomons campaign ruined many reputations and Fletcher got his part of that. King did not like him but Nimitz was a strong supporter.

He was in charge at both the confused Coral Sea battle and the Eastern Solomons draw. He was subordinate to Spruance at Midway. Recent historians, notably Lundstrom, have done much to restore his reputation. His decisions were essentially correct and based on the information available to him at the time.

### Marc A. Mitscher

Mitscher had a bad day at Midway, commanding *Hornet* whose air group ended up contributing absolutely nothing to the battle except having its torpedo bombers massacred. Still, when later in 1943 given another opportunity, he proved himself a very able leader.

CHAPTER 13

# Operation *Pedestal*

## Introduction

Operation *Pedestal* was a convoy of August 1942 with the intention of resupplying the island of Malta, close to starvation and surrendering to Axis powers. Malta was critical as a base for interdicting Axis convoys to North Africa. At this time, Erwin Rommel was advancing toward Egypt and the Suez Canal.

A convoy was assembled, loaded with necessary supplies of food, fuel, and ammunition. Only the fastest freighters available were used, to increase their chances of succeeding in making the run. The convoy was then given an exceptionally strong escorting force. The battle was then on to get as many freighters as possible through to Malta.

The convoy was subjected to intense air attacks, as well as attacks by submarines and small surface crafts. It was not a true carrier battle in that there were no carriers on the Axis side, only land-based aircraft. The operation nevertheless is instructive as to how a multi-carrier RN force operated in a battle against serious opposition.

## Forces Available and Logistics

The British had committed four carriers to this operation. The *Furious* had embarked 38 Spitfires for delivery to Malta. These were flown at an early stage and the ship returned to Gibraltar. HMS *Eagle* was sunk by U-73 early in the operation, only four of its Sea Hurricanes were saved.

| | |
|---|---|
| *Eagle* | 16 Sea Hurricanes |
| *Victorious* | 6 Sea Hurricanes, 16 Fulmars, 12 Albacores |
| *Indomitable* | 24 Sea Hurricanes, 10 Martlets, 16 Albacores |

This leaves us with a defending CAP of 34 Sea Hurricanes, 10 Martlets, and 16 Fulmars. The Albacores were not used, as no attack by major Italian surface units developed. Cruisers *Nigeria* and *Cairo* had been fitted with fighter-direction gear and the intention was that they would direct the fighters operating from Malta.

## Command and Control

RN carriers and cruisers had air-warning radars. No IFF was used. The RN carriers had good fighter direction with *Victorious* probably having the best team. Cruisers *Cairo* and *Nigeria* had been fitted for directing the fighters based at Malta (i.e. the ones delivered by *Furious*). Radar reporting and fighter direction was rehearsed as the convoy departed.

The convoy consisted of 14 merchant ships steaming in four columns with three to four ships in each column. Ahead and to the sides of the convoy was an extensive screen of destroyers. Behind the convoy were the carriers and their escorts. The convoy had exercised emergency turns and change of formation. Communications within the convoy was with both signal flags and short-range radio. Breaking radio silence was accepted.

As the convoy approached enemy waters, all escorts refueled at sea, as there was no longer any oil to be had at Malta if and when they arrived there.

## Visibility and Wind

On August 12, 1942, at latitude 37°N and longitude 10°E, using the UTC+1 time zone, sunrise was at 0534 and sunset at 1916. Nautical twilight began at 0432 and ended at 2018.

Moonrise was at 0546 and moonset at 1930. The night was moonless, perfect for running a convoy through. The date had been chosen with care.

The weather was not much of a factor in this operation, with generally light winds, scattered clouds, and good to excellent visibility.

## Air Operations

The convoy was continuously tracked by land-based reconnaissance aircraft. No attempt appears to have been made to shoot these down. Visibility was good; they only needed to track the convoy and did not need to come close to identify ships. The defending CAP were probably not much faster than the reconnaissance aircraft, so there was little point in trying to chase them off.

Flight decks were in more or less continuous use to keep the CAP aloft. No searches were launched and no strikes were spotted or launched.

The first attack occurred on the evening of August 11. It consisted of 36 Ju-88 and He-111. The Ju-88s did shallow glide bombing and the He-111s dropped torpedoes. No hits were scored and two bombers were shot down by AA.

On the 12th, the first attack of 19 Ju-88 was met by fighters and AA. Four bombers were shot down by the fighters and two by AA.

On the afternoon of the 12th, five waves of Axis aircraft attacked. The first was made up of Savoia bombers releasing a special type of bomb that fell in a zigzag pattern hanging in parachutes but did so from too high an altitude and too far away. No hits were scored.

The second wave consisted of 40 Italian torpedo bombers, but facing very heavy AA they dropped their torpedoes too early and no hits were scored. The third wave consisted of German dive bombers which hit and sank one of the freighters. The fourth wave was two remote-controlled floatplanes but the communications link failed and they flew off and crashed in Algeria.

The fifth wave consisted of two Re.2001 carrying 750kg HE bombs. Looking very similar to returning Sea Hurricanes they were not molested. Both dropped their bombs on the *Victorious*, scoring one hit which failed to explode.

Later in the evening, a group of Savoia torpedo bombers attacked in conjunction with a group of Ju-87 dive bombers. The Ju-87s were instructed to attack the merchants but ignored orders and attacked *Indomitable* instead, scoring two hits that wrecked its flight deck. As previously planned, this was also the time for the carriers to return to Gibraltar, which they did at 1855.

At 1955, both *Nigeria* and *Cairo* were hit by torpedoes from an Italian submarine with *Cairo* sinking and *Nigeria* ordered back to Gibraltar. As these ships had been tasked with fighter direction, the convoy was now without both fighters and fighter direction.

At 2035, an attack by 30 Ju-88 and seven He-111 sank two freighters. During the night to the 13th the convoy was attacked by Italian motor torpedo boats. The cruiser *Manchester* plus four merchants were sunk.

On the morning of the 13th, the convoy was attacked several times by various groups of Ju-87s and Ju-88s that sank two more freighters. By now the convoy was within fighter cover from Malta. Initially the defending fighters did not cause the attackers too much trouble but as the convoy got closer to Malta the fighter defense got stronger. In the afternoon, 16 Spitfires were over the remaining ships at all times, hindering further attacks. At 1818, the first three freighters entered Valletta harbor.

During the 14th, the freighter *Brisbane Star* also arrived. The tanker *Ohio* was still at sea, being towed slowly toward Malta. Some more attacks developed during the day but were beaten off by escorting Spitfires with only one near miss causing some damage. Late in the evening, the *Ohio* slowly crept into

Valletta harbor to cheering crowds. Soon after having been emptied of its cargo, it finally sank and settled on the bottom of the harbor.

Of the original 14 merchants, five had successfully made it into Malta. Despite the heavy losses, the convoy had accomplished its mission. Thus reinforced, Malta resumed attacking Axis supply lines and a few months later Rommel was defeated at El Alamein.

## Analysis

The convoy had 650 planes arrayed against them. The carriers had 60 fighters. There was no way the enemy planes could be kept away from the carriers or the convoy. The armored flight decks were needed and the transports were expendable.

More fighters could possibly have been carried, particularly on the *Victorious*, even more so if deck parks had been used, as they were later in the war against the Japanese.

Fighter direction did not use VHF, only standard HF radios, but still proved effective. However, the number of fighters controlled was quite limited.

The fleet carriers were considered too valuable to accompany the convoy all the way to Malta. A handoff was to be made as soon as the new fighters at Malta could take over. Fighter direction was understood to be very important. The loss of *Nigeria* and *Cairo*, both intended to handle fighter direction after the carriers had returned, significantly weakened the effectiveness of fighter cover late on the 13th and throughout the 14th, but as the convoy came closer to Malta this became less of an issue.

Still, the defense of the convoy was quite successful in beating off the air attacks. AA fire was intense and fighter direction was efficient while it lasted. The attacking aircraft tended to release their bombs and torpedoes too early, and relatively few hits were scored compared to the volume of attacks. The losses due to AA were also relatively low compared to the number of aircraft involved. This all points to the attacks not being pressed home with enough vigor, compared to how many hits the Japanese achieved under similar circumstances and how many losses they accepted.

Both sides played the game as well as could be expected. The British were unable to hide the passage of the convoy but that was pretty much an impossibility anyway. The British were successful in warding off a surface attack by heavy Italian units that would have completely destroyed the convoy.

# Battle of the Eastern Solomons

## Introduction

The Americans had landed on Guadalcanal on August 7, 1942, capturing the airfield there and renaming it Henderson Field. Both fighters and bombers were then quickly flown in, to become what would later be known as the Cactus Air Force, Cactus being the Allied codename for Guadalcanal.

The Japanese immediately counterattacked. A US airfield on Guadalcanal threatened their hold over the entire Solomons. In a surface battle on the night of the 9th, Allied cruisers were badly beaten in the battle of Savo Island. This forced the Americans to withdraw the transports off the landing site at Guadalcanal. The Japanese obviously wanted to recapture Henderson Field but to be able to do that, reinforcements were needed there.

Guadalcanal was a curious situation in that effectively *both* sides had landing sites to defend. With the possession of Henderson Field, the Americans had aerial superiority most of the time, preventing the Japanese from bringing in reinforcements. The Japanese decided to challenge that aerial superiority, at least temporarily, in order to run a proper convoy through.

Tasked with preventing such a convoy coming through, the American carriers were to a degree tied to the general area of Guadalcanal. The Japanese on their side could choose when and where to attack to run a convoy through. Once they had launched such an operation, however, it was up to the Americans to ambush it.

## Forces Available and Logistics

The IJN Carrier Striking Force had carriers *Shokaku* and *Zuikaku* escorted by six destroyers. Operating separately was the Detached Force made up of the small carrier *Ryujo*, cruiser *Tone* with its six floatplanes, and two more destroyers.

The Japanese had additional surface forces involved in this battle but they never played much of a role.

Each of the large carriers had 27 fighters, 27 dive bombers, and 18 torpedo bombers. *Ryujo* had 24 fighters, and six torpedo bombers.

On the US side, Task Force 11 consisted of the carrier *Saratoga* with cruisers *Minneapolis* and *New Orleans* together with five destroyers.

Task Force 16 had the carrier *Enterprise* escorted by battleship *North Carolina*, cruisers *Portland* and *Atlanta*, plus six more destroyers. Each of these carriers had about 27 fighters, 36 dive bombers, and 14 torpedo bombers.

Task Force 18 with carrier *Wasp* and its escorts of cruisers *San Francisco*, *Salt Lake City*, and *San Juan* with seven destroyers had been sent south for refueling on the mistaken information that a Japanese push was not to be expected. They would return to the area two days after the battle. *Wasp* carried 25 fighters, 26 dive bombers, and nine torpedo bombers. It had trouble with its machinery and was limited to a speed of 22 knots.

Before the battle, carrier *Enterprise* had all but one of its quad 1.1-inch AA mounts removed and replaced with four of the new quad 40mm Bofors mounts. It was one of the very first ships to get the new mounts, the battleship *North Carolina* got hers in September. *Saratoga* entered this battle with its new twin 5-inch/38 mounts instead of the old 8-inch guns but would only get its Bofors mounts in October of that year.

The new TBF Avengers had by now replaced the old TBD Devastators. The Avengers were less vulnerable in themselves as they were much faster and could also now keep pace with the dive bombers, which made the coordination and escorting of a strike much easier.

## Command and Control

The Carrier Striking Force was commanded by Vice Admiral Chuichi Nagumo on board the *Shokaku*. The Detached Force was commanded by Rear Admiral Chuichi Hara on the *Ryujo*. Both were under the overall command of Admiral Isoroku Yamamoto on board the *Yamato* operating south of Truk.

As usual the carriers operated together in one large and somewhat loose formation. The Japanese used the small carrier *Ryujo* as bait or diversion, operating separately 100 miles in advance of the main carrier force of the large carriers. The intention was to elicit and absorb the first US strike, after which the Japanese could attack a located enemy that was busy elsewhere.

The ensemble of US carrier task forces was called Task Force 61 and was commanded by Vice Admiral Frank Fletcher on board the *Saratoga*. TF 11 and TF 16 sailed each with their own escorts and separated by 10–15 miles. Within TF 16, the battleship *North Carolina* steamed close to the *Enterprise*, about 1,000 yards away, doing its best to support *Enterprise* with heavy AA fire.

Both Japanese and American carriers could talk to each other using short-range radios. Once launched, radio silence generally prevented the carriers from talking to their planes but sometimes radio messages were sent anyway if they were important enough and if the enemy could be assumed to already know about the carrier.

American carriers had air-warning radar and basic fighter direction but radio discipline remained poor. IFF was installed on a few fighters. For the first time, the Japanese had air-warning radar (a Type 21 installed on the *Shokaku*) but essentially no fighter direction.

## Visibility and Wind

On August 24, 1942, at latitude 7°S and longitude 163°E, using the UTC+11 time zone, sunrise was at 0613 and sunset at 1808. Nautical twilight began at 0527 and ended at 1854.

Moonrise was at 1617 and moonset at 0404. At 2000 the moon was 51° above the horizon and to the east. It was almost full and waxing and was of help with late landings.

The weather was clear with excellent visibility and scattered cumulus clouds. The wind was from the southeast. Toward the night of the 24th the weather worsened with lower visibility and more clouds.

## Air Operations

As dawn broke on the 24th, neither side knew much about the other, neither disposition nor whereabouts. The Americans knew from many signs that a big Japanese operation was under way and that the purpose must be to reinforce Guadalcanal. The Japanese knew that the Americans were going to oppose them. The Japanese had just changed their codes so the code breakers contributed little useful information to Fletcher during the run-up to the battle.

The Japanese were coming down from Truk to the north. During the night, the Detached Force had left the Striking Force behind and steamed south at speed. Hara had orders to attack Guadalcanal, draw attention to himself and provide the Striking Force with targeting data on the US carriers. Nagumo would hit them and the surface forces would then move in and sink whatever was left of the US forces. At least that was the plan. As usual with the Japanese, it was a fairly intricate plan and depended rather heavily on the enemy behaving as expected.

As part of this plan, Nagumo had prepared strikes. The first strike would consist of 54 dive bombers and 24 fighters arranged in two deck-load waves. The second strike would be of 36 torpedo planes and 12 fighters in one deck load. The new policy was that the torpedo bombers should be held back until defenses had been weakened. In previous battles, the torpedo bombers had suffered very heavy losses and the intention was to use them more judiciously.

Both sides were now engaged in a game of hide-and-seek until the enemy carriers had been located. Both sides had elaborate search patterns arranged, by both carrier-based planes, ship-based float-planes, land-based flying boats, and long-range reconnaissance aircraft. Both sides longed intensely for that unanswered first strike that would win the battle, as Midway had demonstrated. One can only wonder how well the various commanders slept the night before the day that would most likely bring forth a major battle.

At 0555 on the 24th, the *Enterprise* launched 20 scouts to search the northern semicircle out to 200 miles. *Saratoga* launched a CAP of eight fighters. Fletcher later instructed *Enterprise* that it would be responsible for search, CAP, and ASW patrols that day. *Saratoga* would be the strike carrier. This made sense as *Saratoga* had the longer flight deck and could house a somewhat bigger strike. It had room for about six more planes in a strike, everything else being equal.

At 0615, the *Shokaku* and *Zuikaku* launched 19 Kates to search the eastern semicircle out to 250 miles.

At 0935, a Catalina patrol plane spotted the small carrier *Ryujo* with escorts. At this point the target was out of range at 281 miles away. Fletcher also knew that this was not going to be the only carrier in the area. He held his fire.

At 0947, expecting its dawn search to come back soon, *Enterprise* launched a CAP of eight Wildcats and eight Dauntless. Another three Avengers were launched as ASW patrol. At 1010, the dawn search had been recovered.

A strike from *Saratoga* the previous day had spent the night at Henderson Field. By 1100, *Saratoga* had recovered this strike consisting of 29 Dauntless and seven Avengers. Before the recovery began, a new CAP of 12 Wildcats was launched.

At 1110, Fletcher received a new sighting report placing the *Ryujo* 245 miles away. He was still reluctant to order a strike. He remembered Coral sea when after having sent off the strike that sunk the *Shoho*, he received a report of the sighting of the *Zuikaku* and *Shokaku* within range. At 1140, Fletcher ordered *Enterprise* to launch a new search as soon as possible. Between 1235 and 1247, *Enterprise* launched 16 Wildcats as CAP plus a search of

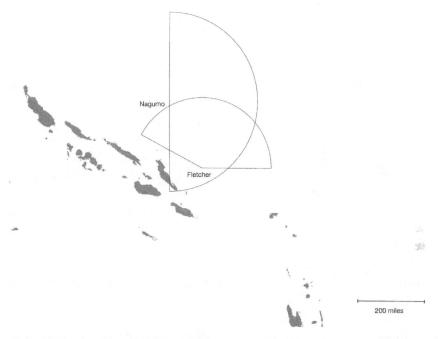

Map of the battle of Eastern Solomons. Positions are as of 0600 on the morning of August 24th, about the time when the morning search was launched. The search patterns flown are shown for both sides.

16 Dauntless and seven Avengers to search the northern semicircle again. Another six Dauntless took over as ASW patrol. At 1307, *Enterprise* recovered CAP including those from *Saratoga*. *Saratoga* had a strike ready to go so in a somewhat unusual display of operational flexibility, Wildcats from *Saratoga* used *Enterprise* instead.

At 1340, Fletcher finally launched a strike on the *Ryujo* using 30 Dauntless and seven Avengers from *Saratoga*. No fighters accompanied this strike, they were retained as CAP for the expected attack from the enemy large carriers. Both US carriers used their flight decks to service CAP while the strike was away. Both carriers also prepared strikes down in the hangar to be brought up and sent off when the large Japanese carriers had been found. At 1403, *Enterprise* launched eight more Wildcats as CAP.

At 1425, a scout floatplane from *Chikuma* sighted the US carriers. The scout was shot down but not before it had sent off the report. It placed the US carriers about 260 miles to the south. Nagumo immediately ordered the prepared strikes to launch and by 1450 the first wave of 27 Vals dive bombers and 15 Zero fighters had been sent off.

At 1515, two US scouts sighted the two large Japanese carriers with plenty of planes on the flight decks but for various communication reasons the report never reached Fletcher. He still did not know that they were now 250 miles north of him. The two scouts did make bombing runs on the *Shokaku* which barely missed. Both carriers immediately reacted by launching the CAP they had on decks, raising the total number aloft to 27.

At 1600, the second wave of the first strike had been sent off by Nagumo's carriers. This consisted of 27 Vals and nine Zeros. Both carriers retained their 18 Kate torpedo bombers in the hangars, reserved for a second strike.

At about the same time, *Ryujo* was found by the strike from *Saratoga*. Its decks were empty—it had earlier sent off a strike on Henderson Field and they had not yet returned. The CAP consisted of only seven Zeros, some of them just launched and unable to gain altitude to intercept effectively. The ships in the formation spread out to give everybody freedom to maneuver. Three bomb hits were scored as well as one hit by a torpedo. *Ryujo* would sink a few hours later. One of the defending Zeros was shot down with no loss to the attackers.

When the first strike from the Japanese large carriers arrived, the strike against the *Ryujo* had not yet returned. A strike was ready to go on the flight deck of *Enterprise* so *Saratoga* handled CAP rotation. The strike numbered 11 Dauntless, eight Avengers, and seven Wildcats.

At 1602, the incoming strike was detected on radar, 88 miles from *Enterprise* and 103 miles from *Saratoga* but both disappeared from the radar screens. The strike on *Enterprise* was launched to clear the flight deck and told to go hunting northwards. More CAP was launched and now there were no fewer than 54 Wildcats circling above the carriers, stacked in three layers. At 1619, the air battle starts. At 1629, the dive bombers began their dives. *Enterprise* was hit by three bombs, a 250kg bomb at the fantail, then a second on the 5-inch guns in the same area, and finally a third hit forward of the no. 2 elevator. The attack was over at 1648. Fires were quickly brought under control and the flight deck was patched. An hour after these hits, *Enterprise* was operational again.

In the final tally, of the 27 Val dive bombers and 15 Zero fighters, 17 Vals and seven Zeros were shot down. Most planes were lost in the massive air battle with relatively few shot down by AA. Defending CAP lost five Wildcats.

The strike from *Saratoga* that sunk *Ryujo* was recovered by 1805. Later, the strike launched just before the attack was also recovered, not having found anything.

The second wave of the first strike approached the US carriers around 1815 but never located *Enterprise*, as it had steamed in circles for a few hours instead of a normal course. The second strike against the US carriers was never launched.

At the end of the battle, Fletcher still did not know how many carriers he had faced. He knew that there had been two large fleet carriers and that they were the ones that had launched the major strike that hit him, but he did not know if there was only one or maybe two additional carriers.

## Analysis

This was the first battle in which the Japanese clearly used a "bait" carrier. The *Ryujo* was placed well ahead of the two main carriers which managed to remain undetected by Fletcher while themselves able to get in an unanswered first strike.

Not knowing where the enemy was, Fletcher played a cautious game. His strike against *Ryujo* was limited and he maintained a very large CAP over his carriers. The strike met weak CAP and had no problems in sinking the carrier, despite somewhat inaccurate bombing. *Ryujo* had its decks clear of planes, but three bombs and one torpedo was just too much for a small carrier. The strike suffered few losses.

Nagumo's strike was the main event of the battle but only involved a third of his attack planes. Nagumo also retained a very significant CAP. His attack ran into heavy opposition in the form of a large CAP. With the attacking fighters totally outnumbered by defending CAP fighters, the dive bombers were badly mauled, both before and after they had made their attack runs. With very dedicated and skilled bombing, three hits were scored on *Enterprise*. With few planes on the deck, the fires were soon put out. A fleet carrier is a big ship and can take some hits as long as the fires can be brought under control.

Fletcher's search did find the two big Japanese carriers. There was nothing wrong with his searches. He was denied the sighting report by a breakdown in communications. Had the report got through, he had medium-size strike ready to go. It would have run into a medium-size CAP contingent over the Japanese carriers. These had the torpedo bombers that had been held back ready to go, fueled and armed, and was in a vulnerable position should the strike have been able to get fires going. Holding back a strike for a better opportunity later on is a gamble. It has the drawback of not using what is available, a form of 'opportunity cost'. It also endangers the carriers they are sitting on.

This was the first battle in which the US carriers played different roles. *Saratoga* was the strike carrier and the *Enterprise* handled search, CAP, and anti-submarine patrols, while also doing fighter direction. This meant that fighters from *Saratoga* sometimes used *Yorktown* for refueling and rearming; this was now done as matter of routine, not just in an emergency. In mid-battle the two carriers also switched roles.

Radar was important in giving defending CAP time to climb to altitude, or the right altitude. This was particularly important for the Wildcat as it needed an altitude advantage to take on the nimbler and faster-climbing Zero. The radar used the distances at which the incoming bogeys were not seen by the radar to determine at what height the bogeys flew through the radar lobes, but the altitude calculated proved to be off by 4,000 feet. The Wildcats were sent to 12,000 feet when the incoming bogeys were at 16,000 feet. The CXAM set was not good at height finding and fighter direction failed.

A problem with radar was the lack of IFF. Fighters had to spend an inordinate amount of time and fuel inspecting friendlies, like the odd returning search plane or land-based search planes that happened to appear over friendly ships.

Another problem was radio discipline. Not just excessive chatter but also who said what at which time, there was a lack of both clarity and brevity in all involved. Fighter-direction methods in general needed to be adapted to work with 100+ planes in intense combat at the same time. VHF radios and the additional frequencies they allowed were requested.

This was also the first battle in which the Japanese used radar. It spotted the two scouts that found them and did attack runs, but the information from the radar was not forwarded to CAP fighters. The Japanese simply did not use the new radar for fighter direction.

In a larger context, the US carriers went north looking for a battle in a way they really did not have to do. They could have stayed closer to Guadalcanal and operated more with the support of planes from Henderson Field. There were advantages with a more aggressive posture and attempting an ambush on the Japanese forces, but Halsey elected to do so at a time when his third carrier was being refueled, leaving room for improvement in how *Wasp* was employed. With regards to refueling, it is not clear if it was *Wasp* that needed to refuel or if it was one of its escorts. Maybe sharing escorts among the task forces and refueling escorts and carriers in separation could have enabled *Wasp* to stay within reach of the battle area.

## Note on *Saratoga*

This was the only carrier battle that *Saratoga* participated in. It missed Coral Sea, being in dry dock after a submarine torpedo hit it, and also missed

Midway, arriving at Pearl Harbor on June 6. At this battle it was not hit but then sat out Santa Cruz after another submarine torpedo hit. Philippine Sea was missed by a refit and Cape Engaño by a collision with one of its escorts.

Several other carriers only participated in one battle but that was usually because they were sunk. *Saratoga* managed to survive the war, including all the desperate 1942 battles, simply by being absent most of the time.

However, it survived the war only to be sunk by an atomic bomb at Bikini Atoll. It is now one of only two World War II carriers that are accessible to recreational divers (*Hermes* is the other). The ship rests in about 180 feet of water, sitting upright. Its flight deck is about 90 feet down and the top of its superstructure is about 50 feet below the surface.

CHAPTER 15

# Battle of the Santa Cruz Islands

## Introduction

The Guadalcanal campaign grinds on. We are now in October of 1942. The Japanese surface forces dominate at night and can reinforce their forces but only using high-speed night runs as they have to be out of range of Henderson Field by daybreak. This is not an efficient or sufficient form of supply. US forces enjoy air cover during the day and can reinforce using regular transports.

The Japanese attempt to break the blockade and to run a proper convoy through to reinforce their forces in order to finally be able to capture Henderson Field. The upcoming battle is in many ways a repeat of the Eastern Solomons battle.

## Forces Available and Logistics

The Japanese Striking Force consisted of the Carrier Group and the Vanguard Group. The Carrier Group consisted of *Shokaku*, *Zuikaku*, and *Zuiho*. The screen consisted of cruiser *Kumano* and eight destroyers. The Vanguard Group had the battleships *Hiei* and *Kirishima*, cruisers *Tone*, *Chikuma*, and *Suzuya*, plus light cruiser *Nagara* and seven destroyers. Planes carried were as follows:

*Shokaku*   20 Zero, 21 Val, 24 Kate, 1 Judy
*Zuikaku*   20 Zero, 22 Val, 20 Kate
*Zuiho*     20 Zero, 9 Kate

The lone Judy dive bomber on *Shokaku* was a pre-production model used for search. The Judy was intended to replace the slow and aging Val but development troubles prevented the type from being used as a dive bomber. With its speed and range it was still very useful in the reconnaissance role.

The Advance Force had battleships *Kongo* and *Haruna*, heavy cruisers *Atago*, *Takao*, *Myoko*, and *Maya* plus light cruiser *Isuzu* and ten destroyers. Carrier *Junyo* acted as screen for the Advance Force and would participate in the battle. *Junyo* was a converted liner with a top speed of about 25 knots which meant that it had trouble operating its Kates in light winds. Sister *Hiyo* was slated to participate in the battle but suffered engine trouble and had to return to Truk. Planes carried were as follows:

*Junyo*   21 Zero, 21 Val, 10 Kate

US Task Force 16 consisted of the carrier *Enterprise*, battleship *South Dakota*, cruisers *Portland* and *San Juan*, plus seven destroyers. Task Force 17 consisted of the carrier *Hornet*, cruisers *Northampton*, *Pensacola*, *San Diego*, and *Juneau*, plus six destroyers. Together these two task forces were called Task Force 61. Planes carried were as follows, with numbers actually operational on the morning of the 26th within parentheses:

*Enterprise*   36(31) Wildcat, 36(30) Dauntless, 14(9) Avenger
*Hornet*        37(32) Wildcat, 36(24) Dauntless, 14(15) Avenger

Both carriers were operating at maximum capacity in terms of the number of planes that could be handled. Both carriers consigned the surplus to act as spares including the extra pilots.

Avengers had replaced the old Devastators and the torpedo planes could now keep pace with the dive bombers. Most Wildcat fighters were now fitted with two 58-gallon drop tanks, effectively almost doubling range. The Wildcats on board *Hornet* were fitted with a smaller belly drop tank that was the first such tank tried but it was only used for a short time, superseded by twin-wing tanks of greater capacity.

The new battleship *South Dakota* was equipped with four of the new quad 40mm mounts, as was *Enterprise* but not *Hornet*. These were the first mounts to enter service, priority being given to carriers and battleships. None of the cruisers or destroyers had any 40mm mounted during this battle. The new dedicated AA cruisers *San Juan*, *San Diego*, and *Juneau* were now available as escorts, having a 5-inch battery with an AA capability almost equal to that of a battleship.

The new VT proximity fuze was not yet available. The first combat use of the VT fuze would have to wait until January 5, 1943 when the 5-inch battery of cruiser *Helena* shot down an attacking Val.

## Command and Control

The Carrier Group was commanded by Vice Admiral Chuichi Nagumo on board *Shokaku*. This force steamed in one large but somewhat loose formation.

The Vanguard Group was commanded by Rear Admiral Hiroake Abe on the battleship *Hiei*. This group operated about 70 miles ahead of the carriers. The intention was to soak up strikes, protecting the carriers. Another advantage was that the float planes on *Tone* and *Chikuma* now started out closer to the enemy and could search faster and more effectively. *Tone* and *Chikuma* were two heavy cruisers that had all the 8-inch guns forward of the bridge, making room for a sort of flight deck aft that carried six catapult-launched Jake floatplanes. These two cruisers usually ran with the carriers, doing searches for them, allowing the carriers to devote all their aircraft to strikes.

The Advance Force was commanded by Vice Admiral Nobutake Kondo on board the cruiser *Atago*. This force operated west of the Striking Force and would support an attack on Henderson Field at Guadalcanal.

The US TF 61 was commanded by Rear Admiral Thomas Kinkaid on board *Enterprise*. The individual task forces for each carrier steamed 10–15 miles apart. The two carriers alternated each day as to which would be the duty carrier, in charge of searches, CAP, ASW patrol, and fighter direction.

Neither commander had had much help from radio traffic analysis and cryptanalysis. They both knew that the other side had carriers in the area, but beyond that not much was known.

Both Japanese and American carriers could talk to each other using short-range radios. Once launched, radio silence normally prevented the carriers from talking to their planes.

American carriers had air-warning radar and basic fighter direction but radio discipline remained poor. IFF was installed on a few fighters. *Shokaku* had air-warning radar but did not use it for fighter direction during the battle, partly by doctrine and partly because the Zeros had problems with their radios.

## Visibility and Wind

On October 26, 1942, at latitude 8°S and longitude 165°E, using the UTC+11 time zone, sunrise was at 0534 and sunset at 1755. Nautical twilight began at 0447 and ended at 1841.

Moonrise was at 1939 and moonset at 0658. The moon was low on the horizon at both dusk and dawn and only marginally useful for late landings. The moon was slightly less than full; once it had risen the moonlight was bright.

The weather was clear with scattered cumulus clouds, some of them large. Visibility was good and the wind was moderate from the southeast.

## Air Operations

On the afternoon of October 25, Kinkaid did something interesting. At 1336, he sent out a search of six pairs of Dauntless scouts to search between 280° and 010°. This was standard. However, right after the search, he also sent out a strike of 16 Wildcats, 12 Dauntless, and seven Avengers. These were to go down the median of the search and would attack immediately anything the scouts had found. They would only go out to 150 miles and if nothing had been found by then, to return. This was quite an unusual gamble, a combined search and strike or "reconnaissance in force." He did not send everything he had, however; it was still a rather small strike but still a good example of the principle of "calculated risk" ordered by Admiral Nimitz.

At 1425, the last plane had departed. Soon after Kinkaid had sent this force, he learned that Nagumo had turned around and gone back north. He now knew the strike would not find anything but since they were under orders to go out only to 150 miles, he did not break radio silence and order them back.

The search element was recovered between 1702 and 1802, but the strike element was nowhere to be seen. The commander had decided to go looking further than 150 miles in a display of excessive zeal. They would have to land in darkness. They also had trouble finding the carrier since it had moved on from the intended point of recovery. The carriers had been going southeast, into the wind to recover planes. In the ensuing mess one Wildcat, four Dauntless and three Avengers were lost, either ditched or damaged beyond repair. The pilots were angry but they had not followed an order that was based on information they were not privy to. Pilots were generally only told what they needed to know, as they could very well be captured by the enemy and subjected to torture. Later in the war, American pilots were told even less and when captured were told to immediately say everything they knew. This was done to spare them from the torture they would not be able to withstand anyway.

As the moon rose it shone brightly. It was a beautiful night, almost like daylight. It was tempting to launch a moonlight strike. A strike of eight Wildcats, 15 Dauntless and six Avengers was spotted on the *Hornet* with preliminary orders to attack and strafe enemy carriers assumed to have their flight decks full of planes ready to be launched in the morning. At the last moment, the strike was canceled. At 0001, a report from a radar-equipped Catalina found

Nagumo in the bright moonlight about 300 miles to the northwest and it was realized that they were out of range. The pilots were relieved; they were not looking forward to a night mission knowing full well that during the hours of the strike, the weather might well change with clouds moving in which then would have meant ditching in the dark. At 0250, another Catalina dropped four 500lb bombs next to *Zuikaku*, also dropping a flare to blind the enemy AA gunners before hightailing it out of there. This Catalina duly sent a contact report but in yet another communications breakdown, it never reached Kinkaid.

During the night, Nagumo changed course back toward the Americans. On board his carriers, search, CAP, and the first strike wave were arranged on the flight deck. The second wave was being readied in the hangars. On their side, the Americans had turned north to look for the enemy. Both forces were now steaming at high speed toward each other. Having closed during the night, at 0500 on the 26th, the opposing carrier forces were only 200 miles apart. Major action was imminent.

At 0445, an hour before sunrise, just as nautical twilight began, Nagumo launched a search of the sector to the east and south, from 050° to 230°, out to 300 miles. The planes used were 13 Kate torpedo bombers with each of the three carriers contributing a third of that number. At 0520, *Zuiho* launched the first CAP of the day, three Zeros.

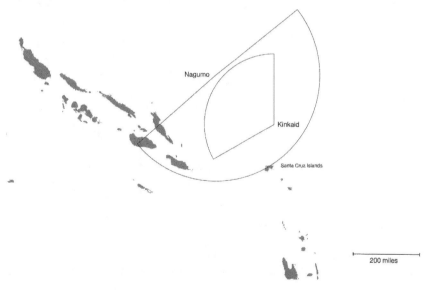

Map of the battle of Santa Cruz Islands. Positions are as of 0500 on the morning of October 26th, about the time when the morning search was launched. The search patterns flown are shown for both sides.

At 0512, the *Enterprise*, as the duty carrier of the day launched a CAP of seven Wildcat, four Dauntless as ASW patrol, plus 16 Dauntless in eight pairs as scouts. The scouts were to search from 235° to 000° out to 200 miles. Had Kinkaid got the contact report from the Catalina a few hours before, he probably would not have had to commit so many dive bombers to searching. At 0551, *Hornet* added eight Wildcats to the CAP.

At 0645, one of the American scouts found and reported the Japanese carriers and at 0658, one of the Kate search planes found and reported the *Hornet* task force.

Both sides now scrambled to launch strikes. Getting in the first strike was critical to winning the battle. As it turned out, both would strike at about the same time, the strikes sighting each other as they passed toward their respective targets.

Between 0732 and 0743, *Hornet* launched the deck-load strike originally prepared for the moonlight mission. The strike had eight Wildcats, 15 Dauntless and six Avengers. A second wave of eight Wildcats, nine Dauntless, and 10 Avengers sat ready in the hangar. They now had their engines warmed up and hurriedly spotted on the flight deck, departing at 0755. The *Hornet*, the strike carrier of the day, was now empty. It should be noted that this is one of the few accounts of aircraft engines being warmed up in the hangar.

At 0747, *Enterprise* launched another 11 Wildcats to reinforce the CAP. At 0750, it then launched a modest contribution to the attack consisting of eight Wildcats, three Dauntless, and nine Avengers. They were shown placards to proceed without joining up with the planes from *Hornet*.

At 0740, the first wave of 21 Zeros, 21 Val dive bombers, and 20 Kate torpedo bombers had left the flight decks of Nagumo's carriers, heading for the US carriers. CAP needed rotation and returning search planes needed to land. A second wave was then brought up on the flight deck.

At 0740, as the Japanese carriers were busy rotating CAP and bringing up the second wave, one pair of US scouts found them steaming about 100 miles from the US carriers. The scouts had not been detected or identified as hostile, and no CAP opposed them. Both commenced attack runs on the *Zuiho* and each scored a hit with a 500lb bomb. With most of its planes away on duty, the fires were put out but the flight deck was out of action for the duration of the battle. This sudden attack caused major confusion with all flight operations but at 0818 an additional 19 Val dive bombers and five Zeros had left for the US carriers. The Kates that had been used for search had been recovered and by 0900, 16 Kates and four Zeros had left for the US carriers. The carriers were now largely empty and the CAP above them

Avengers on *Enterprise* about to take off are given bearing to and speed of target. They are also told to proceed without joining up with the planes from *Hornet*. These placards were used to give last-minute orders. USN carriers were notoriously bad at coordinating their strikes.

numbered 23 Zeros, layered at different altitudes to defend against both dive and torpedo bombers.

At 0840, the new Type 21 radar on board *Shokaku* detected the incoming attack at a distance of 78 miles.

At 0927, the dive bombers of *Hornet*'s first wave turned from a northwesterly direction heading to a northerly and soon spotted Nagumo's carriers. They radioed for the Avengers down low to do the same but they never heard the calls. The Avengers continued on their original course and finding nothing, eventually turned back. The dive bombers and their escorts fought their way through the defending CAP and did their attack runs. *Shokaku* was the nearest carrier and was hit by three 1,000lb bombs. Its flight deck was wrecked and fires started that took five hours to put out. Two out of three carriers were now out of action, only *Zuikaku* remained.

Now it was time for the strike from *Enterprise* to do its turn. It had been decimated by Zeros from the *Zuiho* but did not hear the call from *Hornet*'s dive bomber to take a turn to the north. One of the *Enterprise* Avengers carried an ASB-1 radar that would have been useful in locating enemy ships but that particular aircraft was shot down by the fighters from *Zuiho*.

The third group of US attackers that day, the *Hornet*'s second wave, also did not hear the call. Having nothing else to do they descended on the cruisers *Tone* and *Chikuma*, scoring two hits and two near misses with 1,000lb bombs, badly damaging *Chikuma*. Tone was attacked with torpedoes but all missed. An Avenger dumped another 500lb bomb on the hapless *Chikuma*.

Thus ended the morning's strikes by US aircraft. By 1000 all were heading back. The strikes had lost five Wildcats, two Dauntless, and two Avengers. Of the CAP, five Zeros had been shot down.

*Enterprise* handled fighter direction and 37 Wildcats made up the CAP. The selection of *Enterprise* to do the fighter direction was probably a mistake; the fighter pilots from *Hornet* thought their own flight direction officer (FDO) was more experienced.

At 0855, the Japanese strike was detected by radar at 40 miles, a much shorter detection range than the usual 70–80 miles. Both carriers had the same problem while the radar on cruiser *Northampton* functioned normally and detected the bogeys at 70 miles. The fighters had been placed at 10,000 feet with the expectation that the radar would provide enough warning to allow the fighters to go up to any altitude where oxygen was needed (Wildcats had problems with their oxygen equipment). As it turned out, the Japanese were approaching at 14,000–17,000 feet and without enough warning, the Wildcats were at a severe disadvantage, not being good climbers in the first instance. The CXAM radar was poor at resolving altitude so it was late until the fighter director urged the fighters to start clawing for altitude. For the Wildcat to be successful against the Zero, it needed an altitude advantage. As it was now, the Wildcats were climbing and at low speeds, the type of combat where the Zero excelled. The escorting Zeros ripped into the defending CAP trying to reach the bombers, which many of them did, but the Wildcats simply had numbers on their side.

As the attack developed, *Enterprise* hid in a rain squall while a very well-coordinated attack began on the *Hornet*. The only defense *Hornet* now had was its AA battery. Unfortunately, it had not received the same upgrade that *Enterprise* had, and so had to rely on the old 1.1-inch and the short-range 20mm, neither of which were effective at discouraging a determined attack.

One 250kg bomb hit the flight deck forward. Another bomb landed aft next to the starboard gun battery. Then a third bomb hit the center of the flight deck aft. Two suicide bombers crashed, one forward and one near the stack. The torpedo attack was also pressed home with great courage. Despite violent evasive maneuvers and heavy AA, the attacks were pressed on into very close range and suffering grievous losses, two torpedoes hits were achieved. They proved very destructive. *Hornet* lost power and went dead in the water. The fires from the bomb hits were eventually put out.

The attackers lost three Zeros, 11 Vals, and 10 Kates. Returning, two Zeros, six Vals and six Kates later ditched from battle damage or lack of fuel. Only seven Zeros, four Vals, and four Kates returned to the carriers. The defenders lost six Wildcats.

Beginning at 0930, with the strike over, *Enterprise* began recovering search and ASW patrol planes that by now were very low on fuel. The plan was to quickly refuel and rearm the dive bombers and get an attack launched that would then land on Henderson Field. CAP also needed to be rotated; only eight were at altitude while 13 circled at low altitude.

At 1008, the second wave of the Japanese strike arrived. These were the 19 dive bombers launched as the first group of the second wave, escorted by five Zeros. Most of the CAP was sent to the wrong place and/or wrong altitude by the fighter director. The Vals began their dives largely unmolested.

*Enterprise* had emerged from the rain squall and was now the focus of the attack. Both it and *South Dakota* put up enormous amounts of AA, both making good use of their new Bofors mounts. Still, one 250kg bomb hit forward, penetrating the flight deck and exploded outside of the hull near the bow, causing minimal damage. A second bomb hit just behind the forward elevator, jamming it in the up position.

Reorganizing CAP, the fighter director now had 11 at altitude and 14 circling above *Enterprise*. At 1035, radar spotted more incoming planes and 1040 it resolved to a group of incoming bogeys. This time the CAP was sent to the right place and altitude.

In the incoming strike, 16 Kates and four Zeros, saw the stopped *Hornet* but pressed on, as they wanted to hit *Enterprise*, the only remaining carrier. This was not really in line with the original reason as to why they were held back, to wait until defenses had been worn down and to finish off a damaged carrier. Now they bypassed the cripple and selected the fresher and better defended *Enterprise*.

At 1045, an anvil attack developed with eight on each side. Nine torpedoes were launched but all are successfully evaded.

Of the 19 Vals, 10 were shot down. Of the 16 Kates, eight were shot down. None of the escorting Zeros was shot down.

At 1115, the flight deck of *Enterprise* was again operational. The first strike planes had begun returning as the Kates attacked. Many were low on gas and some were damaged; they badly needed to land. CAP also desperately needed to be rotated, and all congregated over the *Enterprise*. Excess planes were pushed over the side.

Steaming with Kondo's Advance Force was carrier *Junyo*. It had heard all radio messages about the found US carriers. At 0904, and from a distance of 280 miles, launched a strike consisting of 12 Zeros and 17 Val dive bombers. A second strike of seven Kate torpedo planes was then readied.

The CXAM radar on *Enterprise* had by now quit completely. The SC radar set on *South Dakota* picked up the bogeys at 45 miles but this information never reached fighter direction on board *Enterprise*. The CXAM on *Northampton* picked up the bogeys at 25 miles on its radar but Kinkaid thought they were friendlies. Finally, at 1115, the radar on board *Enterprise* was functioning again and bogeys were detected at 20 miles. Apparently the antenna was out of alignment mechanically, possibly by bomb blast. Someone went up to repair it, lashing himself to the antenna. At this point the inevitable happened. Somebody noticed that the radar was not working and that the antenna was not rotating. Using his excellent powers of deduction, he switched the antenna on again. With a major battle raging all around him, the poor repair guy found himself on a merry-go-round, hanging on for dear life. At least he got a good overview of the battle. Finally, some considerate crew mate switched off the antenna rotation and repairs could continue.

At 1121, 17 dive bombers attacked *Enterprise*. The flight deck was in disarray and the guy who repaired the radar antenna still up there. All available AA cut loose and succeeded in downing three of the Vals. The rest succeeded only in scoring one near miss on *Enterprise*, as many in the low clouds ended up attacking *South Dakota* or one of the cruisers instead. There were plenty of Wildcats at low level and many were low on both ammo and gas but they still succeeded in shooting down another five Vals. AA fire was by now very confused with all kinds of planes darting in and out of the clouds. Eventually the attack wound down, gunners and fire directors could relax a bit, and recovery could resume.

Of the 17 Vals, eight were shot down and three later ditched. Only six of the original 17 managed to land back at the carrier. No escorting Zero was shot down, nor any of the Wildcats.

At 1139, no fewer than 73 aircraft were waiting to land on the *Enterprise* and this with its forward elevator *hors de combat* and with its forward flight deck already stocked with 15–20 planes. It withdrew to the southeast, steaming into the wind. Forty-seven planes were landed in 43 minutes. Landings were done with the number two elevator busy, meaning that if the plane did not catch an arresting wire, it would crash on top of whatever was on the elevator. The last few planes, after catching the arresting wire, did not taxi forward as there was simply no room. The last plane to land caught the first arresting wire and was chocked right then and there. Flight operations had to be temporarily suspended until some planes had been moved below. With the recent bomb hits, the hangar was a grisly scene with many dead, dying, and wounded lying around. The last to land were the big Avengers. While waiting to land, they had to make do as CAP and investigated a bogey that turned out to be a PBY Catalina. Between 1251 and 1305, a new CAP of 25 Wildcats was sent aloft. At 1322, recovery process was complete. During this process 14 planes had run out of gas and ditched. To relieve congestion, 14 Dauntless were refueled and told to go to Henderson Field. By now *Enterprise* was also out of range of the enemy carriers. After all this, *Enterprise* had the following planes on board:

*Enterprise*   41 Wildcat, 33 Dauntless, 10 Avengers

Likewise, on the Japanese side, between 1140 and 1400, the two undamaged Japanese carriers *Zuikaku* and *Junyo*, recovered the few planes that returned from the morning's attacks.

At 1307, *Junyo* launched a second strike of eight Zeros and seven Kate torpedo planes. At about the same time, *Zuikaku* launched a third strike of five Zeros, two Vals, and seven Kates (six of which had 800kg bombs instead of torpedoes).

At 1535, *Junyo* launched a third strike of six Zeros and four Vals.

The second strike from *Junyo* found and attacked the crippled *Hornet*. There was no CAP over *Hornet*. At 1523, one torpedo hit caused heavy flooding and eventually the decision was taken to evacuate the crew. Defending AA extracted a price in shooting down two Kates. Also, five of the escorting Zeros were later ditched for various reasons.

The third strikes from both *Zuikaku* and *Junyo* also attacked Hornet, scoring a hit with a 250kg bomb and another with an 800kg bomb from one of the Kates. *Hornet* was then abandoned. Escorting destroyers pumped several torpedoes into it but *Hornet* refused to sink. Later in the night, Japanese surfaces arrived, looking for cripples, and put several more torpedoes into it. The ship finally rolled over and sank at 0135 on the 27th.

After all returning planes had been recovered, the Japanese had at their disposal the following:

*Shokaku* -
*Zuikaku* 38 Zero, 10 Val, 19 Kate
*Zuiho* -
*Junyo* 12 Zero, 12 Val, 6 Kate

*Shokaku* had to return to Japan for repairs. *Zuikaku* was used for training to rebuild the shattered air groups. Only *Junyo* remained to threaten Guadalcanal. The blockade continued and eventually the Japanese decided to evacuate their forces from Guadalcanal. The fight was over. There would be no more carrier battles until the US had rebuilt its carrier force enough to go on the offensive. This would have to wait until 1944.

## Analysis

The disposition of Japanese surface forces is interesting. The Vanguard Group, operating ahead of the carriers, acted as a sort of bait. This was risky. These ships had no air cover and Japanese AA was weak. Against an air strike, all they could do was evasive maneuvering. Still, it worked reasonably well. They soaked up a minor strike while having cruiser *Chikuma* badly damaged.

From a communications and coordination point of view, the Americans really made a mess of this battle. Only half of the first strike group made it to the target. Search contacts were lost and not maintained. The available radar-equipped plane was shot down.

It is known that the Japanese were listening to the American networks and both jammed the frequencies and most likely also injected spoofed messages. No particular jamming equipment was needed—all you needed to do was to transmit something on the same frequency and any competent radio operator could do that. This is not enough to explain all the failures, however.

Both radar and fighter direction failed to live up to expectations and backup procedures failed. In the aftermath of the battle, many Wildcat pilots complained bitterly about poor fighter direction.

As the distance to target was quite short, there was time to do better strike coordination but both commanders had cold feet, not wanting to be caught with planes fueled and armed on board, as had happened at Midway. Planes should be used to blow up the carriers of the enemy and not your own carriers. That was the lesson of Midway.

The Wildcats in their role as escorts, had a difficult time in protecting the bombers from marauding Zeros. Also, the way the Japanese strikes approached at a high altitude was entirely correct; they knew the Wildcat was a slow climber and that weakness was exploited.

The battle saw the first use of air-warning radar by the Japanese, not for fighter direction, but merely to provide warning of an incoming attack. The warning gave the *Shokaku* the time to empty its gas pipes and fill them with $CO_2$ instead which probably saved the ship when in the ensuing action it was hit by a bomb in the avgas area.

With the recent improvements in AA capability on the USN ships, mainly the new quad 40mm Bofors mounts but also the presence of both battleships and the new *Atlanta* class AA cruisers, the number of planes shot down by AA had started to become a real factor. Up to this time, AA mostly had the task of ruining attack runs and throwing off the aim but now planes were actually being shot down with some regularity. There were stories of IJN pilots who on returning to the carriers were so badly shaken that they were barely coherent.

The Japanese carrier planes suffered heavy losses and it is often said that these losses crippled Japanese naval aviation. This is true but is perhaps more a consequence of the Japanese deficiencies in training and in providing replacements. Pilots and planes are expendable, should be handled as such, and quickly replaced. The important thing is to sink the enemy carrier. The Japanese did and the Americans did not.

The first and strongest of the Japanese attacks focused on one target, the *Hornet*. Had they attacked both carriers then both might have been put out of action. Concentrating on one had the effect of overloading the local defenses so it was probably correct, at least not an obvious disadvantage.

Like Midway, this battle illustrates well how difficult it is to operate a carrier in a prolonged engagement. The problem of how to continuously update defensive CAP and to land and launch both search and deck loads of strike planes, while under constant attack, has no solution. Flight operations require steaming a steady course into the wind which is out of the question while under attack. The carrier is also the most vulnerable, with planes on its decks in various stages of refueling and rearming. How to split up functions among the various flight decks, and how to conduct strike operations in general was at this stage a largely unsolved problem.

The *Shokaku* took a real beating in this engagement. It suffered at least three and possibly up to six bomb hits but it still survived. Only HMS *Illustrious* took more bomb hits in the mauling it suffered by Luftwaffe Ju-87s around Malta in January 1941.

## Aftermath

Both sides had now effectively run out of carriers. They also operated at the end of very long logistics chains. With the carriers and their escorts now gone, logistics now permitted the deployment of battleships.

Any Japanese battleships had to be able to reach Guadalcanal during the night while staying outside the range of the bombers at Henderson Field during the day. They selected the *Hiei* and *Kirishima*, two of their fastest. The US deployed the brand-new *Washington* and *South Dakota*. The USN had recently taken delivery of no fewer than six modern fast battleships, the *North Carolina* and the *South Dakota* classes. The four new battleships of the *Iowa* class were also on their way, either launched or on the slipways. The USN was very well supplied with modern battleships. They could afford to send their latest and greatest into a battle where they risked losing them.

Two night-time brawls ensued. *Hiei* was damaged by US cruisers and ultimately caught and sunk by the bombers at Henderson, while the *Kirishima* was sunk by gunfire from US battleships. The battle for Henderson Field had turned into a battle of attrition, something the Japanese wanted to avoid, exacerbated by a very poor logistical situation for them. Ultimately they decided to cut their losses and evacuate. The Guadalcanal campaign was over.

With only the *Saratoga* and *Enterprise* left as carriers in the Pacific, the Americans asked the British for a loaner. The British agreed and HMS *Victorious* was transferred to the Pacific, converting to use America planes and procedures along the way and referred to as USS *Robin*. After a few months in the southwest Pacific, *Victorious* returned to the Atlantic in the fall of 1943, re-training to use RN equipment. This is interesting as the *Ranger* was also available, having just completed the Operation *Torch* landings. It would have been much less of a problem to have *Ranger* operate with *Saratoga* and *Enterprise*, yet the trouble was taken to use a British carrier instead.

The argument that *Ranger* was too slow to operate with the fast carriers is not really valid, as the *Wasp* was about as fast, as were the battleships that operated with the fast carriers. The Japanese also thought 28 knots was enough, for example with the *Kaga*.

The seaworthiness of the *Ranger* was also questioned. It had a very slender cruiser-like hull that made it prone to pitching in long swells. If indeed seaworthiness was a problem, then it should have been kept out of the

North Atlantic and be allowed to enjoy the much more placid waters of the southwest Pacific.

Another argument against the *Ranger* was that it was too fragile for operations in the Pacific. Yet there it would have met some very similar carriers operated by the Japanese.

*Ranger* was built to operate a large air group. The reasoning behind the *Essex* class vs. the armored carriers of the RN has always been that in the Pacific it was more important with a large air group than with other defensive qualities. If so, then this should apply to *Ranger* as well. It might have been a bit slow and small to operate torpedo bombers in light winds but it would have been a good "duty carrier," handling search, CAP, and ASW patrols.

Disregarding the "slow" or "not seaworthy" or "fragile" arguments, what then remains is the fact that in 1943 the USN would not trust a larger air group to defend a carrier, instead preferring a smaller air group and an armored flight deck. Probably a correct assessment given the limitations of fighter direction at the time. The implication is that in 1943 there were serious doubts about the correctness of the *Essex* design.

# CHAPTER 16

# Battle of the Philippine Sea

## Introduction

Both the Japanese and the Americans spent 1943 rebuilding their carrier forces. The Japanese were on the defensive. The Americans had waited until they had enough of the new carriers to begin a serious push into the Japanese perimeter. In a series of landings, the Marshall Islands had been captured without the IJN coming out to give battle. It was now a question of what the next step would be.

On June 15, 1944, US forces landed on the island of Saipan in the Marianas. The landings took the Japanese by surprise, as they had expected an attack further south in the Carolinas. Attacking the Marianas directly meant bypassing Truk, their major naval base in the Carolinas, about 600 miles to the southeast.

The Japanese knew that B-29s could reach Japan from bases in the Marianas. If this invasion was allowed to proceed, it would only be a matter of months before the Japanese homeland would be subjected to the same devastating bombing campaign that was being waged against Germany. The Combined Fleet had to sortie and did so in full force with the intention of winning a large and decisive victory. Comparisons were being made to the battle of Tsushima.

The US priority was to defend the landings. Winning a victory over the Japanese carriers was only a secondary consideration. The fast carriers were used mainly to provide air cover for amphibious forces, they were "tied to the beaches," to the frustration of some in the USN. In the grand scheme of things, however, it was the amphibious forces that did the real attacking, not the carriers.

The Japanese plan was to stay out of range of the US carriers and to launch shuttle attacks using the airfields on the islands they still held. Planes would be launched from the carriers, attack the enemy, and land on the islands to refuel and rearm, then attack enemy carriers, and then return to their carriers. US planners expected this—similar tactics had been used at Guadalcanal—but the overall consideration was still that priority should be given to defend the landings.

The airfield on Saipan was captured on June 18, two days before this battle. On July 9, Saipan was declared secure. The landings on the neighboring islands of Guam and Tinian began on July 21 and 24 respectively. The island of Rota was left untouched and the small garrison there surrendered at the end of the war. During the upcoming battle, Saipan was not yet operational as a US base, and Guam, Tinian, and Rota all had Japanese-held airfields.

## Forces Available and Logistics

US Task Force 58 operated as four task groups with a grand total of 15 carriers, seven fleet carriers and eight light carriers, plus a huge number of escorts:

| TG 58.1 | |
| --- | --- |
| Yorktown | 46 Hellcat, 40 Helldiver, 17 Avenger, 4 Dauntless |
| Hornet | 41 Hellcat, 33 Helldiver, 18 Avenger |
| Belleau Wood | 26 Hellcat, 9 Avenger |
| Bataan | 24 Hellcat, 9 Avenger |

TG 58.1 was escorted by the cruisers Boston, Baltimore, Canberra, and Oakland, plus 14 destroyers.

| TG 58.2 | |
| --- | --- |
| Bunker Hill | 42 Hellcat, 33 Helldiver, 18 Avenger |
| Wasp | 39 Hellcat, 32 Helldiver, 18 Avenger |
| Cabot | 26 Hellcat, 9 Avenger |
| Monterey | 21 Hellcat, 8 Avenger |

TG 58.2 was escorted by the cruisers Santa Fe, Mobile, Biloxi, and San Juan, plus nine destroyers.

| TG 58.3 | |
| --- | --- |
| Enterprise | 31 Hellcat, 3 Corsair, 21 Dauntless, 14 Avenger |
| Lexington (F) | 41 Hellcat, 34 Dauntless, 18 Avenger |
| San Jacinto | 24 Hellcat, 8 Avenger |
| Princeton | 24 Hellcat, 9 Avenger |

TG 58.3 was escorted by the cruisers Indianapolis, Reno, Montpelier, and Cleveland, plus 13 destroyers.

| TG 58.4 | |
| --- | --- |
| *Essex* | 42 Hellcat, 36 Helldiver, 20 Avenger |
| *Langley* | 23 Hellcat, 9 Avenger |
| *Cowpens* | 23 Hellcat, 9 Avenger |

*TG 58.4 was escorted by the cruisers Vincennes, Houston, Miami, and San Diego, plus 14 destroyers.*

*TG 58.7 consisted of the battleships Iowa, New Jersey, Washington, North Carolina, South Dakota, Indiana, and Alabama, with cruisers Minneapolis, New Orleans, San Francisco, and Wichita, plus 13 destroyers.*

Looking at this very impressive fleet, not many of the ships were in commission at the outbreak of the war. Nearly all had entered the navy after the Guadalcanal campaign, a result of the massive shipbuilding effort the US had engaged in. The downside of this was that most of the crews did not have much experience and many had not had the time to train on everything they might be asked to do (from 1939–45, USN manpower expanded 28 times). On the Japanese side the only major new ship was the *Taiho*.

On board US ships, 5-inch guns now could use the new VT proximity fuze which roughly tripled their efficiency against aircraft. All ships were also well equipped with massive batteries of 40mm and 20mm AA guns.

On the US carriers, the Wildcat had now been replaced by the more powerful Hellcat. The SBD Dauntless had also largely been replaced by the SB2C Helldiver that not only could carry a bigger bomb further but also had folding wings. The increased room made it possible to have more fighters.

*Enterprise* had been selected as the carrier that would specialize in night operations. Many of its Avengers had the AN/APS-3 (ASD) radar installed that could detect surface targets at 40 miles. Many of its Hellcats had just been fitted with the AN/APS-6 radar that could detect ships at 25 miles but was mainly intended for night-time interceptions.

The Japanese had nine carriers. The brand-new *Taiho* had an armored flight deck, a first for IJN carriers. The *Junyo* and *Hiyo* were converted liners which, although almost as powerful as a large carrier, were limited by a relatively slow design speed of 25 knots. They also had only two elevators, slowing down flight operations somewhat. The smaller *Chitose* and *Chiyoda* were converted seaplane tenders and had a design speed of 28 knots. The carriers were organized in the following groups:

| A Force | |
| --- | --- |
| *Taiho* (F) | 26 Zero, 23 Judy, 17 Jill, 2 Val |
| *Shokaku* | 26 Zero, 24 Judy, 17 Jill, 2 Val |
| *Zuikaku* | 27 Zero, 23 Judy, 17 Jill, 3 Val |

The A Force was escorted by cruisers *Myoko, Haguro,* and *Yahagi,* plus seven destroyers.

| B Force | |
| --- | --- |
| *Junyo* | 27 Zero, 9 Val, 9 Judy, 6 Jill |
| *Hiyo* | 26 Zero, 18 Val, 6 Jill |
| *Ryuho* | 27 Zero, 6 Jill |

B Force was escorted by the battleship *Nagato,* cruiser *Mogami,* and eight destroyers. *Mogami* had been badly damaged at Midway and had since been rebuilt in the same style as *Tone* and *Chikuma,* with no stern turrets and its aft deck instead used to handle floatplanes, typically about six Jake floatplanes.

| C Force | |
| --- | --- |
| *Chitose* | 21 Zero, 3 Jill, 3 Kate |
| *Chiyoda* | 21 Zero, 3 Jill, 6 Kate |
| *Zuiho* | 21 Zero, 3 Jill, 6 Kate |

C Force was escorted by the battleships *Yamato, Musashi, Kongo,* and *Haruna,* with the cruisers *Tone, Chikuma, Suzuya, Kumano, Atago, Chokai, Maya, Takao,* and *Noshiro,* plus eight destroyers.

The IJN had a history of operating their carriers in pairs, often with an extra small carrier thrown in. We can see the same pattern here with the exception of the First Carrier Squadron. *Taiho* was built as the single ship in its class and an improved version was intended to be built in larger numbers.

About half the Zeros on board the carriers were equipped as fighter-bombers, carrying a 250kg bomb instead of the centerline 330 liter drop tank. This bomb was the same as was carried by the old Val dive bombers from 1942 but that does not mean that a Zero could operate as a true dive bomber since it lacked dive brakes. The intention was to use a shallow glide approach which was not going to be as accurate.

## Command and Control

Commander of Fifth Fleet was Admiral Raymond Spruance flying his flag on cruiser *Indianapolis* (steamed with TG 58.3). The carriers were commanded by Vice Admiral Marc Mitscher on carrier *Lexington,* the battleships by Vice Admiral Willis Lee.

Each task group sailed in a formation with one carrier in the center, the other carriers in an inner circle with a radius of about 2,000 yards, and then the escorts on an outer circle with a radius of about 4,000 yards. Each carrier had a plane guard destroyer following close astern to pick up the crew of any plane that ditched.

TG 58.7 did a variation of this, with the battleship *Indiana* in the center, then the other battleships and escorts on a 4,000-yard circle.

During the battle, TG 58.1 employed another variation in order to save fuel for the destroyers. Preparing for flight operations the carriers would build up speed going westward/downwind while the escorts continued as usual. The carriers would then turn into the wind and go ahead with flight operations. Once finished, the carriers would turn around and catch up with the escorts again. This meant much less going back and forth at high speed for the destroyers, saving considerable amounts of fuel, at the cost of taking the risk of operating the carriers without escorts, if only for a short while and while steaming at high speed.

Each of these task forces then sailed about 10–15 miles from the others. The Americans placed the battleship group nearest the enemy. This meant that those Japanese planes that managed to get through the CAP mostly attacked the battleships instead of the carriers. In front of the battleships were two destroyers to act as pickets, the *Yarnall* and the *Stockham*, both sporting the standard SC air-search radar but no special height-finding radar.

Vice Admiral Jisaburo Ozawa commanded the Japanese forces on board the *Taiho* in A Force. His carriers were divided into three groups. The C Force was positioned about 100 miles closer to the enemy acting as picket, bait and to soak up strikes. This force was outstretched in a picket line. The battleships and cruisers were placed in the C Force so they could effectively use their floatplanes for search. Behind the C Force were the two other forces with the larger carriers, separated by about 10 miles.

The Japanese continued with their tradition of operating their carriers in a large but somewhat loose formation but by now there were more escorts nearer to the carrier. The formation was also closed up when under air attack to enable the escorts to more effectively protect the carriers with their AA, but the emphasis was still on being able maneuver and less on mutual AA protection.

This battle saw the use of the Zero in the role of a fighter-bomber, carrying a 250kg bomb instead of the drop tank. Zero pilots did not have good navigation facilities, so to help them navigate, Kate torpedo bombers were sent with them to act as pathfinders. These Kates did not have any surface search radar.

Both sides had air-warning radar with the capability to detect an incoming strike at a distance of 50–100 miles. The USN had VHF radios fitted to all aircraft; they had four channels and radio discipline was enforced. One of the VHF channels was reserved for fighter-direction communication between the task forces. Fighter direction was efficient with Combat Information centers (CIC) on all ships.

## Visibility and Wind

On June 20, 1944, at latitude 13°N and longitude 138°E., using the UTC+10 time zone, sunrise was at 0622 and sunset at 1916. Nautical twilight began at 0531 and ended at 2007.

Moonrise was at 0545 and moonset at 1851. The moon was below the horizon at night and was also new so there was very little moonlight to assist with late landings.

The weather was clear with scattered cumulus clouds. Visibility was excellent which facilitated target location for both bombers and CAP. The wind was from the east, a steady trade wind of 9–12 knots. The easterly wind meant that flight operations involved steaming eastwards. During the day it was therefore difficult to move westwards to any large extent. Any significant move westward would have to be done during the night.

## Air Operations

On the morning of June 18, three days after the initial invasion, US forces were positioned about 50–100 miles west of Saipan. Saipan itself was guarded by old battleships and many CVEs. The Japanese were approaching from the west-southwest and were now about 650 miles from the American carriers.

At 0535, the Americans launched a regular morning search westward out to 325 miles. Avengers were used; in particularly dangerous search sectors each was escorted by a Hellcat.

At 0600, the Japanese launched a search eastward out to 425 miles using Kate torpedo planes and Jake floatplanes from the cruisers.

Another search westward out to 420 miles was launched at 1200 from the Japanese carriers using Judy dive bombers and Jake floatplanes. The Japanese fleet had steamed eastward during the morning and this search produced the first sightings of the US ships. Four sighting reports were made between 1525 and 1640. The Japanese now knew where the US carriers were.

At 1330, the US carriers sent out a search westward out to 325 miles. They missed the Japanese fleet by about 60 miles. Submarine *Cavalla* had the day before sighted the Japanese fleet so the US knew they were coming and at approximately what time. The night between 18th and 19th might bring a night surface battle. Spruance asked Lee if he was interested in a night battle and Lee said no: the battleships lacked training for night battles. Spruance decided against moving west during the night. Mitscher was not happy with this: he wanted to tangle with the enemy carriers and now found himself defending a beach, out of position for an attack against Ozawa.

Ozawa, on his side, reversed course to stay about 400 miles away from the US carriers. He intended to stay out of range of the enemy, both in his searches and attacks.

The Japanese kept tabs on US movements by periodically checking on their positions. US searches did not find anything, as Ozawa stayed out of range. There were reports from land-based radio direction finding stations that had picked up transmissions from the probable area of the Japanese carrier and there were also (garbled) reports from a submarine but neither of these were felt to be reliable.

During the night, a radar-equipped PBM flying boat operating from Saipan had picked up 40 ships in two groups but was unable to transmit the report by radio and the report did not reach Spruance until some time after the plane had landed at 0845.

At 0200, a night search of 14 radar-equipped Avengers was launched from the *Enterprise*. They flew together on a course of 255° for 100 miles and then fanned out in a search westward to 225 miles. They missed the vanguard C Force by about 50 miles.

On the morning of the 19th, Spruance had little knowledge of Ozawa's whereabouts but Ozawa had a pretty good idea of where Spruance was.

By 0445, Ozawa's battleships and cruisers in C Force had launched 16 Jake float planes to search eastward out to 350 miles. A second search by 13 Kate torpedo planes and a Jake was launched between 0515 and 0520—they were to search eastward out to 300 miles. As had happened the previous day, search planes from the two sides often sighted each other. This usually meant that a Kate or a Jake bumped into a Hellcat with predictable results. No fewer than seven Japanese search planes were lost that morning, either by running into other search planes or by being spotted on radar and dispatched by CAP.

Contrary to standard practice, the Japanese did not launch any ASW patrols this morning. Since some strike planes would be busy with searches and since it was imperative that as many planes as possible would be available for the

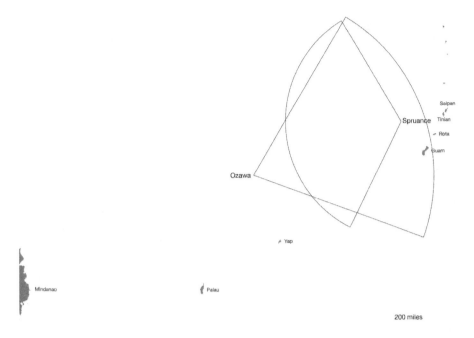

Map of the battle of the Philippine Sea. Positions are as of 0530 on the morning of June 19th, about the time when the morning search was launched. The search patterns flown are shown for both sides. Ozawa knew where Spruance was and was careful to stay out of range. Spruance knew roughly where Ozawa was but could not prevent being outranged. For clarity only the 0530 long range searches are shown. There were other searches flown that morning, notably by Japanese floatplanes.

strikes, this precaution was skipped. This would have disastrous consequences later.

At 0530, the USN dawn search was launched westward out to the usual range of 325 miles. The search was made up of nine Avengers with five Hellcats escorting those in the middle of the search fan pattern.

Also at 0530, carrier *Shokaku* launched 11 Judy, accompanied by two Jakes from the cruiser *Mogami*, to search eastward out to 560 miles. In total then, the Japanese had no fewer than 43 search planes in the air before sunrise. The Americans had only nine search planes in the air. At least they kept their ASW patrols running.

At 0730, a Jake spotted the US carriers and survived to file the report which was confirmed by another search plane 4 minutes later. Now Ozawa knew everything he needed to know.

Spruance and Mitscher discussed what to do about enemy air activity over Guam and Rota. Mitscher was against a strike there and wanted to focus on the enemy carriers. A bit later, he seemed to have gotten cold feet. Seeing both as threats he now wanted to get that threat out of the way before the inevitable incoming carrier strikes started to fill up his radar screens.

At 0824, 36 Hellcats arrived over Guam and shot down about 30 fighters and five bombers, many of which had recently flown in from Truk. Guam was now much reduced as a threat.

At 0800, C Force started launching the first strike of the day: first, two Kates to act as pathfinders, then 45 Zero fighter-bombers each armed with a 250kg bomb, then 16 Zero fighters as escorts and eight Jills armed with torpedoes. Launching was complete by 0830. Flight leaders were instructed to land at Guam if they did not have fuel to return to the carriers.

At about 0830, the large carriers of A Force started launching a second strike of two pathfinder Kates, 48 Zeros, 54 Judys, and 27 Jills. By 0856, the launching was complete. Ozawa now headed west to keep his distance to the enemy. *Taiho* also launched a lone Judy to proceed to the northeast of the US carriers and to drop "Window" chaff to try to draw CAP to that area, away from the incoming strike. Nice little trick here: Ozawa was trying to use the Americans' radar against them.

At 0909, the *Taiho* was hit by a torpedo from the US submarine *Albacore*. The damage seemed minor and it was able to maintain its place in the formation.

At 1000, B Force started launching the third strike of the day consisting of 15 Zero fighters, 25 Zero fighter-bombers and seven Jill torpedo planes. This was directed to a fresh contact, placing the enemy about 50 miles north from the target of the two earlier strikes.

At 1010, a large number of bogeys started to appear on the radar screens, first detected by battleship *Alabama* at 124 miles away. The new SK-2 radar was proving its worth. As the bogeys approached their altitude was estimated to be 24,000 feet. This was the strike launched by A Force. All available CAP was launched. Bombers ranged on the flight decks were sent off and told to circle to the east, awaiting further orders. All aircraft in the hangar decks were degassed and disarmed.

Strangely, the strike did not fly straight in, but paused for 10 minutes to regroup for the attack. This gave the fighters extra time to get into position. The attack was met about 70 miles from the carriers.

Each carrier handled its own fighter direction but was in contact, on a separate channel, with the other carriers. Newly launched Hellcats began by taking up CAP station above the carrier, climbing to altitude, freeing those Hellcats that already were there to be vectored on to the enemy.

The Japanese first strike was met by about 50 Hellcats. Of the original 69 planes in the strike, about 30 were shot down at the cost of three Hellcats. Of the remaining 40 planes, some attacked the radar picket destroyers but 3–6 managed to get through to attack the battleships despite intense AA. One Zero hitting *South Dakota* with a 250kg bomb caused casualties but no serious damage. Only eight Zero fighters, 16 Zero fighter-bombers, and six Jills returned to the carriers. The Japanese air attack coordinator watched the intense AA and advised against attacking this group of ships in the future, which might explain why later strikes were directed to a different target.

At 1107, the Japanese second strike of 100+ planes from A Force was detected on radar at 115 miles away. Again the attackers paused to regroup before continuing the attack, giving the defending fighters valuable time to get prepared. They were met about 60 miles out. Most that got through attacked the battleships but a few went past and headed for the carriers. One Judy managed to drop a bomb on *Wasp* causing only minor damage; another Judy got a near miss on *Wasp*. Two other Judys got near misses on *Bunker Hill*. All but two of the attackers were shot down. A small group of about six torpedo planes went after TG 58.3 but no hits were scored. Only 16 Zeros, 11 Judys, and four Jills returned from this strike of the 131 originally launched

At 1110, Mitscher approved using the orbiting bombers for an attack, despite not knowing where the enemy was. Avengers from *Enterprise* would search westward out to 250 miles and the bombers would follow 30 miles behind and along the search median. This attack was never carried out; instead the bombers were ordered to hit Guam if fighter cover was available.

At 1120, a long-range PB4Y Liberator based at Manus Island found A Force.

At 1130, the fourth Japanese strike of the day had finished launched from B Force. This was their second wave of the day and they now had nothing left to send. The strike consisted of 30 Zero fighters, 10 Zero fighter-bombers, nine Judy dive bombers, 27 Val dive bombers, and six Jill torpedo planes.

At 1220, the *Shokaku* was hit by three or possibly four torpedoes from the submarine *Cavalla*. Damage was heavy. Fires were initially handled but eventually became uncontrollable. The ship sank at 1501

At 1300, the third Japanese strike of 47 planes from B Force had arrived over the revised target coordinates but not having found anything, appeared to be in orbit. They were observed on radar about 50 miles away and intercepted by 40 fighters. Only seven were shot down and the rest managed to return to the carriers.

At 1320, the fourth Japanese strike of the day was picked up on radar 134 miles out. It had arrived at the same coordinates as the third strike and again, not finding anything, started a search pattern. Still not finding anything, they headed for Guam and Rota and were met by Hellcats. Some found the carriers that were now in the process of recovering fighters. Both *Wasp* and *Bunker Hill* had to maneuver to evade bombs. Most of this group made their way to Guam where Hellcats later found about 40 circling at low altitude over the airfield. The Hellcats pounced and shot down about 30 of them. Of the 82 planes in the fourth strike, 73 were shot down.

At 1400, US carriers launched a new search westward out to 325 miles, still finding nothing. Ozawa remained out of range.

At 1532, the *Taiho* suffered a huge explosion caused by gasoline vapor from what had been initially thought to be minor damage from the torpedo that hit it at 0909. The ship sank at 1828. Ozawa was picked up by an escort and temporarily set up his flag on cruiser *Haguro*. The next day he transferred his flag to *Zuikaku* (which had better radio communications facilities).

During the aerial battles of the day, US fighter direction received unexpected help from a Japanese air attack coordinator. His transmissions were monitored on board *Lexington* by one in the team who was fluent in Japanese, and knowledge of his orders was used to vector CAP. It was proposed to send some fighters to shoot him down but Mitscher vetoed it, saying, "no indeed, he did us too much good!"

Throughout the day, US searches had failed to find the Japanese carriers. Spruance still did not know where Ozawa was. His only reliable reports were the sighting by the PB4Y Liberator at 1120 and the attack by *Cavalla* on the *Shokaku* at 1220.

As the day drew to a close, the Americans knew they had scored a major victory, having shot down about 318 enemy aircraft while only losing 23 of their own. The Combined Fleet had ceased to be a major threat to the landings. The intense flight operations of the day meant that the formations had gradually migrated eastward, closer to Guam and away from the enemy. During the night TG 58 now sailed west, looking for a complete victory by sinking the Japanese carriers before they withdrew.

But Ozawa was not defeated. Heavy losses among the air groups were the norm and his pilots had reported many hits on enemy ships and many "Grummans" shot down. He expected many of his planes to have landed and refueled at Guam and returned to the carriers. He intended to continue the battle the next day. Initially he moved eastward toward the US carriers, but then at 2345 he changed course to a northwesterly direction to reorganize his forces. He did not know it at this time but his retreat had started and he was further north than Spruance knew.

At 0530 on the 20th, the Americans launched the usual dawn search but found nothing. They still only searched out to 325 miles and missed the Japanese fleet by about 75 miles. An extra mid-day search also found nothing. Steaming was westerly or slightly to the south of that, looking for the damaged *Shokaku*. Only later was the course changed to northwest, the direction in which the Japanese were retreating. Both sides now had serious worries about their fuel, particularly on the destroyers, but the chase was on and proper refueling would have to wait.

At 1512, a search plane from *Enterprise* finally found the fleet 275 miles away and steaming westward at 20 knots. The sighting report was garbled but was verified at 1540.

A strike had been spotted on the decks of the large carriers. The engines had been kept warm by periodically running them. As soon as the engines were turned off, the fuel was topped off. The strike was ready to go.

At 1624, a strike was launched against the target about 300 miles away. The strike had 96 Hellcats, 51 Helldiver, 26 Dauntless, and 54 Avenger torpedo bombers of which only 12 carried torpedoes, the others had four 500lb bombs. Planes proceeded as launched and only formed up in formations while en route. A second deck-load strike was pondered but ultimately canceled and the planes degassed and disarmed.

The strike arrived over the Japanese fleet at 1838 as daylight was fading. They were met by about 68 Zeros. The pilots appeared to be better now—it seemed like these were good ones, those who had survived the Turkey Shoot the previous day. They were still overwhelmed by the sheer size of the attack. A rather hurried and uncoordinated attack was made that succeeding in sinking the *Hiyo* by torpedoes. Bomb hits were scored on the *Zuikaku, Junyo,* and *Chitose* but without planes on board, the fires were soon extinguished and the getaway could continue. The attack was over by 1910, just before sunset. As night fell many of the returning planes ran out of fuel but most managed to make a night-time landing back on the carriers.

When it was all over, the Combined Fleet was down to 35 carrier-based aircraft and 12 float-planes, compared to 450 and 45 before the battle.

## Analysis

Both sides had more carriers than was practical in a single steaming formation so they divided them into three and four formations respectively. Both sides employed so many carriers that the old discussion of whether or not to separate the carriers was no longer relevant.

In this battle, the Japanese used a whole group of small carriers to act as a picket line and to soak up strikes. In the end, they did not to have make a sacrifice, as the Americans never found the bait. The Americans used their battleships in a similar way, to defend the carriers by soaking up strikes which they did without too much harm done.

Long-range land-based search planes were useful but as usual too few in numbers to have much of an impact once a battle was imminent. This applied to both sides.

Going into this battle, the goal at the tactical level was to get in the first strike. The experience of the 1942 battles showed that conclusively. Scouting and intelligence was critical and both sides were very much aware of this.

Spruance had the same problem as Nagumo at Midway: he had two enemies, planes based on the islands and planes based on the Japanese carriers. Attacking one meant exposing himself to the other getting in an unanswered first strike. Happily for Spruance, the Japanese had not anticipated his attack and he could deal with each threat in succession.

The Japanese did not have the advantage of having broken the enemy's code. They also knew that the Americans had air-warning radar, largely eliminating the possibility of a surprise attack. They instead planned to attain the unanswered first strike by simply staying out of range through the use of shuttling tactics. This would ensure the first strike both by being able to spot the Americans first and by the American inability to strike back. The prevailing wind out of the east also meant that Spruance had problems closing with Ozawa, as flight operations meant steaming away from the Japanese.

The Japanese succeeded in staying out of range of both searches and strikes. They were allowed to use all day of the 19th to launch strike after strike without the Americans ever knowing where they were and thus unable to counterattack. This was despite the advantage the Americans had in radar, including surface search radar on board search planes.

Spruance could have searched more aggressively but if he could not attack what he found, what would the point be? One can argue that it would still be useful to know where the enemy was but he already knew that to the extent he needed to know in order to accomplish his mission.

Spruance's decision to avoid a night battle was also correct. It is easy to forget the limitations that came from having a brand-new navy not yet trained for night battles, a type of warfare the Japanese had repeatedly shown that they had mastered. One can argue that the US advantage in radar would have compensated for the lack of training but, then again, if you are not trained on the tools, the risks are considerable no matter how good the tools are.

Spruance could have made a dash westward during the night to get to a position within range of the Japanese carriers. The price he would have to pay was the possibility of a night action he did not want or need. As soon as

Ozawa saw that move, he would again move out of range and the only thing that would have happened was that Spruance was now outranged in a position further to the west and thus in a weaker position to protect the beaches. It could take some time before Ozawa had moved out of range again and that was the window of opportunity that Spruance could have aimed for, but it came at a price in positioning and Spruance was not willing to pay it. It should be remembered that at this stage in the war the IJN remained a most dangerous enemy and the American superiority was not yet so great that it allowed abandoning an essentially attritional strategy.

Ozawa knew that Spruance knew all this and Spruance knew that Ozawa knew. Thus the shuttle tactics, Spruance's decision not to go west, Ozawa's maintaining a position out of range of Spruance, and Spruance's decision to allow that.

The situation of 1942, in which both fleets had carriers that were essentially eggshells armed with hammers, had by now changed in favor of defense. The USN combination of large numbers of fighters, aided by well-trained fighter-direction teams using accurate and long-range radar and with capacious radio networks, proved very effective. With hugely improved defensive capabilities, the first strike became much less important. The first strike was simply shot down.

That the Americans had so vastly improved their defensive capabilities was no accident. They knew that once they were on the offensive, they would be at a disadvantage tactically, as the Japanese knew which island was being invaded and that the US carriers would be tied to defending the beachhead. It was understood that in the overall strategic offensive, the fast carriers were now basically a defensive force with the main task of ensuring local aerial superiority, despite aircraft being shuttled in from neighboring islands. This is why so much attention was paid to improving defenses and why the number of fighters had been increased by so much. The old days of scouting and raiding was over: the rise of air power had forced the fast carriers into a basically defensive but strategically much more important role. The carrier admirals did not always like what success had granted them, and so we have the debate as to whether carriers really should be "anchored to the beaches" as Spruance allowed them to be, a debate that at times became quite heated, as it was used as a tool in the rivalry between aviators and non-aviators.

The Japanese did not increase the number of fighters nor did they do much to improve their fighter direction. Both these measures were essentially defensive in nature and, being the attacker, were not of much use. For defense, the Japanese carriers depended on outranging the Americans, which they knew they could do using shuttle tactics with islands they were defending.

On the level of the tactics of flight operations, the Japanese failed to foresee how much defenses had improved. There were not enough escorting fighters to handle the masses of Hellcats the strikes had to fight their way through. It was also felt that Japanese fighter pilots lacked aggressiveness and that bomber formations were relatively easy to break up and that, once broken up, individual bombers were easy to shoot down.

The Japanese attacks were also structured in a way that suited American fighter direction. They were nicely bunched up in a small number of large attacks that were easy to track and to intercept. The Japanese were even so cooperative as to circle for some minutes, just after they had been detected, so the American fighter could get into position.

In this the first great battle of the island-hopping campaign, the Americans knew that they had superior forces but that the Japanese were far from defeated and that anything could happen. It then made sense, as a first step, to attrition the Japanese and to do this without taking any more risks than needed. This called for someone like Spruance. In the next battle, once the threat had been blunted, the US could afford to be more daring with Halsey in command.

Interviewed after the war, Ozawa said that they knew that Spruance's temperament was more toward the cautious side. This was a factor in going for the outranging plan. The plan succeeded. They had played a near perfect game. Still they lost and badly so. They had to do something. For the next battle, they completely changed tactics. Against the aggressive Halsey, it was going to be interesting.

# CHAPTER 17

# Battle of Leyte Gulf

## Introduction

On October 20, 1944, US forces landed at Leyte in the Philippines. The Japanese knew that if the Philippines was lost, the war was lost. They had to defend it.

In what turned out to be the biggest naval engagement in history, carriers did *not* play much of a role. The Japanese carriers were reduced to being used as bait while the US carriers were limited to chasing that bait, leaving us with two battleship actions as the main events.

The battle of Leyte Gulf consisted of several actions, and, for purposes of carrier operations, the focus will be on the battle of Cape Engaño. It was actually not much of a battle but it is where the last carrier force of the IJN was sunk.

The landings at Leyte depended entirely on carrier-borne fighters for air cover, despite being a landing on a large land mass with plenty of land-based air power available to oppose it, either available in situ or shuttled in from Formosa, China, and Japan. The initial plan was to invade Mindanao first, establishing airbases there before tackling Leyte. However, a series of probing carrier raids by Halsey had met little opposition, so the decision was taken to skip Mindanao and head straight for Leyte.

## Forces Available and Logistics

Task Force 38 had four task groups with a grand total of 17 carriers. Before this battle, TG 38.1 had been detached to Ulithi to refit. The following remained:

| TG 38.2 | |
|---|---|
| *Intrepid* | 44 Hellcat, 28 Helldiver, 18 Avenger |
| *Cabot* | 21 Hellcat, 9 Avenger |
| *Independence* | 19 Hellcat, 8 Avenger |

*Escorted by the battleships Iowa and New Jersey, cruisers Biloxi, Vincennes, and Miami, plus 16 destroyers.*

| TG 38.3 | |
|---|---|
| *Essex* | 51 Hellcat, 25 Helldiver, 20 Avenger |
| *Lexington* | 42 Hellcat, 30 Dauntless, 18 Avenger |
| *Langley* | 25 Hellcat, 9 Avenger |
| *(Princeton* | 25 Hellcat, 9 Avenger) |

*Escorted by the battleships Massachusetts and South Dakota, cruisers Santa Fe, Mobile, and Reno, plus 14 destroyers.*

| TG 38.4 | |
|---|---|
| *Franklin* | 37 Hellcat, 31 Helldiver, 18 Avenger |
| *Enterprise* | 39 Hellcat, 34 Helldiver, 19 Avenger |
| *San Jacinto* | 19 Hellcat, 7 Avenger |
| *Belleau Wood* | 25 Hellcat, 9 Avenger |

*Escorted by the battleships Washington and Alabama, cruisers New Orleans and Wichita, plus 11 destroyers.*

Facing this fleet were the survivors *Zuikaku, Zuiho, Chitose,* and *Chiyoda* with a total of 52 Zero fighters, 28 Zero fighter-bombers, 25 Jill, and four Kate torpedo bombers, plus seven Judy dive bombers for a grand total of 116 planes. At the battle of Philippine Sea these carriers operated a total of 157 planes so the carriers clearly had less than normal complement but it was still a decent force.

| | |
|---|---|
| *Zuikaku* | 20 Zero, 25 Jill, 7 Judy |
| *Zuiho* | 20 Zero, 4 Kate |
| *Chitose* | 20 Zero |
| *Chiyoda* | 20 Zero |

The allocation of the planes to the individual carriers is still an educated guess. It is known that smaller and/or slower carriers had problems operating the Jills. *Zuiho* normally carried a few Kates for search and as a modest strike capability. The Zeros depended on torpedo planes for navigation but that does not mean that they had to be stationed on the same carrier. The Judys were often used for search, and being more of a high-speed design also operated best from a fast carrier with a long flight deck. *Chitose* and *Chiyoda* were converted seaplane tenders and were slower than the purpose-built carriers.

This force was escorted by the two hybrid battleships *Ise* and *Hyuga*, light cruisers *Oyodo*, *Tama*, and *Isuzu*, plus nine destroyers.

## Command and Control

The commander of the Third Fleet was Admiral William Halsey on the battleship *New Jersey*. In command of Task Force 38 was Vice Admiral Marc Mitscher on the *Lexington*. Halsey was very much in charge.

Each task group sailed in a formation with the 3–4 carriers together in the center with a common screen of cruisers and destroyers around them. The battleships were part of the screen at daytime but sometimes separated and formed a battle-line at night, in preparation for a possible night action. The task groups were kept about 10–15 miles apart.

Vice Admiral Jisaburo Ozawa commanded the Japanese carriers, flying his flag on board the *Zuikaku*. The four carriers operated as a loose group with escorts around them. Vice Admiral Takeo Kurita commanded the main battleship force.

Both sides had air-warning radar with the capability to detect an incoming strike at a distance of 50–100 miles. The US had four-channel VHF radios fitted to all aircraft and radio discipline was enforced. Fighter direction was efficient with Combat Information centers (CIC) on all ships. One of the VHF channels was reserved for fighter-direction communication between the task groups.

## Visibility and Wind

On October 25, 1944, at latitude 18°N and longitude 126°E, using the UTC+9 time zone, sunrise was at 0632 and sunset at 1808. Nautical twilight began at 0545 and ended at 1856.

Moonrise was at 1319 and moonset at 0050 (on the 26th). At 2000 the moon was 50° above the horizon and to the south and southwest. It was half and waxing and could be of help with late landings.

The weather was clear with a few scattered cumulus clouds. The wind was a brisk 13–16 knot trade wind out of the northeast. Steaming northeast, as was done during most of the battle, meant steaming straight into the wind.

This simplified flight operations, as no major change in course was needed to launch or recover aircraft. Hurrying back to defend the transports, it complicated flight operations.

## Air Operations

Ozawa went into battle fully cognizant that he was a decoy and that he should expect to be sunk. During interrogations after the war, he was not fatalistic about it. He knew his force was too weak to effectively defend Kurita's battleships, so the mission made sense to him. He was skeptical of his chances in succeeding as decoy, rating them 50/50.

During the 23rd, Ozawa broke radio silence to bring attention to his presence. He did not know if it had any effect.

At dawn on the 24th, Ozawa launched a strike of 75 aircraft against TG 38.3. This strike was met by CAP and many were shot down with most of the survivors landing at Luzon (because of the weather). After this strike his carriers were down to 19 Zeros, five Zero fighter-bombers, four Jills, and one Judy.

At 0938, a lone land-based Judy scored a hit with a 250kg bomb on the middle of the flight deck of the light carrier *Princeton*. This happened while it was rearming and refueling aircraft. Six Avengers were in the hangar, fully fueled and armed. The damage from the bomb was manageable but an avgas fuel line had been cut and one of the Avengers had a drop tank punctured. Avgas fires erupted which in turn put out of action some of the firefighting equipment. Damage-control teams were not able to put out the fires and soon explosions started, probably the warheads of the torpedoes of the Avengers. At 1524, a major explosion occurred, at 1749 an even bigger one, and at 1750 the ship sank. A classic case of a carrier being hit while having armed and fueled planes in the hangar.

At 1530 and 1635 on the 24th, Ozawa's carriers had been spotted by US search planes. Halsey took a while to decide but he finally made up his mind and at 2022 Mitscher turned north to deal with them. The carrier *Independence* then recalled those of its aircraft that had been shadowing Kurita. Nobody was now looking after Kurita and no one was left to guard San Bernardino Straits, not even a lone guard destroyer.

At this point Ozawa had received sighting reports of the US carriers. He was convinced that he had been spotted. He turned northwest, expecting to be chased. At 1930, he despaired about having been spotted and turned southeast again. In the early hours of the 25th, he again turned north as befitted a tasteful lure. Ozawa did not know it but this meant that the surface forces would not collide during the night. The chase was certainly on, however.

At 0100, *Independence* launched five radar-equipped Hellcats to search the sector 320° to 10° out to 350 miles. At 0205 and then at 0235, the Japanese force was found. The distance was reported as 120 miles but they were actually 210 miles away.

At 0240, Mitscher deployed the battleships about 10 miles ahead of the carriers in expectation of a gun battle the next day to finish off cripples.

Between 0540 and 0600, a dawn search plus a strike of 60 Hellcats, 65 Helldivers, and 55 Avengers was launched. The strike was told to orbit ahead of the carriers.

At 0710, the American dawn search placed Ozawa's ships 150 miles ahead or 70–90 miles away from the orbiting strike.

At 0800, the attack commenced. The CAP over the carriers turned out to be 12–15 fighters of which about nine were shot down.

At 0835, a second strike of 14 Hellcats, six Helldivers, and 16 Avengers was launched. They attacked between 0945 and 1100.

At 1115, in response to mounting pressure from Nimitz, the battleships turned round and headed south to deal with the crisis off Samar. The cruisers *Santa Fe*, *Mobile*, *Wichita*, and *New Orleans* plus nine destroyers stayed with the carriers.

Between 1145 and 1200, a third strike of 200+ planes was launched at a distance of 102 miles. This strike started attacking at 1310. *Zuikaku* was hit by at least three torpedoes and sank at 1414. The last of the Pearl Harbor attackers had now been sunk, the Avengers having done what they were named to do.

At 1315, the fourth strike of 30–40 planes took off. It soon attacked but bombing was not very accurate.

At 1610, a fifth strike departed, consisting of full deck loads from all five large carriers. This was the third strike of the day for many of the pilots and bombing was again not very accurate.

Finally, at 1710, the sixth strike departed, consisting of 36 planes. It accomplished very little, but then there was not that much left to accomplish.

The last ship to sink was *Chiyoda*: having already been abandoned, it was finished off by gunfire and torpedoes from US cruisers and destroyers. The battleships *Ise* and *Hyuga* were able to escape by a combination of intense AA gunfire, adroit evasive maneuvering, and poor bombing.

# Analysis

The Japanese carriers had a decent number of planes going into this battle. The standard description of the battle says which that "the Japanese carriers did not have any planes and were only used as bait" is not really correct. The planes they had were used early in the battle to make an attack and to announce the presence of the decoy; thus they were quickly used up and out of the battle. The planes had planned to return to the carriers but the weather forced them to go to land bases instead. Hence, when the US carrier planes attacked the carriers, they had only a token force of fighters on them and the decks were empty, but that was not how they entered the battle.

The carrier battle itself was rather predictable, as the Japanese were hopelessly outclassed in every respect. It was basically target practice for the by now very experienced and seasoned US aircrews.

Outside of the carrier battle, two flank attacks by surface ships were attempted by the Japanese. One attempted to go through Surigao Straits but was stopped by defending surface forces—the battleships sunk at Pearl Harbor had now been repaired and were used successfully as point defense. The other flank attack was successful, the carrier decoy having worked very well, but was kept busy by some small escort carriers and their escorts in the action off Samar.

The result of the action off Samar was that Kurita thought that he had destroyed a significant part of the American carriers. He could have gone after the transports but that meant sacrificing the core of what was left of the IJN for some transports that were by now unloaded and would have been quickly replaced. If the enemy had been denied supremacy, he would be forced to withdraw the transports anyway, as happened after the US defeat at Savo Island. By turning around, the situation remained desperate and odds were poor, but at least Japan had something to play with in case something happened that turned the war in its favor.

Halsey had to choose between guarding the San Bernardino Straits or to go after the carriers. US doctrine dictated that he keep his forces together to avoid being defeated in detail. The underlying strategy was that of the superior force to focus on numbers and attrition and not make mistakes. The Japanese knew this and exploited it in the overall plan of the battle.

Had he stayed and guarded the straits, Kurita would have seen that he was met by a superior force and most likely turned around after having fired off his torpedoes. Halsey could have pursued the fleeing Kurita but that would have meant exposing the transports to a threat from the decoy force.

Had Halsey left a token force to guard the straits and to act as a trip wire, Kurita would still have pushed through and the transports would still be threatened; the only difference is that Kurita would have been caught by Halsey as he would have had to turn back before sinking the carriers.

The choice Halsey actually made meant sinking the Japanese carriers at the cost of giving Kurita the opportunity to sacrifice his battleships in order to sink some transports. In the short term this would have caused problems for the ongoing invasion but once Kurita's battleships were gone, there would have been nothing left of the Japanese navy.

Halsey could have separated his battleships from his carriers but that would have left the carriers vulnerable to a night attack by Japanese surface forces and left the battleships with weak air cover. The decoy force included two old battleships, so having his carriers escorted only by cruisers and destroyers would have entailed a certain risk.

Behind all this was the tension within the USN over the role of the carriers. The carriers started the war as raiders and scouts but ended up as a basically defensive force, providing air cover for an amphibious operation. Should the fast carriers be anchored off a beach or should they be allowed to have a more mobile and aggressive role? The carrier captains wanted to roam free like a pack of wolves, hunting down their prey with that 30-knot speed in their whiskers, not babysitting plodding transports. Boring. But it was the transports that did the real attacking.

Overall, the Japanese plan for this battle was to act as underdog. The plan was complex and quite risky in the way the fleet was split up and in the use of a decoy force. Ultimately, the plan did not succeed in splitting up the US forces, in defeating them in detail, or in changing the status quo.

The battle had a point target, the transports. In all previous carrier battles, the carriers were free to roam and did so, usually at long range and with very little contact between surface forces. The existence of a point target tended to focus and then compress everything, making it much more of a battleship action. The interplay between carriers and battleships made it a very complex battle.

After Ozawa successfully had extended the OODA Loop of Halsey, Kurita had no problems in getting inside it. The way Halsey was forced into unplanned and risky reactions is a nice illustration of what John R. Boyd meant by "getting the enemy to fold on himself." One of the more interesting aspects of that was how the US carriers had trouble making their way back from the trap. When steaming downwind, flight operations meant turning into the wind, back into the trap.

On the other hand, Kurita had his own problems. His *Observe* and *Orient* phases suffered: he mistook his opponent off Samar for a greater force than it really was. He did not have a clear picture of the enemy's dispositions. He knew very little of what Ozawa was up to. He feared a trap by the Americans, partly correct as the six old battleships commanded by Admiral Jesse B. Oldendorf were getting ready to greet him at the entrance to Leyte Gulf. His *Decide* and *Act* phases also suffered: he was in a largely reactive frame of mind and quite exhausted after days of intense action. One should always keep in mind the enormous pressures these admirals faced: they all understood very well the consequences of poor decisions and on how much it would be debated by future historians.

In the end it did not matter. The Japanese were by now simply too weak to exploit the opportunities. All this battle achieved was to show how hopelessly outclassed they now were. The USN ended the battle with undisputed mastery of the seas, a mastery that remains to this day.

## Note on the Zuikaku

The name *Zuikaku* means "Lucky Crane" or "Auspicious Crane." It was indeed a lucky ship. At Coral Sea it was sister *Shokaku* ("Soaring Crane") that took the hits. At Midway neither was present and at Eastern Solomons neither was hit. At Santa Cruz it was again sister *Shokaku* that took the hits. At Philippine Sea it was yet again *Shokaku* that was hit by torpedoes and sunk, *Zuikaku* took a bomb hit, but with its decks empty the fire was soon put out. Without her sister to take the hits for her, *Zuikaku*—the last of the Pearl Harbor veterans—was finally sunk in this battle.

Of the prewar fleet carriers, the *Lexington, Yorktown, Wasp, Hornet, Hermes, Eagle, Courageous,* Glorious, *Ark Royal, Kaga, Akagi, Hiryu, Soryu, Shokaku* and now *Zuikaku* had all been sunk. Only *Furious, Saratoga, Ranger,* and *Enterprise* remained. When the war ended, *Furious* had been paid off, *Saratoga* and *Ranger* had been relegated to training, leaving *Enterprise* as the only fully operational prewar carrier.

# CHAPTER 18

# Carrier Operations in a Larger Context

## Economic Fundamentals

This table below shows how much the various nations spent on the war (in billions of US wartime dollars). These numbers are not exact and the sources differ but they should provide a good idea of the relative sizes involved:

| | | |
|---|---|---|
| 1. | United States | 296 |
| 2. | Germany | 272 |
| 3. | USSR | 192 |
| 4. | Britain | 120 |
| 5. | Italy | 94 |
| 6. | Japan | 56 |

Interestingly, in 1941 the GDP of Germany, including the occupied territories, was roughly equal to that of the US. Germany remained at that level, however, while the US economy expanded rapidly during the war years, more than doubling in size. Today the GDP of Germany, Britain, and Italy appear in the same order while Japan has passed Germany into second place while Russia has fallen dramatically in relative power, lagging well behind Italy.

## The British Eccentric

One of the most intriguing aspects of the RN in World War II is how it ended up with such an eclectic mix of ships, aircraft, and guns. Both the battleships and the carriers were quite disparate collections, a mix of new ships, rebuilt ships, and outdated ships, all quite different in thinking and armament. The most egregious example was the mix of medium gun calibers used within the RN. There were of course various historical reasons why this situation developed, and once the conflict had started the pressures of war forced further improvisations and there was just never enough time and resources available for proper development and for efficient production and logistics. The Americans and Japanese had the advantage of having a two-year period during which they could study the experiences of the RN before they themselves were committed to battle.

Somehow though, this quite fascinating mix of tools was put to remarkably good use with impressive adaptability in how to use these tools under varying circumstances. The RN had to fight a three-front war (Atlantic, Mediterranean, Far East) but despite having resources very thinly stretched, the job was eventually done in a most admirable way.

## The Japanese Gambler

As we have seen, the Japanese carrier force was entirely geared toward offensive warfare. In this role it was very good, the best in the world at the time of Pearl Harbor.

It is easy to criticize Japan for its various failings in how to fight a war of attrition, the slowness to change, the deficiencies in logistics and in pilot replacement, but all that is to an extent beside the point. Had resources been diverted toward a more attritional and/or defensive kind of war, there would have been less focus on the offensive and those initial successes would not have been quite so devastating for the Allies.

The Japanese entry into the war was essentially a gamble. They gambled that a democratic USA would not go to a full-scale war with all the sacrifices that that would entail. A necessary part of the gamble was to increase the apparent cost of going to war by inflicting spectacular defeats. Everything was geared to winning that gamble. Once it had failed, the war was lost. However, in going for an all-out offensive, the Japanese played the game as well as they could have.

They hoped that the attack on Pearl Harbor would be a knockout blow. The reality is that the Japanese did not have the resources to mount anything close to a knockout blow. They did what they could and hoped it would suffice, even though it was in reality only a raid on an outpost.

Once it was clear that that basic gamble had failed, the Japanese adopted plan B: defend so successfully that the Americans got tired and lost interest.

In the execution of plan B, their main hope was to win a decisive battle, avoiding the war of attrition they were certain to lose. The only problem was that to the extent that these decisive battles were fought, they lost them.

## The American Giant

One can only be impressed by the speed and skill with which the American giant responded once awoken. There were many deficiencies in the 1942 battles but by 1944 things had been sorted out, everything was in place, and a huge and very efficient carrier task force had been formed. A good example is the breakneck speed with which the USN was expanded and equipped with 40mm AA, radar, and more powerful aircraft.

The Americans outspent the Japanese by a factor of about 6–10 during the war, depending on the type of expenditure. It showed. Some of the slightly frivolous expenditures were the VT fuze and the *Iowa* class battleships, both of which cost large sums of money with quite little to show for it. The simple truth was that the US could afford it. It spent about $300 billion on the entire war effort (out of a GDP of about $100 billion in 1940 and $215 in 1945). This is equivalent to about 5,000 *Essex* class carriers. One of the most expensive projects of the war was the B-29, costing $3 billion in total with similar amounts spent on the B-17 and B-24. Each of these projects was then the equivalent of about 50 *Essex* class carriers. To put things in perspective, a hundred or so fleet carriers was simply within the margin of error of the overall war effort. During the same time, Japan was hard pressed to build a handful of carriers. After 24 *Essex* class carriers had been built, the US could easily have kept building them by the dozens but there was simply no need for more.

The massive air power that all these new carriers brought with them could dominate not only the Japanese fleet but also Japanese land-based air power. This was not understood in 1942 but became clear during 1944. By then it was realized that the slog up the Solomons, along New Guinea, through the Philippines, and along the Chinese coast was no longer necessary. After the Marianas, Okinawa or even Kyushu could have been the next target. This would have been in the spirit of Mahan but was famously opposed by MacArthur who used his political influence to get his way. Roosevelt was up for re-election in November 1944 and MacArthur was the only person with any real chance of challenging him, being the anointed War Hero and having won the GOP primaries of both Wisconsin and Illinois. After the Marianas, the two met in Pearl Harbor and appear to have struck a deal, MacArthur got his return to the Philippines and Roosevelt got his support for re-election.

The huge US fleet of 1945 could go basically anywhere. Not even land-based air power could stop it. As the ultimate Mahanian expression of sea power, the entire Western Pacific could have been bypassed with the fleet sailing straight from Pearl Harbor into Tokyo Bay in what would have effectively been a repeat of the Perry Expedition.

This might not have been an optimal strategy, however, as it would have involved substantial risks. Toward the end of the war, the US knew they would win. All they had to do was not to lose. A possibly faster end to the war hardly outweighed the risk of a defeat, even if that risk was small. The strategy chosen was probably quite optimal, a reasonably speedy advance, if somewhat predictable and attritional, but without taking any major risks. A much faster advance would also have been of limited value, as the invasion of Japan was still constrained by the policy of Germany First.

Still, the best strategy would probably have meant not having to go to war in the first place. Had the American public been willing to spend more on defense at a much earlier stage, willing to show that it was ready to go to war, it would never have had to. As it was, Roosevelt did not "speak softly and carry a big stick," he very explicitly ordered Japan out of China while the stick was still being built. Japan was not amused but also not impressed. Hence the war.

## Ending the War

The ending of the war necessarily revolves much around the use of the atomic bomb, however horrible that weapon is. Whatever happened in the carrier battles in the Pacific, atomic bombs would start dropping on Japan in August 1945. The bombs would then continue to drop at a tempo of about one every ten days, increasing in tempo toward the end of 1945 to one every three days.

Had the Japanese been successful against the American fleet, perhaps by catching several carriers at Pearl Harbor and/or by sinking the rest at Midway, they might at most have succeeded in delaying the defeat by 6–12 months, but in the end this would just have resulted in more atomic bombs being dropped on them.

Japan could do nothing to stop these atomic bombs from being dropped. A B-29 operating out of Midway could reach Japan, but carrying a nuclear device it would not have had enough fuel for the return trip. It would have to ditch about half way back, with the crew picked up by a submarine. As soon as the Japanese figured out that a lone B-29 could be just as dangerous as a large formation, then that single B-29 would need to have a large formation to hide in. The defenders would not know which bomber carried the device and which bombers carried the fuel needed to return to Midway. If Midway was not available, then B-29s could make one-way trips from the US West Coast. Finally, even if the carriers could not act as a launch platform for heavy bombers, they could still provide fighter escorts for those bombers (as was done on occasion, before Iwo Jima was captured).

Japan formally started developing an atomic bomb in April 1941. The basic physics of the bomb was known before the war, so building it was mainly an exercise in producing the fissile material together with the engineering challenge involved in building a practical device. Funding was minimal, however, and the project never made much progress. The cost of the Manhattan Project was about $1.8 billion, of which something like 90 percent was spent building the plants that produced the fissile material—plants large enough to produce the fissile material needed for one bomb every three days. The cost also included the development of two designs, both developed with great haste. A less ambitious project would have cost much less. As an example, the British developed their bomb at a cost of about $200 million. A major consideration for the Japanese was access to uranium. After a geological search, uranium deposits were found in Hungnam in what today is North Korea, but by then it was very late. Uranium is actually quite a common element in earth's crust, more common than, for example, tin, cadmium, mercury, and silver. The problem is to find a concentration of it to make extraction cheaper. As a last-ditch effort, the Japanese tried to import uranium from Germany by submarine but the attempt failed. The fact remains that the Japanese never made a serious attempt to build an atomic bomb, and the comparative lack of resources certainly played a part in that decision. As with almost everything in this war, the Japanese had the technology but not the industrial capacity. They could have developed the bomb but could never have kept pace with the US capacity to build them in quantity. As an aside, Germany could well have afforded both the development and large-scale production of the bomb. The budget of the V2 project exceeded that of the Manhattan Project (with the bomb delivering "a much better bang for the buck"). Using the British figure, developing the bomb would have cost about the same as building the *Bismarck* and *Tirpitz*.

Then there is the question of a delivery vehicle for the bomb. Japan possessed few heavy bombers; the closest they got was the Nakajima G8N prototypes. Delivery by carrier-borne aircraft then becomes an obvious solution but that would have required a purpose-built bomber, most likely twin-engine, and a relatively light-bomb design.

The Japanese decision to go to war was essentially one huge psychological gamble. The atomic bomb could have been used as part of that gamble. After Pearl Harbor, or instead of Pearl Harbor, Japan could have announced that it was on its way to building an atomic bomb. The implied message would be that they were going to grab what they wanted and anybody that tried to take it back would risk a nuclear war. That would have immediately touched off a race to be the first to build the bomb, a race that most likely would decide the war. On the other hand, the race was already on—it just was not public. With the race public, it would now be difficult to make the case for the Americans to embark on a conventional campaign, including against Germany, as the war would effectively be decided by the scientists and engineers anyway. In the short run, whether or not Japan actually had the resources to win that race does not really matter. In the long run, how interested would the American public be in exposing itself to the possibility of a nuclear war in order to roll back what was now a well-established fact on the ground in some country far away? If America won the race to build the bomb and if the American public was willing to use it, taking into account the risk of a possible counterstrike, then Japan had lost the war. The operative word here is "if." With the world on the brink of the atomic age and with the general public largely unaware of it, a simple press release could have changed the psychology of the whole war, something any democracy is quite vulnerable to.

In retrospect, the Japanese decision to go to war was an utterly disastrous one taken by a group of culturally isolated individuals constrained by their own group dynamics. The only person that could take on the group, with any hope of success, was Emperor Hirohito himself. He eventually did and that ended the war.

The end of the war came as a surprise to many. The general expectation was that the Japanese would fight to the last man. Fighting to the last man made sense in the relatively minor battles outside of the Home Islands, as it made clear to the attackers that victory would be expensive. But if the attacker persisted and an attack on the Home Islands was imminent, then fighting to the last man ceased to make sense, as it would involve complete annihilation of the Japanese people. It had to be a bluff. The bluff was called and Japan folded.

# PART III

# The Art and Evolution of Carrier Operations

# CHAPTER 19

# Combat Models

## Introduction

The first part of this book was a presentation of the tools of the trade. The second part was a walkthrough of the carrier battles of World War II. The next part will be an evaluation of how carrier battles were fought, in a more general sense, together with how the fighting techniques evolved or could have evolved. To do this, the concept of the combat model is used.

Combat modeling explores the various trade-offs in offensive firepower, defensive firepower, staying power, numbers, and qualitative advantages.

Combat models can be arbitrarily complex, but that complexity has to be kept reined in. It has to serve a useful purpose and not become an exercise in itself. The models used here are kept simple.

## Lanchester's Laws

These are a set of equations to model attrition in combat. Formulated in 1916 by Frederick W. Lanchester, an English mathematician and engineer, they were originally intended to model aerial battles but quickly applied to trench warfare as well.

Battles are assumed to consist of many small interactions, and that for each unit of time, the firepower of one side will cause a level of attrition on the other side and vice versa. When fire is not aimed and the number of hits also depends on the density of targets, the result is Lanchester's Linear Law. This applies mainly to ancient combat.

Applied to modern combat, where fire is aimed and the density of targets can be assumed to have no effect, the result is Lanchester's Square Law. What it says is that the superior force will inflict heavier losses on a force that has less ability to absorb those losses and that the situation will only worsen as the battle grinds on. After it is all over, the superior force will have won a victory that is much better than initial relative strength. In essence, it is much more advantageous to concentrate forces and to defeat the enemy in detail. In terms of carrier battles, all the carriers should be kept together and then be used against a part of the enemy carrier fleet. At least this is the theory.

In the Square Law, the stronger force's advantage is equal to its numerical superiority *squared*. If the numerically inferior force wishes to compensate by superior quality, that qualitative superiority must compensate for the numerical superiority *squared*. This should be kept in mind when looking at how the Japanese tried to compensate their numerical and industrial inferiority by superior technology and/or warrior spirit.

## Salvo Combat Models

Lanchester's equations, as originally formulated, are a poor fit for modern naval combat using missiles. Missiles are typically fired in salvoes at discrete time intervals and the number of salvoes fired is small. This is quite different from the original scenario of many salvoes being fired more or less continuously. The discrete time model for salvo combat was introduced by USN Captain Wayne P. Hughes in his landmark study *Fleet Tactics* published in 1986.

A discrete time model can be seen as using game turns. In each game turn each side fires off a number of missiles. Each missile has a probability of hitting a target ship and will cause a set amount of damage. Each ship has a certain capability to withstand damage. When that damage has been received, the ship sinks. This then continues until only one side is left floating. This basic model can then be refined and adapted to the situation in various ways.

The standard salvo combat model is completely deterministic—there is no element of luck. A variant using statistical properties and concepts is known as the stochastic salvo model. Another variant allows different types of missile and different types of ship and is known as the heterogeneous salvo model. We could then combine the stochastic model with the heterogeneous model but by now it is probably more mathematics than modeling.

Carrier combat is quite close to missile combat. The main difference is that the "missiles" are manned and are expected to return to the carrier after their ordnance has been released.

Salvo combat models have been applied to the five major carrier battles of the Pacific War with refinements made to the basic models. The interesting thing here is not what will happen. We know already what happened and we can use that to calculate the various probabilities. The interesting thing is to see how sensitive the outcome was to changes in what went into the battle, to explore various what-if scenarios. This enables us to better understand the dynamics of the battles.

The basic salvo combat model needs to be adjusted for the peculiarities of the carrier battles of World War II. The model will model the technology and conditions of a strike on a carrier but will not necessarily reflect what happened during the actual battles, that is, the various tactical choices that were made. As an example, judging from the loss rates, the US torpedo bombers were very vulnerable. But this loss rate was largely due to the poor strike coordination at Midway, not because they were inherently more vulnerable than other torpedo bombers. Therefore, the historical loss rate is not necessarily fully reflected in the model.

The model is also kept as simple as possible. There are a number of historically perfectly valid distinctions that could be made but are *not* made; only those that matter to the discussion are made.

## The Importance of '42

The year 1942 was the critical year in the history of aircraft carriers. Not only was it in 1942 that the only major multi-carrier battles were fought in the Mediterranean, but more importantly it was also the year that saw four major carrier battles in the Pacific. These four battles give us an opportunity to study carrier battles as a group without having the details of one individual battle hiding the underlying and generally applicable truths.

## Combat Model

Drawing from the statistics of these four battles, the following combat model will be used for the 1942 battles in the Pacific, with a change in effectiveness of fighters for the 1944 battles.

The assumed situation is a coordinated attack by both dive and torpedo bombers, both of which are escorted by fighters. Opposing this attack are the defending CAP fighters on patrol above the carriers.

Each CAP fighter that attacks the dive bombers has a 20 percent chance of downing a dive bomber. Each CAP fighter that attacks the torpedo bombers has a 40 percent chance of downing a torpedo bomber.

To account for escorting fighters, one is assumed to engage one CAP fighter and by doing so halves the effectiveness of that CAP fighter. This is what most often happened and the above hit rates then becomes the more historical 10 percent and 20 percent.

Actual percentages are higher but have been lowered to reflect the fact that not every CAP fighter managed to get in position to attack the bombers, being out of position for some reason. In 1942, about 50–70 percent of the CAP fighters successfully engaged the attackers. The Japanese had the advantages of their carriers operating together, of the Zero being able to go where it was needed relatively quickly, and mostly being used to defend against US torpedo bombers that were relatively easy to find and attack. The Americans had the advantage of radar warning but much of that was wasted in poor fighter direction and by sometimes being out of position when the carriers operated separately.

The model ignores how many fighters were shot down in the battle between escorts and CAP. It is only what happened to the carriers that matters, the number of bomb and torpedo hits that were scored. In a standard salvo combat model, these exchanges of strikes would then continue for some number of times. In carrier combat, there was usually only one or maybe two exchanges of strikes, so follow-on effects of planes lost before the next strike can be ignored in the interest of simplicity.

In this model nothing gets shot down by AA. Apologies to the AA gunners of the time but their effect was mainly to distract the bombers, to scare them into early and/or ineffective release, and in that role they were quite effective. Only the odd lucky hit resulted in a bomber actually being shot down, at least before releasing its ordnance. It was only in the last battle of 1942, at Santa Cruz, that USN AA had improved to the point where losses due to it started to become a real factor.

Each remaining dive bomber will then have a 10 percent chance of scoring a hit on a carrier. Each remaining torpedo bomber will have a 5 percent chance of scoring a hit on a carrier. If the carrier is taken by surprise and/or has only weak AA available by itself or on nearby escorts, hit percentages are higher. Furthermore, torpedo bombers need a minimum number of attackers to be able to set up a successful anvil attack, something like 8–12 bombers. Much less than that and the target will likely be able to avoid the torpedoes and the hits percentage will be lower (such as 0 percent).

Finally, each bomb is considered to equal 0.2 carriers sunk and each torpedo hit is considered to equal 0.5 carriers sunk. This way the number of hits can be converted to number of carriers sunk.

## Combat Model Extended to 1944

In the 1942 model, no distinction is made between US and Japanese fighters. The Zero and the Wildcat were quite different as designs but the end result in combat effectiveness was similar. In 1944, the Hellcat was considerably more effective than the Zero as a design. More importantly, the Hellcat now enjoyed effective fighter direction which dramatically increased its effectiveness defensively. The Hellcat now had the time, speed, and ammunition to wreak havoc among attacking Japanese bombers and their escorts. How much the effectiveness should be raised is somewhat arbitrary but can be estimated to be four-fold. The probabilities for shooting down a dive bomber and a torpedo bomber are now raised to 80 percent and 160 percent respectively.

In 1944 the Japanese started to use Zero fighters as bombers, blurring the distinction between fighters and bombers in the model. Since such a fighter-bomber is not going to be very good as a bomber, and if facing serious opposition can be assumed to behave like a fighter, it is treated as a fighter.

In 1944, the AA on board US ships had dramatically improved since 1942. As an estimate, 50 percent of attacking Japanese bombers were shot down.

## Modeling Luck

Take 15 dive bombers making an attack with each bomber having a 10 percent chance of scoring a hit. Treating it as non-random, we would end up with 1.5 hits. This is what the model above is: it is a deterministic model. Treating it as a series of events with some probability, we have the possibility of zero, one, two or more hits with each number of hits having a probability.

Treating a carrier battle as a series of events with some degree of randomness will tell us about the variability of the battle. The average outcome will be the same but we will get information on how much the outcome will vary around that average. Since the purpose of the analysis is not to predict future battles or to engage in alternative histories, variance is not included in the model. Variance, the randomness of battles, will still be discussed. It is just not part of the model.

CHAPTER 20

# Concentration vs. Dispersion

## At the Strategic Level

The trade-off between concentration and dispersion exists at several levels. At the strategic level, a nation only has a limited number of carriers. How should they be employed? Should they be concentrated in order to achieve a certain objective at minimum cost while attriting the enemy carriers, or should they be divided and thus possibly achieve more objectives?

A good example is the Japanese defeat at Midway and the run-up to that battle. Japan had six fleet carriers but only four were present at Midway. Before Midway, the *Shokaku* and *Zuikaku* were sent south to the Coral Sea to cover the invasion of Port Moresby. At Coral Sea, the *Shokaku* was hit by bombs and both ships suffered losses to their aircrews. Neither was present at Midway. Had they been, Japan might have won the battle. At least that is the conventional wisdom.

To oppose them, the *Lexington* and *Yorktown* were sent south. *Lexington* was sunk and *Yorktown* was damaged. If the Japanese erred by splitting their carrier force by sending two south to the Coral Sea, then the Americans also erred by opposing them with only two carriers of their own. If the Americans had not opposed the Japanese at Coral Sea, then *Shokaku* and *Zuikaku* would have been present at Midway. It was only if the Americans also split their carriers that anything would likely happen that would stop *Shokaku* and *Zuikaku* from participating at Midway.

If both sides had two carriers knocked out, this would have been quite advantageous for the Japanese. They would have gone from a ratio of 6:4 to 4:2 in carriers. What happened of course was that the Americans knew about the upcoming battle. The *Yorktown* was hastily repaired and managed to participate in the battle. The ratio was now 4:3 but not through poor deployment decisions by the Japanese but because the Americans basically cheated. Had they not, the decision to send *Shokaku* and *Zuikaku* south to support that invasion would have been seen as a good move. Had the Japanese won decisively at Coral Sea, it could have been 6:2 at Midway and the move south would have been seen as brilliant.

The argument that the Japanese divided their carriers at Coral Sea can be made against the Americans as well. If the Americans had not divided their carriers by sending two off on the Doolittle Raid, then they might have been present at Coral Sea and the US carriers might not have been defeated there.

The Japanese had the initiative and for them it was a question of grabbing what they wanted before the US started to bring in superior resources. By splitting the carriers, they could attack more targets and get all they wanted in a shorter time. The Americans responded largely in kind. Neither side adhered strictly to the principle of force concentration. Both tended to split their carriers into two task forces with 2–4 carriers in each task force, at least before Midway, before they started to run out of carriers.

Setting the strategic level considerations aside, now look at the tactical level. The forces have been allocated and the battle is about to begin. How are the available forces best used?

## At the Tactical Level

There are several good reasons for concentration. Defensively, steaming together facilitates sharing the CAP and there is also mutual support from AA. Offensively, it makes the coordination of strikes easier, as the planes can form up without wasting too much time before proceeding.

The main reason for dispersion was the realization that carriers were "egg shells armed with hammers." If it was effectively impossible to stop an attack, it was better not to have all the eggs in one basket. If a strike had the capability to disable more than one carrier but only a single carrier was presented as a target, then the attacker would waste firepower. It was therefore argued that the carriers should be split up in different formations sailing some distance apart. The distance would be as great as needed to make it probable that the attacker would only target one of them.

The weakness in this argument is that it assumes that the enemy will cooperate in wasting its firepower. There is nothing fundamentally against the attacker finding out about the second task force and then allocating his strikes in a way that is optimal for the attacker, not the defender. Doctrine and training might get in the way but that would only be temporary.

An alternative to dispersing the task forces is to use one carrier as a bait. The intention here is for the carrier to soak up the strike and by doing so protect the others. Since it is going to be sunk anyway, a small or otherwise less valuable carrier is selected. The bait carrier can also do searches. Good search is particularly important for the side that can outrange the enemy, as it improves the odds that this advantage can be put in play with a possible huge payout in the form of an unanswered strike against the enemy fleet carriers. Thus we have the Japanese being more interested in using bait carriers, as they had longer-range strike aircraft.

A subtler variation of the bait carrier is to place the carriers with one of them in the direction of the enemy, along the likely avenue of approach, and the other carriers further back. The attacker will find the advance carrier and presumably attack it without attacking those further back. This is not necessarily a bait in the express meaning of the word: everything is done to protect that carrier. It is just a way of placing task forces one in front of the other, instead of side-by-side, in the direction of the enemy with an awareness of the likely consequences. For the Japanese, this tactic had the additional advantage that it played against the shorter range of US aircraft. Running short of fuel, it was very tempting to attack what was available even if not the main target.

Another variant is to use a surface force as bait, or advance force, instead of a carrier. Battleships are heavily armored and can take a beating while cruisers and lesser ships are simply expendable. A cruiser might not be a tempting enough target but a battleship would be. Any type of advance force also acts as radar picket, but then it is also more difficult to provide with CAP; forces to the rear of the picket are better protected. But if your battleships are well armored, fast, maneuverable, and well-endowed with AA, they should survive.

## Results from Combat Modeling

The first stage of this analysis assumes that the attacker will only target one of the dispersed carrier groups. If the attacker has spotted both or all carrier groups and his doctrine and training allows splitting up the attack, then this analysis will not make sense.

Assuming two carriers against two carriers and that half the fighters are sent as escorts with the strike while half is retained as CAP. Also assume that all available planes are sent as one strike.

This gives something like 40 dive bombers and 40 torpedo bombers plus an escort of 20 fighters. Assume that is met by 30 fighters in the CAP. Furthermore, assume that both escorts and CAP concentrate on the torpedo bombers.

The dive bombers will then score an average of 4.0 hits and the torpedo bombers will score 1.4 (losing 12 torpedo bombers to CAP before weapons release).

On the average, this would sink about one carrier. It is not enough to sink or seriously damage both carriers and dispersion does not appear to be worth it.

Scaling things up to four against four carriers or even six against six, we have two or three carriers sunk and the case for dispersion looks better. Midway is a good example. This is the battle where the Americans divided their three carriers into two task forces operating widely separated, over the horizon at 20–40 miles apart. Only one task force was found and attacked. This should then be compared with the Japanese plan of having all four carriers in one large formation. They were found and caught in a vulnerable state: three out of four of them were lost with the lone survivor saved simply by being the carrier in the formation that was furthest away from the attackers, by having its colleagues acting as baits.

## Best Balance

For battles of the size typical of 1942, dispersion does not make sense. For a larger battle with four against four carriers, dispersion looks like a viable disposition.

In an uneven battle, it is the number of carriers on the enemy side that matters. For two carriers facing four carriers, it makes sense to disperse the two carriers. For four carriers facing two carriers, concentrating the four carriers will be better.

Of course, if the carriers are in a very vulnerable situation with fueled and armed planes on the decks, then dispersion makes very good sense. This implies that doctrine should allow for different tactical dispositions for different stages of flight operations.

The cost of a risk has not been accounted for, as luck cannot be factored into the model. Taking luck into account, a better case can be made for dispersion, as it lowers the maximum loss possible.

# CHAPTER 21

# Fighters vs. Bombers

## Introduction

A carrier can have only a limited number of planes on board. There is a choice between carrying fighters or bombers. With more fighters available you will be better able to escort and protect your own bombers and/or protect your own ships against incoming attacks. With more bombers, the strikes against the enemy carriers are more likely to be successful.

## Size of Air Group

Bombers and fighters are not necessarily of the same size and the total number can depend on the mix. However, that effect is small. The portion of the flight deck that needs to be empty to enable take offs depend on what the fighters need. Those fighters used for CAP can be assumed not to be loaded with extra fuel tanks. With more fighters present, the total capacity will be slightly more. On the other hand, this can be compensated for by how heavily loaded all types of planes can be. To an extent, then, there is a small tradeoff between strike range and the size of air group.

## Results from Combat Modeling

Looking at the model it is immediately clear that in 1942, fighters were not very good investments. Each fighter contributed less, in both offense and defense, than it deducted from the offense by taking up room aboard that could otherwise have gone to a bomber. A more numerous CAP would certainly be useful, and better escorting of the very vulnerable torpedo bombers would certainly have led to lower losses. However, it would not have led to a better exchange ratio of hits to enemy versus friendly carriers. At the end of the battle that is what matters.

The model ignores the role CAP fighters had in disrupting attack formations and hence in keeping hit percentages low. Fighters also have a very important function in chasing off or shooting down enemy search planes. Even if the model does not show this, it still makes sense to retain a limited number of fighters. Their number should not be allowed to subtract too much from the number of bombers available though.

Before the war, when carriers were still seen as an adjunct to the battle line, fighters were regarded as critical to protect your own spotting planes as well as shooting down enemy spotting planes. The side that had spotting planes in the air above the enemy battle line, to spot the fall of shot, would most likely win the gunnery duel. Before the war, knowing well that heavy AA was largely useless against high-level bombers, fighters were also seen as the only effective defense against them. As the war progressed, it was understood that high-level bombing was ineffective against maneuvering ships and that threat subsided.

The US did increase the number of fighters during 1942. The number of bombers stayed constant; the increase was made possible by new Wildcats that had folding wings.

The situation in 1944 was different. Firstly, the US now had efficient fighter direction. It also had a significant advantage in the number of carriers. This heavily affected the mix and will be explored in the following scenarios.

## An Even Carrier Battle in 1944

Assume a battle with both sides having two carriers steaming as one formation. As a simplification, assume that each side simultaneously launches strikes using all available bombers, with half the fighters sent as escorts, while the other half are retained as CAP. When acting as escorts or as CAP, assume that half go with the dive bombers and half go with the torpedo bombers.

Japanese carriers are assumed to operate 28 fighters, 24 dive bombers, and 16 torpedo bombers each. These numbers are held constant throughout. They are close to the historical but have been tweaked slightly to simplify calculations. American carriers are given a complement of 90 planes each that can then be used for any mix of fighters and bombers.

American carriers are now assumed to operate an historical mix of 40 fighters, 32 dive bombers, and 18 torpedo bombers:

|  | Bombs | Torpedoes | Carriers sunk |
|---|---|---|---|
| Hits on American carriers | 3.8 | 0.6 | 1.0 |
| Hits on Japanese carriers | 6.3 | 1.7 | 2.1 |

Now assume that the American carriers instead used a more offensive loadout more similar to that used in 1942, that is 24 fighters, 42 dive bombers and 24 torpedo bombers:

|  | Bombs | Torpedoes | Carriers sunk |
|---|---|---|---|
| Hits on American carriers | 4.2 | 1.1 | 1.4 |
| Hits on Japanese carriers | 8.2 | 2.2 | 2.8 |

Now assume that the Americans went for a more defensive loadout with 64 fighters, 18 dive bombers, and eight torpedo bombers:

|  | Bombs | Torpedoes | Carriers sunk |
|---|---|---|---|
| Hits on American carriers | 3.2 | 0.0 | 0.6 |
| Hits on Japanese carriers | 3.5 | 0.7 | 1.0 |

To make valid comparisons, the above numbers do not take into consideration bombers shot down by AA (before releasing ordnance). Taking the very effective AA on the US side into account, using the model presented, all Japanese hit numbers should be halved.

## An Uneven Carrier Battle in 1944

Assume a battle with the US having four carriers while the Japanese have two. American carriers operate an historical mix of 40 fighters, 32 dive bombers, and 18 torpedo bombers:

|  | Bombs | Torpedoes | Carriers sunk |
|---|---|---|---|
| Hits on American carriers | 2.2 | 0.0 | 0.4 |
| Hits on Japanese carriers | 12.7 | 3.5 | 4.3 |

Now assume that the American carriers used a more offensive loadout of 24 fighters, 42 dive bombers, and 24 torpedo bombers:

|  | Bombs | Torpedoes | Carriers sunk |
|---|---|---|---|
| Hits on American carriers | 3.4 | 0.2 | 0.8 |
| Hits on Japanese carriers | 16.7 | 4.7 | 5.7 |

Now assume that the Americans went for a more defensive loadout of 64 fighters, 18 dive bombers, and eight torpedo bombers, again employed as a single deck-load strike:

| | Bombs | Torpedoes | Carriers sunk |
|---|---|---|---|
| Hits on American carriers | 0.0 | 0.0 | 0.0 |
| Hits on Japanese carriers | 7.1 | 1.5 | 2.1 |

Again, to make valid comparisons, the above numbers do not take into consideration bombers shot down by AA (before releasing ordnance). Taking the very effective AA on the US side into account, using the model presented, all Japanese hit numbers should be halved.

## An Asymmetrical Uneven Battle in 1944

Now for a scenario approximating to the historical sequence of events at the battle of Philippine Sea. Two Japanese carriers are able to get in an unanswered strike against four US carriers with all fighters available as strike escorts. The US carriers absorb that strike with all fighters available for CAP, then launch a counterstrike with all bombers meeting no defending CAP over the Japanese carriers. Both sides use the historical mixes:

| | Bombs | Torpedoes | Carriers sunk |
|---|---|---|---|
| Hits on American carriers | 0.0 | 0.0 | 0.0 |
| Hits on Japanese carriers | 12.8 | 3.6 | 4.4 |

In this model, 160 fighters defend the US carriers and all attacking Japanese bombers are shot down. That said, the dive bombers come quite close to getting a few past the fighters (although they still have to face the AA). With a good size counterstrike meeting no defending CAP, nor very effective AA, the Japanese carriers are sunk.

Very interestingly, this scenario with American carriers quite passively absorbing a Japanese strike actually provides better results than the standard exchange of simultaneous strikes. The dream of any carrier captain was always to get in an unanswered strike and the Japanese did everything to achieve that. In the Philippine Sea battle they succeeded but it actually worked against them. By having all fighters available for CAP, hits on US carriers were reduced to nil. Facing fewer Japanese fighters on CAP, the counterstrike now provides slightly better results. Having played a perfect game, the Japanese still lost. They would have to play a different game.

## Best Balance

With a small number of fighters, improving fighter direction increases defensive capabilities at no cost in offensive capabilities, but since the number of fighters is relatively small, the net effect is only a marginal increase in defensive capabilities.

Fighter direction is key to the trade-off, however. With good fighter direction, a CAP fighter has opportunity to, on the average, shoot down more than one attacking bomber. The CAP fighter is now profitable, as it costs the enemy more in reduced offensive power than it costs by reducing the number of bombers available for a strike.

Increasing the number of fighters *and* improving fighter direction yields a dramatic effect on defensive strength. The fleet is now very much able to defend itself effectively even against a substantial attacking force. There is no longer a need for a sacrificial carrier; the carriers can now operate together and the effect of mutual support is now very tangible. The drawback is that with comparatively fewer bombers the offensive strength is reduced but should still be able to inflict substantial losses on the enemy.

As can be seen from the scenarios above, the historically chosen mixes seem to be close to optimal. On the other hand, the exact mix seems to be relatively non-critical in terms of who wins the battle and the exchange ratio in doing so. This is somewhat surprising as the types of planes operated is such a fundamental characteristic of a carrier. It turns out that the mix is much more a question of how bloody the battle will be. With a larger number of fighters on CAP, fewer hits will be suffered but with fewer bombers, fewer hits will also be inflicted on the enemy.

This is of course what happened in 1944 during the Philippine Sea battle. Many more fighters meant fewer hits were scored for both sides. By 1944, the USN carriers also had a different role. The primary purpose of the carriers was now to achieve air superiority over a landing site. The carriers did not attack; the amphibious forces did the attacking and the role of the carriers was essentially defensive, to protect the landings. This meant that fighters were the primary weapon. Bombers were still useful but there were alternatives to bombers for indirect fire support, for example, naval gunfire or land-based artillery once ashore.

The Japanese increased the fighter ratio somewhat but essentially stayed with the 1942 mix. The role of the carriers also stayed much the same during the war, essentially that of attacking enemy carriers. In the 1942 battles, the Japanese largely succeeded in that. With a clearly offensive stance, not developing good fighter direction was understandable since they never had a large number of defensive fighters to direct. Another point to consider is the actual usefulness of the longer engagement times that fighter direction provides. With the limited ammunition supply of the Zero, combined with how much ammunition was required to bring down the more rugged American planes, the additional time available might not have been of much use anyway. If so, what we are actually seeing here is the limitations of the Zero and its philosophy of being lightly built.

Disregarding various special factors and going back to the core problem of fighters against bombers, it appears that we have in fact two distinct solutions (or "Nash Equilibria" in game theory parlance). If fighters are not profitable compared to bombers, then we are going to see a mix with a minority of the planes being fighters. If on the other hand, fighters are indeed profitable compared to bombers, then we are going to see a mix with a majority of the planes being fighters. In the first case, it will be a bloody battle and it will be a case of who finds and attacks the enemy first—a pretty nerve-wracking and very tactical battle. In the latter case, it will first and foremost be a battle for air supremacy and once that battle has been won or lost, a quite one-sided affair. It will most likely be a more pedestrian battle of attrition and much less tactical.

## Fighter-Bombers

Having to choose between fighters and bombers is not easy. It would obviously be nice if fighters could also be bombers. The total numbers of planes does not increase but we have greater operational flexibility. For any one given task, more planes are available.

Fighters and dive bombers are quite similar in size and behavior. A fighter could often carry a bomb and a dive bomber was often reasonably useful as a fighter. Torpedo bombers tended to differ though, as they were typically bigger and slower than both fighters and dive bombers, having to lug that heavy load.

As engines became more powerful during the war, it became possible for fighters to carry a heavy bomb and even a torpedo. The Hellcat, Corsair, and Fw 190 fighters were all tested carrying a torpedo. The major problem was usually that the torpedo was quite long compared to a small and nimble fighter and adjustments had to made to the undercarriage.

The main disadvantage with the fighter in the role of the bomber was that it did not have a rear gunner. This made it easy to break up an attacking formation, effectively ruining the attack. As a dive bomber, the fighter was also less accurate. Then there was the problem of the pilot handling navigation, the radio as well as everything else. A major problem was simply training—the fighter pilot had to learn various types of bombing on top of being a good fighter. Training would become more time consuming as well as resulting in pilots not becoming true specialists.

While attacking, the fighter-bombers would initiate the attack on the enemy ships, suppressing AA. Then they would pull back to regroup and act as escorts to those carrying torpedoes. Theoretically it allowed planes to be recycled in the attack but it also introduced problems of range and coordination that had to be solved.

While defending, all the planes on board could be used as fighters. Here we have a clear and unambiguous advantage with the fighter-bomber.

In the early years of the war, fighter direction had not yet evolved and it was generally better to have more bombers and relatively few fighters. In that setting, the drawbacks of the fighter-bomber outweighed the advantages. Fighter engines also had not yet become powerful enough to carry heavier loads.

Later in the war, we have to distinguish between carrier battles and ground support. In a late-war carrier battle, with good fighter direction, most of the planes were pure fighters anyway. Having an even higher number of fighters available was still useful but should be weighed against the deficiencies of the fighter-bomber on the attack. In a carrier battle, aircraft losses are not important, as there is only one or maybe two strikes and planes are basically to be considered ammunition anyway.

Doing ground support, the fighter-bomber looks much better, particularly using rockets that do not require the fighter pilot to be re-trained. The main historical reason for fighter-bombers instead of dive bombers—their much higher survival rate—also very much applied to the daily grind of doing ground support.

# CHAPTER 22

# Battleships vs. Carriers

## Introduction

Most naval battles involve a point target, either a convoy or a landing site. Some large battles have been about enforcing or breaking a blockade, notably battles like Tsushima and Jutland, but in World War II by far the most common reason for having a battle was the presence of a point target.

Battleships are very well suited for attacking or defending a point target, having a high sustained firepower and high survivability. They are slower than aircraft and can only project their firepower out to a short range, but both of these drawbacks are less important around a point target.

Carriers have less sustained firepower and lower survivability. They are not very good at attacking or defending a point target. They are best for area domination. Carriers, however, can project their high instantaneous firepower over much long ranges.

A surface fleet could very well sneak up on a carrier formation. It happened during the Norwegian Campaign and again off Samar. In basically all the 1942 battles between Japanese and American carriers, the Japanese tried to seek a surface engagement and the inferior US surface forces invariably withdrew. It was a major consideration in all these battles even if no surface action actually happened.

The carrier had the advantage in daytime in an area with predominantly nice weather, the Central Pacific being one such area. In areas with poor weather and at night, the battleship had the advantage. Radar technology was critical in enabling carriers to avoid being caught in a surface battle, negating much of the advantages of the battleship. Radar only helps the carrier to avoid being caught by surface forces but is not of much help if the carrier has to stand and defend a point target.

## Battleships Attacking Carriers

Now, to resolve the question of which of the two is the supreme expression of a nation's naval power, use a scenario where battleships are pitted against carriers, "mano a mano," so to speak.

If both fleets are just sailing around with nothing particular in mind, then the carriers will win, as they can simply stay out of range and pound the battleships.

A more realistic scenario is around a point target. If the battleships are the defenders then we have the same situation as before: the carriers will stay out of range and attrition the target. If the carriers are defending and the battleships are attacking, then we have an interesting situation.

Assume that the carriers have a striking range of 200–300 miles and that they are defending a point target—a convoy or a landing site. Assuming a night of ten hours and that the battleships can approach this target at 24 knots, the battleships could conceivably reach the target without the carriers being able to get in a strike.

Assuming that the carriers can have some wiggle room, either by being placed closer to the approaching battleships than the target or by being able to retreat with the target at some slow speed, then the carriers will be able to get in a strike or two before the battleships reach the target.

## Results from Combat Modeling

Assume a single carrier defending against a single battleship. Assume the carrier is carrying 20 fighters, 20 dive bombers, and 20 torpedo bombers and assume that there is no fighter cover above the battleship.

Assuming that this engagement takes place in 1942. Using those hit rates, then we get two bomb hits and one torpedo hit. No planes are shot down and the next strike will achieve the same number of hits. Assuming two strikes, we get a total of four bomb hits and two torpedo hits, which will most likely disable the battleship, allowing the strikes to continue. Effectively, the carrier will wear down the battleship and the target will be defended, although perhaps in an indirect way, not directly and definitely.

Now assume that this takes place in 1944. The main difference is the much improved effectiveness of AA. Half the bombers will be shot down and then one bomb hit and 0.5 torpedo hit will be scored. The next strike will launch with the remaining planes and half of those will be shot down (assuming that the available AA was not affected by the bomb hits). There will be 0.5 bomb hit and 0.25 torpedo hit. If the carrier is able to get in a third strike, we get a grand total of slightly less than two bomb hits and perhaps a torpedo hit but by then the carrier has lost most of its aircraft.

This means that a surface fleets built around battleships, heavily armed with effective AA and maneuverable, might not be stopped by air attack alone and should be able to reach a point target with acceptable losses. The only effective way of stopping the battleships is then with another fleet of battleships. Supremacy has now, at least partially and for this type of situation, reverted back to the battleship. This was never tested in combat, although both Surigao Straits and Samar showed the general principle. A similar flank attack done by the US battle fleet could probably not have been stopped by any Japanese carriers employed to stop them. This can be seen from the Philippine Sea battle in just how successful the US ship formation was in defending itself against those of the Japanese air attack that had managed to get past the fighters. This situation would have been further reinforced with radar-directed AA.

The situation in 1944 is then what it was thought to be before the war: that a battleship would be hard to stop by aircraft alone. This situation will not last for long, though. The advent of effective guided bombs would then tilt the balance in favor of the aircraft, at least until effective surface-to-air missiles arrived. Also, as aircraft technology evolved and ranges and bomb loads increased, the kill zone the battleship had to traverse before reaching its point target was extended and becoming more dangerous: the battleship became effectively non-viable as a capital ship.

It should also be noted that the above conclusion, that a battleship will wear down the attacking aircraft faster that these will wear down the battleship, breaks down if expanded into a series of such engagements. The carrier will be able to replace its planes very quickly while the battleship will take a long time to repair or replace.

## Best Balance

Setting that thought experiment aside, the trade-off between carriers and battleship depends on many factors. That the carrier was the new "Queen of the Seas" and that the battleship was obsolete is just too simplistic. In many ways it depended on circumstances—in many ways the battleship and the carrier were complementary and should be used as combined arms.

The carrier had a certain fragility to it. It was not generally well armored. In poor weather and visibility, the air group was grounded. As an example, escorting convoys to Russia, the carrier had limited usefulness. In poor visibility and against point targets, it was all about battleships.

Carriers also had problems facing superior land-based air power. In the European theater of operations, major landings against a near-peer enemy could not be based on carriers. If so, there was little need to build the ships that would only be marginally useful. In the Pacific, it was a different story. Isolated Pacific islands could be conquered with carrier-based air power. Here, a naval power with ten times the industrial capacity of its enemy could impose its will on any land-based opposition.

All nations invested in battleships. Up until 1940–41, the IJN probably had the highest proportion of spending on carriers, the USN the smallest, with the RN somewhere in between. Americans really do like their guns; the Japanese were the upstarts, betting on a new technology while the British tried to be sensible about the whole matter.

The USN got a very poor return on the investment in its *Iowa* class battleships. Mainly babysitting carriers, they together shot down a grand total of about 15 enemy planes, about the same number as a reasonably successful Hellcat ace. For an expenditure of $400 million for the four battleships, the enemy lost planes worth about $1 million. Shore bombardment was their other main task, but the USN had plenty of other gunships to do that, to the extent that shore bombardment actually achieved much against defenders that were well dug-in.

The huge investment in the two *Yamatos* was seen as a necessity in order to give the IJN a chance against the numerically superior battle line of the USN. The three ships built, that is the *Yamato*, *Musashi*, and *Shinano*, together cost about $400 million. It is very doubtful if this investment was cost-effective compared to the more normal battleship designs or to carriers (or even compared to the development of an atomic bomb). The *Yamatos* still proved rather useful in an indirect way, as the backbone of the Japanese surface fleet that the Americans were unwilling to meet in a night battle. Having to avoid a night surface battle quite severely limited the US carrier movements during the night in many engagements. It also meant that US carriers had to be careful not to get too close to Japanese forces, which increased the likelihood that the Japanese would be able to use the longer range of their strike aircraft to outrange the US carriers.

The RN certainly needed their battleships: the main areas of operations suited them. The main problem was huge areas to cover and a general shortage of resources. Instead of building the *Nelsons*, *King George Vs*, and *Vanguards*, a more cost-effective solution would probably have been to take the 15-inch turrets from the *Revenge* and *Courageous* classes and recycle them on a series of eight new battleships each armed with three twin 15-inch guns, of 35,000 tons and capable of 30 knots to be able to match that of the modernized battlecruisers. The RN would probably also have been much better off by standardizing on twin 4-inch mounts for secondary armament and heavy AA, including using the same twin 4-inch mounts as the main armament for all the various destroyers and escorts. This is all in splendid hindsight of course. It also assumes that national pride—around the issue of having battleships that were not quite as powerful as those of the enemy—would not get in the way.

# CHAPTER 23

# Armored Flight Deck vs. Size of Air Group

## Introduction

The purpose of having the deck armor at the level of the flight deck, as opposed to the level of the hangar deck, is to protect the aircraft inside the hangar. This is not really to protect the aircraft per se; it is to prevent a bomb from penetrating into the hangar and causing uncontrollable fires and explosions among the fueled and armed planes in the hangar. Additionally, if a bomb lands among fueled and armed planes up on the flight deck, the resulting fires and explosions will not spread into the hangar. Finally, with an armored flight deck, the carrier is much more likely to be able to remain operational after a bomb hit on the flight deck.

Traditionally, placing the armor at the level of flight deck led to a decrease in the size of the air group. The tradeoff between having an armored flight deck and the size of the air group has been a big topic, with Limeys and Yanks arguing back and forth in a quite animated debate.

HMS *Formidable* showing off her armored deck. Note two small elevators, a consequence of the emphasis on survivability, and the planes lining up to use the forward elevator. Note also the planes stored on outriggers on the starboard side, enabling additional planes to be carried—planes that did not have to fit on the elevators.

## Design Considerations of Armored Flight Decks

It should be noted that when talking about armored flight decks, the whole flight deck is typically not armored and the thickness of its parts can vary. The hangar is not the only part of the ship that is protected but armor does not have to be at the level of the flight deck. The total amount of armor carried is also a different question.

A 3-inch armored deck covering 3,400 square meters weighs about 2,000 tons. This weight can be placed either on the hangar deck or on the flight deck or perhaps both. If placed on the flight deck, for reasons of stability, then the flight deck normally has to be lower in the hull. This then leads to a decrease in available ship volume which then leads to a decrease in the volume available for the hangar.

Then again it might not. The designers may decide to change some other parameter. As an example, a wider hull would provide both the stability and the required volume. It might also be noted that hangar volume in itself does not weigh anything, it is just air.

Having two hangar decks halves the amount of armor needed to protect them. This is simply because both decks can now be under the same sheet of armor. On the other hand, the lower hangar will be quite low in the ship which precludes having large side openings and thus deck edge elevators. Comparing the hangars of armored carriers like *Implacable* and *Taiho* to that of the unarmored *Essex*, they were of roughly comparable width but considerably shorter. The shorter hangar was still more than enough to cover the machinery and magazine spaces with the same armor. As a single hangar deck typically runs for most of the length of the ship, covering it all with armor will mean that the ship's spaces underneath the ends of the hangar are protected to an extent that is not normally considered efficient.

The weight penalty of having an armored flight deck also depends on to what extent the sides of the hangar must also be armored, that is, having an armored box around the hangar, not just an armored roof. In the early days, the range of aircraft was modest and carriers ran a very real risk of bumping into enemy surface ships. This necessitated protection against guns, typically cruiser caliber guns. As ranges increased and radar became common, that danger faded and the hangar sides could be left thinly armored, reducing the total weight of the flight deck.

Finally, the size of the hangar is not necessarily the limiting factor on size of air group carried. The use of deck parks, having aircraft permanently parked on the flight deck, allows for a bigger air group than can be stored in the hangar.

## History of Carrier Design

Before going into a comparison of the various carrier designs, it might be useful to give a brief history of how design of fleet carriers evolved before the war.

The first generation of fleet carriers were the battlecruiser conversions. The Americans built the *Lexington* and *Saratoga*, the Japanese the *Akagi* and *Kaga* (the latter actually a battleship). These were large ships with traditional armor for their type. They also carried cruiser-type guns and were expected to be able to fend for themselves if running into enemy surface forces. The British converted the battlecruisers *Furious*, *Glorious*, and *Courageous*. These were very lightly armored, known as "Fisher's Follies," and depended on speed to escape a scuffle. Their bows had a very fine entry and could not support the weight of a flight deck; hence the flight decks did not extend over the bows.

Next followed the first true fleet carriers. The Americans built the *Ranger* and the Japanese built the *Soryu* and *Hiryu*. The British built the larger and more ambitious *Ark Royal*. These were all lightly armored with an emphasis on aircraft-carrying capacity.

Then we have the prewar generation of fleet carriers. The Americans built the *Yorktowns* and the smaller *Wasp*. The Japanese built the *Zuikakus* and the British the *Illustrious* class. These were all more balanced ship with the British leading the way in having armored flight decks, sacrificing hangar space, at least initially.

Finally, we have the wartime fleet carriers. The Americans built the *Essex* class as enlarged *Yorktowns*, sticking to unarmored flight decks. The Japanese elected to follow in the path of the British and built the *Taiho* with an armored flight deck. The British built the *Implacable* class, continuing with armored flight decks but expanding the hangar space.

## Hangar Sizes

The following table lists some carriers, their standard displacement, hangar floor space in square meters, hangar heights in meters (upper and lower hangar), number of hangar decks and thickness of any flight deck armor:

| | Displacement | Area | Height (U+L) | Decks | Armor |
|---|---|---|---|---|---|
| *Furious* | 22450 | 4957 | 4.6+4.6 | 2 | - |
| *Courageous* | 22500 | 5095 | 4.6+4.6 | 2 | - |
| *Ark Royal* | 22000 | 5690 | 4.9+4.9 | 2 | - |

| | Displacement | Area | Height (U+L) | Decks | Armor |
|---|---|---|---|---|---|
| *Illustrious* | 23000 | 2638 | 4.9 | 1 | 3-inch |
| *Indomitable* | 23000 | 3606 | 4.3+4.9 | 1½ | 3-inch |
| *Implacable* | 23450 | 3857 | 4.3+4.3 | 1½ | 3-inch |
| *Lexington* | 37681 | 2920 | 6.10 | 1 | - |
| *Ranger* | 14575 | 3330 | 5.77 | 1 | - |
| *Yorktown* | 19875 | 3194 | 5.25 | 1 | - |
| *Wasp* | 15752 | 3055 | 5.23 | 1 | - |
| *Essex* | 27208 | 4247 | 5.35 | 1 | - |
| *Independence* | 10622 | 1313 | 5.30 | 1 | - |
| *Midway* | 47387 | 6095 | 5.33 | 1 | 3.5-inch |
| *Soryu* | 15900 | 5647 | 4.6+4.3 | 2 | - |
| *Hiryu* | 17300 | 5647 | 4.6+4.3 | 2 | - |
| *Shokaku* | 25675 | 7000 | 4.8+4.8 | 2 | - |
| *Taiho* | 29300 | 6840 | 5.0+5.0 | 2 | 3.1-inch |
| *Unryu* | 17150 | 6405 | 4.9+4.9 | 2 | - |
| *Graf Zeppelin* | 28090 | 5648 | 5.7+5.7 | 2 | 0.8/1.8-inch |

Numbers are from NavyPedia.org. Some of the hangar sizes are believed to be inaccurate, most likely depending on how that size is calculated. Sources often differ on the exact number. Using a single source for all numbers, relative sizes should hopefully be accurate which is what is needed for the comparison here. Still, caution is advised, as figures vary, particularly for Japanese carriers. One reason seems to be the way Japanese hangars had very irregular shapes. As an example, the book about *Taiho* by Goralski gives the dimensions of the hangars as 150×18 and 150×17m, yielding a total area of 5,250m². The *Akagi* and *Kaga* have not been listed, as sources differ, with reputable sources giving numbers that are obviously wrong.

As an aside, modern USN carriers have a hangar size of about 6,900m². The new RN *Queen Elizabeth* class has a hangar size of about 5,200m². Both have armored flight decks but *QE* appears to have thicker armor on what is a smaller size ship. Old habits die hard but then geostrategic and economic realities remain largely the same.

What is apparent from this table is that there is not really a clear and unambiguous correlation between hangar size and having an armored flight deck, at least not between navies. There is a correlation but it is mixed up with other factors such as the US philosophy of having only a single hangar deck. As an example, the armored *Taiho* had a considerably larger hangar than the unarmored *Essex*.

With most of the planes of the day being "taildraggers," the hangar height required was determined by the height of the propeller. As an example, the three-bladed propeller of a Hellcat needed 4.4m if a blade pointed straight up but the minimum height was only 3.5. The Corsair needed 4.6 with one blade straight up, but with the four-bladed propeller the minimum was 4.0. It might be noted that on the Corsair, the wings folded upwards, requiring a hangar height of 5.0 which is why the RN had to clip them 20cm to make them fit into their 4.9m hangars. This does not imply that RN hangars were too cramped for modern planes, only that the Corsair was designed to make use of a height that was there for reasons not applicable to RN carriers (being able to warm up engines and overhead stowage of disassembled aircraft). The Japanese Kate torpedo bomber also had wings that folded upwards but these required less headroom than the Corsair. The Corsair, as well as the Helldiver, could have been designed with the folding mechanism placed more like on the Kate but might then have needed more floor space. The Seafire went with a double fold mechanism that kept it below the 4.3m limit on many RN carriers while still not being too wide to fit on their narrow elevators.

USN carriers had hangars with more headroom than any other navy. They also used their hangars to warm up the engines. This does not appear to have been the actual reason for that increased height—being able to stow spares hanging from the ceiling seems to have been the main driver. However, one reason does not exclude the other.

Toward the end of the war, the armored *Implacable* carried about 80 planes while an unarmored *Essex* carried about 100. Given that the *Essex* was a bigger ship, they carried a roughly equal number of aircraft per ton of displacement. The comparison in size of air group between the *Implacable* and the *Essex* is particularly valid since they operated much the same types of aircraft, even more so as those types were not designed to fit inside the hangars of *Implacable*.

The *Taiho* carried fewer aircraft, despite its large hangars. That was because neither its fighters nor its dive bombers had folding wings. Not having folding wings made them lighter and better as aircraft. Accepting the weight and performance penalty of folding wings, the *Taiho* could have operated more planes than an *Essex*.

To save on the amount of armor needed, those with an armored flight deck tended to have two hangars. Somewhat counter-intuitively then, those with armored flight decks tended to have *larger* hangars. This reflects differences in operational philosophy more than the constraints of naval architecture. The British wanted to have their aircraft in the hangars and not up on the flight deck while the Japanese wanted to operate aircraft that did not have folding wings.

Disregarding operational philosophies and looking at this strictly from the viewpoint of naval architecture, how did the designers of the *Taiho* do it? How could they design a ship with an armored flight deck, a larger hangar, and the same speed as an *Essex*, all on roughly the same displacement? That question should perhaps be put to the designers of the *Essex*. Their answer would probably be simple—lack of time. Tank designers face much the same problem of combining firepower, armor, and mobility. Maybe the *Taiho* was the equivalent of a Panther tank while an *Essex* was a Sherman, a design that was available and could be produced quickly and in large numbers but with better designs soon to follow. The Americans were not alone in having to sacrifice quality for quantity. After Midway, the Japanese had to abandon building more of the *Taiho* or planned *Taiho-Kai* (improved *Taiho*) classes, concentrating on the quickly built *Unryu* class instead.

## Experience from Battle Damage

An armored flight deck of any reasonable weight will not provide full protection against everything. For example, a 1,000lb AP bomb will most likely penetrate successfully. Its value lies in forcing the attacker to use that kind of ordnance: a simple 250lb HE bomb will not suffice and fewer bombs will be available to score hits. Using an AP bomb, the explosive charge is smaller and less destructive. To achieve penetration, the bomb will also usually be released from a higher altitude, resulting in fewer hits. Having to carry the heaviest bomb possible will also reduce the range of the attacking aircraft. Furthermore, an armored deck placed at the hangar-deck level will probably be penetrated in the same manner and having the armor higher up will most likely also cause the bomb to detonate higher up in the ship, causing less damage to the vitals.

Both Val and Dauntless dive bombers normally carried 500lb bombs although the Dauntless sometimes carried a 1,000lb bomb. Later aircraft models with more powerful engines like the Barracuda and Helldiver could carry 1,600 or 2,000lb bombs. This bomb could then be carried a long distance over water, together with the fuel needed, while being able to take off from a carrier deck. This meant that it could be quite difficult for a dive bomber to carry a bomb heavy enough to penetrate an armored flight deck, especially for early dive bombers.

Battle experience for both the Japanese and the Americans was fairly straightforward. Torpedoes are good at sinking ships. The Japanese were better at executing coordinated and escorted torpedo bombers attacks, and all three US carriers sunk by aircraft were at least partly as a result of torpedoes.

As expected, the light construction of US and Japanese flight decks meant that bombs penetrated easily, as did kamikazes. All four Japanese carriers sunk at Midway were gutted by fires started by bombs penetrating the unarmored flight deck. The *Shokaku*, *Lexington*, *Yorktown*, and *Hornet* all suffered disabling bomb hits (in case of *Shokaku*, twice). The new *Essex* class was just as vulnerable, as can be seen by how both *Bunker Hill* and *Franklin* were badly damaged by single bomb hits that touched off massive fires. The *Essex*, *Intrepid*, *Ticonderoga*, and *Hancock* all needed lengthy repairs after being hit by bombs or kamikazes. The older *Saratoga* and *Enterprise* also suffered kamikaze hits that required lengthy repairs. This is a grand total of eight fleet carriers that were put out of action for significant periods of time. Out of a fleet of about 12 *Essex* carriers that saw real combat, together with the two older carriers, this is a quite substantial degradation that has to be attributed largely to the lack of armored flight decks. The *Randolph* and the new *Lexington* also suffered damaging hits but neither would have been helped by an armored flight deck.

In the absence of fueled and armed planes on the decks, carriers of both navies proved quite difficult to sink. The flight deck was fairly easy to put out of action, however: one or two bombs would often suffice. Sometimes the damage could be quickly patched up or repaired but usually lengthy repairs were needed.

Now for the armored carriers of the RN. Early battle experience in the Mediterranean, where both *Illustrious* and its sister ship *Formidable* were repeatedly hit by bombs but both survived and returned to service, showed the effectiveness of armored flight decks. The comparison suffers since these hits were largely with bombs so heavy that the flight deck could not withstand them. Had these hits been by the typical 250kg Japanese bomb, released from a dive bomber, then these flight decks would most likely have been able to withstand them and damage would have been minimal.

Kamikazes proved ineffective against carriers with armored flight decks, being basically too slow to penetrate any armor. As the USN liaison officer on the *Indefatigable* commented: "When a kamikaze hits a U.S. carrier it means six months of repair at Pearl. When a kamikaze hits a Limey carrier it's just a case of 'Sweepers, man your brooms.'"

## Results from Combat Modeling

The combat model presented was based on the carrier battles of 1942 when neither the US nor the Japanese had carriers with armored flight decks. With an armored flight deck, the model needs to be adjusted. The effect of attacking dive bombers should be reduced by some percentage. This number is hard to estimate, but judging from British experience, it is not marginal. Assume that the number of hits should be reduced by 50 percent. This is the number of *effective* hits. The main effect of an armored deck is to increase the likelihood that a bomb hit will not put the flight deck out of action, at least not for a period that significantly affects the outcome of the battle.

Now assume that we have a choice between having an armored flight deck and a larger air group. The defensive value of having an armored flight deck will be compared to the defensive value of having more fighters, disregarding the offensive value of a larger air group.

On a carrier with poor fighter direction, fighters are less effective and the defensive value of these extra fighters is therefore limited. Most of the bombers will still get through. The value of the extra fighters is therefore limited.

On a carrier with good fighter direction, the defensive value of having some extra fighters is much greater. On the other hand, since fighters are now more valuable, a carrier has more of them to begin with, regardless of total capacity. The relative increase in the number of fighters available is therefore limited and consequently their effect on how many bombers will get through. Again, the value of the extra fighters will most likely be less than the value of an armored flight deck.

The attacker will react to the armor by carrying heavier bombs, to the degree that this is possible. It will to be paid for by carrying less fuel and range will be shorter. The destructive power of AP bombs will be less, including when exploding in the water as near misses. Hitting the armored flight deck first, the AP bomb will likely penetrate less deeply into the vitals of the ship. This is normal in warfare; the point is not necessarily to be able to withstand anything the enemy can attack with. The point is to, in an overall sense, be better optimized than the enemy.

In some ways it is ironic that an armored flight deck was most useful at the beginning of the war, when relatively small bombs were being used. As aircraft got more powerful and heavier bombs could be used, usefulness was more limited, as the flight deck could not withstand these heavier bombs. As it was understood that the armor should be at the level of the flight deck, bombs were outpacing the capability of the armor and thus its usefulness. The exception is the kamikazes, as they often did not carry the heaviest bombs and also impacted at relatively low speeds.

Finally, having armored flight decks can affect the composition of air groups. If dive bombers become less effective by not having juicy targets like unarmored flight decks, then the number of torpedo bombers might be increased. Since torpedo bombers are very vulnerable, more fighters will be needed as escorts.

## Best Balance

The debate around the value of the armored flight deck has ended in a bit of an anticlimax. If the correlation between armor and air group is quite weak, then why the debate? To an extent, the debate might have its roots in how different navies initially approached the problem. This they could do because everybody was unsure about the true role of carriers and nobody had much combat experience. At the outset, for various reasons, the RN appears simply to have not been greatly interested in a large air group. Likewise, in the Pacific, the parties there were simply not that interested in protection. In both cases, this was not so much because conditions differed—they really did not. It only looked that way because the role of carriers was still in flux. Yet there was never any major reason why no one could have both an armored flight deck and a large air group. Perhaps we have been asking the wrong question: perhaps we should ask if the large side openings, typical of USN carriers, were worth it.

The main advantage with large side openings was that it allowed the warming up of engines while in the hangar. On the other hand, this possibility does not seem to have been used extensively and, even if used, did not make strike launches all that much faster. Finally, engines could be warmed up by using oil heaters, without the need to run the engines. An additional advantage was that it allowed having deck-edge elevators. This was certainly an advantage: they proved very practical, but from an overall combat effectiveness viewpoint, they were no game changer. In conclusion then, if the large side openings meant leaving the flight deck unarmored, they were most likely not worth it.

This is a somewhat unusual conclusion. The typical conclusion in a situation like this is that each design was best for the requirements it was built for. Here we can say, with some degree of objectivity, that one design was better than the other. As usual, however, it was less the fault of the designers and the builders than a result of operational philosophy and requirements.

# CHAPTER 24

# Effectiveness of Heavy AA Guns

## Heavy AA Gunnery

The main reason for having heavy AA is to reach higher altitudes. Heavy AA shells leave the muzzle at roughly the same velocity as a smaller caliber gun but the heavier shell is slowed down less by air resistance. The heavier the shell the higher up you could reach.

A 5-inch shell takes about 6 seconds to reach 12,000 feet, about 10 seconds to reach 18,000 feet, and about 22 seconds to reach 30,000 feet. The time it takes for the projectile to reach altitude means that it is only effective against aircraft flying in a relatively predictable path, for example, large formations of four-engine bombers. Even these large formations could evade much of the AA by regularly changing altitude, just enough so that the shells exploded harmlessly above or below the formation.

On average, it took the Germans between 3,400 and 16,000 heavy shells to shoot down a single four-engine bomber at high altitude. The British used similar numbers during the Blitz. With 5-inch ammunition stowage on a major warship typically being around 500 shells per barrel, it would take every 5-inch shell stored on the ship to bring down a single bomber.

Bombing from a high altitude cuts both ways, however: as your altitude goes up, your accuracy becomes worse and worse. High-level bombing was notoriously inaccurate.

A large and easy-to-hit target like a city still had to be defended from high-altitude bombing and heavy AA was needed. Defending a ship, a much smaller and mobile target, it is much less clear that heavy AA is really needed.

A high-angle capability adds cost and weight to a mount. Heavy AA needs not only high-angle elevation, but also power traversing and elevation coupled to a good AA fire-control system. Against torpedo bombers, a standard low-angle mount is not necessarily useful. Torpedo bombers come in close and can have considerable angular speed, even if slow compared to other planes, requiring much faster traversing and elevation than a ship at long range.

The shell of a heavy AA gun is an overkill against carrier-based planes, being more appropriate against multi-engine heavy bombers. Heavy machine gun bullets (.50 caliber etc) are too light to be efficient, requiring many hits for a kill and thus very close range—somewhat the same situation for 20mm during the war. The 40mm was a more efficient projectile: one hit was often enough. After the war, with heavier and faster aircraft operating further out, some people replaced the 40mm with 57mm or even 3-inch.

Time fuzes need to be set before the shell is fired. The time it takes to set the fuze can slow down the rate of fire. Not setting a time fuze can improve rate of fire enough to compensate for the lack of time fuze. A drawback of the VT fuze was that if it did not detect a target, it just whizzed by without exploding and thus did nothing to distract the pilot. VT fuzes were normally mixed in with normal fuzes used as tracking rounds to see where they were firing.

## USN Statistics

The big problem with any statistics about the effectiveness of AA gunnery is that everything depends on the attack profiles. These vary wildly. The best AA guns were those that did not shoot down anything at all because the enemy did not dare to attack.

The most relevant source available is the USN statistics from World War II (USN Information Bulletin No. 29: Antiaircraft Action Summary – World War II):

| | weight | RoF | shell | shells/AC | kg/AC | min/AC | min/weight |
|---|---|---|---|---|---|---|---|
| 1×5 inches | 15 t | 20 | 25kg | 654 | 16350 | 32 min | 480 min |
| 1×5 inches VT | | | | 340 | | | |
| 1×40mm | 2.5 | 150 | 0.9 | 1713 | 1539 | 11 | 28 |
| 1×20mm | 0.77 | 300 | 0.12 | 5287 | 634 | 18 | 14 |
| (Phalanx | 6.1 | 3000 | 0.10) | | | | |

The first weight is that of the mount in tons per barrel. Minutes/AC is how many minutes one barrel must be firing per aircraft shot down. Minutes/weight is how many minutes it takes to shoot down an aircraft per ton of mount weight.

Percentages of kills achieved were 25/50/25 for 5-inch/40mm/20mm. During Santa Cruz, the battleship *South Dakota* claimed 5/30/65 against carrier planes while mounting four quad 40mm and 5 quad 1.1-inch together with 32 single 20mm (and no VT fuzes for the 5-inch). With more 40mm on board we would probably have seen something like 5/65/30.

The numbers above are against Japanese planes that were often lightly built and employed in aggressive attack profiles, such as kamikazes. They are also averages for the whole war from 1942 to 1945. Generally speaking, they should be taken with a pinch of salt. Applied to a different set of conditions, they should be taken with a very large dose of salt. Still, these numbers are the best we have and will be the basis for much of the following discussion.

## Relative Effectiveness

One quad 40mm mount was about six times more likely to shoot down an attacking aircraft than a twin 5-inch mount. This is per unit of time and ignores the fact that the 5-inch, with its longer range, possibly could engage for a longer time. Also, since a quad 40mm mount weighs only about a third of a twin 5-inch, in terms of topside weight a quad 40mm was about 18 times more efficient.

A twin 5-inch mount cost about $400,000. A quad 40mm mount cost about $67,000, and a single 20mm cost about $2,000 (these figures are without fire-control equipment). Nothing could beat the 20mm in terms of raw cost-effectiveness but that effectiveness depended on the enemy pilot obliging by coming within its very short range. None of these numbers include the cost of the ship itself, and from an overall systems point of view the cost of the mounts might not really matter that much. The key limiting factor was normally deck space with good arcs of fire and in some cases topside weight.

A VT fuze cost initially about $40–50, dropping to $18 in 1945. As a rough estimate, the ammunition involved cost about $2 per kg projectile. With the VT fuze increasing kills by only about 2–3 times, VT fuze ammunition was more expensive per kill.

The US spent about $1 billion on VT fuzes during the war, equivalent to 15–20 large fleet carriers or 20,000 single-engine aircraft (or tanks). VT fuzes made up one of the biggest outlays of the war for what was effectively a subsystem with a relatively minor effect on the outcome of a battle. Yes, it was useful. Yes, it was impressive engineering. But no, it was not a cost-effective weapon. VT fuzes were mainly used against the Japanese, notably the kamikazes attacking the US fleet, the Luftwaffe being in more or less a purely defensive posture before the fuzes became available in 1944. VT fuzes were also used by army artillery for air bursts against infantry in the open, proving very effective. This was the reason why some USN cruisers had VT fuzes available for their 6-inch shells, they were mainly for shore bombardment and not really intended for use against aircraft but were used in that way as well on occasion. VT fuzes intended for use against ground targets did not have the self-destruct feature needed for AA work.

VT fuzes were vulnerable to jamming. As a large number of VT fuzes fell into German hands when they captured an army supply dump, there was a need to develop protection against the Germans cloning the technology. In just two weeks, a jammer was developed by modifying a standard AN/APT-4 jammer. The jammer was then tested in a B-17 against live ammunition with a live crew in the bomber. The crew was very pleased to report that the shells exploded prematurely, well away from the bomber.

VT fuze technology had now been rendered mostly harmless. This applies to VT fuzes in general, as a new variant of the same basic radio technology would simply have been met with a new jammer. It is basically the same situation as for radio-guided bombs like the German Fritz-X: once the jammers were in place, the weapon was ineffective.

Even as 5-inch guns were provided with effective VT fuzes, it would still have been better to replace the 5-inch mounts with 40mm gun mounts. This would not only have saved the cost of the VT fuzes but also much of the cost and weight of the 5-inch gun mounts.

The 40mm had a maximum ceiling of 23,000 feet. Sources differ on what could be considered "effective range" but it could be defined to be anything between 8,000–12,000 feet altitude (assuming a suitable director) depending on target characteristics and behavior. Against carrier-borne single-engine aircraft, with their attack profiles, the 40mm had all the range it needed to have. Against level bombers, flying at high altitude and in predictable paths, heavy AA was still useful. On the other hand, those bombers had a very low probability of hitting a ship and did not represent a major threat to carriers.

It is simply not efficient to shoot down single-engine aircraft with 5-inch shells. It is just as sub-optimum as sinking a large warship by pelting it with 40mm fire. Either approach will eventually succeed, given enough time and ammunition, but at the end of the day aircraft and ships are very different targets and should be fought with different tools.

A heavy AA battery still made eminent sense when high-level bombing was considered an effective threat and combined with limited-range guns like the 25mm and 1.1-inch guns.

The rationale for dual-purpose guns is easy to understand but it is less clear that it really is the optimum solution, or even a reasonably cost-effective solution, when level bombing turned out to be much less of a threat than was thought when the dual-purpose guns where designed into major warships. As secondary armament on a battleship, it might have made better sense to use the more powerful 6-inch guns for those rare night battles. Taking this line of thought to its extreme, screening a battleship against those rare surface threats might be left to the cruisers and destroyers, and the battleship can then do away completely with secondary armament and mount nothing but 40mm medium AA.

Likewise with carriers, only twin/quad 40mm should have been mounted and upwards of 40 mounts could have been fitted. The *Saratoga* held the record: it ended the war with 23 quad and two twin mounts while still retaining its 5-inch battery. In terms of raw combat efficiency, 5-inch mounts are a poor use of valuable deck space and topside weight. A carrier will very likely never be tasked with fighting anything bigger than a single-engine carrier-borne aircraft which makes heavy AA relatively pointless.

Mounting heavy AA on escorts still makes good sense, however, as on the *Atlanta* and *Dido* classes of cruisers or on the *Akitsuki* class of destroyers. They can be seen as an insurance against any threat that might develop from high altitude, like guided bombs. If a carrier needs to be protected using heavy AA, it makes better sense to have it on the escorts, since given that the target is going to be high up it might as well be fired at from an escort, as opposed to medium- and short-range defenses which are best mounted on the ship being attacked.

The author has practical experience firing both the 20mm and the 40mm Bofors guns. On the 20mm the gun mount shakes around quite a bit but one quickly learns to ignore that and the noise is not an issue. The ring sight takes practice to use effectively. Shooting down towed targets is difficult at any kind of range, the target has to be close before the gun will start to land hits, unless the gunner is really proficient. Some gunners are, some just had a knack for it.

Firing the 40mm is a very different experience. Very different. The 40mm is one wicked gun. The bangs are just vicious and literally take your breath away. Standing next to it while firing at the full rate of fire, breathing becomes somewhat staccato. The rate of fire is also about the same as the heart rate which makes it a particularly unpleasant gun to be around. Focusing on the task at hand requires an effort. The noise level of multiple quad mounts firing away must have been fantastic, like not being able to hear yourself screaming at the top of your lungs. Larger-caliber guns obviously have a more massive boom but not the same rate of fire. Having experienced the 40mm, the 20mm becomes a toy, not taken very seriously but kept around anyway, somewhat like a pet.

After Midway, Captain Buckmaster of USS *Yorktown* recommended the following: "Replacement of 5-inch guns, 1.1-inch guns and 50 caliber machine guns, by a large number of 40mm automatic guns. While smaller caliber automatic guns have proven effective at short ranges, their range is too short to offer effective opposition to attacking planes prior to delivery of their attack. 5-inch caliber guns are very effective at long ranges and should be retained in ships which are used as anti-aircraft screening vessels." The 40mm had not yet entered service on any USN ships but he was most likely aware of the power of the Bofors.

The most cost-effective AA gunnery of all time was probably courtesy of a Browning M1911 .45 pistol. Second lieutenant Owen J. Baggett, a B-24 bomber co-pilot, had just bailed out and was hanging in his parachute. Zero pilots were going from parachute to parachute killing the aircrews. The pilot of one Zero wanted to check if Baggett was dead and put his plane in a vertical stall very close to him. Baggett then pulled out his pistol and shot down the Zero with a bullet to the head of the pilot. Do that five times and you are an ace.

## Automatic Loaders and Water-Cooled Barrels

Water-cooled barrels are required for a very high rate of fire. Heavy AA have the longest engagement ranges and times and stand to gain the most from water-cooling. Heavy AA also cannot easily add more barrels. Light AA have shorter engagement times and can do without. Medium AA could certainly use water-cooling but could compensate by having more barrels without increasing the weight of the mount too much.

Water-cooling was introduced in World War I for heavy and medium machine guns. It was also used in the British 2-pounder AA gun. The 40mm gun was used in water-cooled versions by both the RN and USN. Water-cooling was also used by the twin 3-inch AA mount developed by USN after World War II. In modern naval guns, in the 76–130mm size bracket, water-cooled barrels are now more or less standard.

Water-cooling is well suited for naval guns for fairly obvious reasons— running out of water being rather unlikely. Furthermore, weight is not a problem since the gun is stationary. Land-based AA is more weight-conscious and access to water can be an issue. There is also a lot of space available if a larger number of guns is required. The cost of developing water-cooling technology thus had to be paid for by the various navies without assistance from an army or air force.

It would take time and money to develop 3–4-inch heavy AA with a rate of fire of 60–100 and both the automatic loaders and the water-cooling. The basic technology was there before the war and it could have been accomplished in time for the war had it been seen as important enough, as perhaps with much of the technology developed during the war. The first heavy AA gun with an automatic loader and a water-cooled barrel appeared in 1950, a 120mm gun by Bofors that had a rate of fire of 42–45 rounds per minute, more than twice that of the otherwise excellent 5-inch/38 of the USN.

## Directors

Fire control needs to be more sophisticated the further away the target is. Heavy bombers doing level bombing have a longer effective range and so a large complicated (and slower) director makes good sense. Small carrier-based planes have a short effective range, particularly so if the pilot is jinking, and thus simpler and faster-reacting directors made more sense.

A related subject is how the gun layer gets feedback about where the shells are actually going in relation to the target. On heavy AA, it can be seen from the shell bursts. Light and medium AA use automatic fire and there is no time for fuze setting; tracers are used instead but there is a limit to how far out tracers can be observed. The tracer burn time for the shells of the 40mm Bofors was around 10 seconds giving a range of 5,000 yards horizontally or 15,000 feet vertically.

Another problem is how to separate shell bursts and tracers from different guns. The Japanese used air bursts of different colors. Tracers are easier to separate as the tracer stream is continuous and can be traced back to the gun firing.

## After the War

Postwar the focus was on combining the advantages of heavy and medium AA, that is to increase the rate of fire and muzzle velocity of heavy AA while still having a shell large enough to provide a definite kill and to house a proximity fuze. However, there are fundamental limitations to what unguided projectiles can achieve against fast and agile targets, and eventually AA guns were replaced by missiles as the primary defense against aircraft.

# CHAPTER 25

# World War II Carrier Design Revisited

## Introduction

Using the experience gained during the war, how should have a World War II carrier have been designed? The context here is strictly what would have been ideal in 1940–44, not what would have been needed after the war.

Considerable experience was gained during the war, and the role and handling of a carrier changed quite dramatically. The next generation of carriers, however, were designed for the next generation of planes, notably jets. The optimum World War II carrier was therefore never designed or built—things were just moving too fast.

The requirements are assumed to be the same for both the European and Pacific theater of operations. Either theater has areas of operations that are confined by land masses and in close proximity to large numbers of enemy land-based aircraft. The logistics are different but that does not necessarily have a major impact on carrier design itself, more on the logistics chain.

The total size of the carrier force can have an effect on carrier design. A very large carrier force can be expected to achieve local air superiority over land-based aircraft and a more offensive design might be better suited. Likewise with a force with only a single or very few carriers, a more defensively oriented design might be better.

## Speed

The original role of the carrier, as envisaged before the war, was that of a scout or a raider, much the same as a battlecruiser in World War I. In this role, speed was certainly essential. Most of the early carriers were also converted battlecruisers and got their speed from that.

Speed was also useful for aircraft operations, as it made for a greater wind speed over the deck. On the other hand, the much slower escort carriers also successfully operated the same aircraft types as the faster fleet carriers, so it could obviously be done.

Japanese and US fleet carriers were designed around deck-load strikes. As many planes as possible were spotted on the flight deck, warmed up, and then sent off as one strike. The size of the strike was limited by how much runway the foremost planes had. If the wind speed over the deck was slightly less, then a slightly longer runway was needed and the strike would have to be with fewer planes. On a fleet carrier, this is the disadvantage of having a slower carrier.

Assuming no wind and the carrier steaming at 28 vs. 32 knots, the additional runway length required for take off is about 30–35 feet, or the length of one aircraft. Assuming that these are spotted three abreast and interleaved, this means that the additional runway needed is the equivalent to the parking space taken up by about six planes. These will then have to be launched using a catapult instead. A catapult launch takes 40 seconds instead of the usual launch interval of 20 seconds, meaning that the launch of a deck-load strike takes some additional minutes, which should then be factored into the 3–5 hour length of a typical strike mission. Thus a slower or faster carrier is very much a factor in the way flight operations are conducted. However, from an overall weapons systems point of view, the effect is quite marginal.

Another way to maintain strike size is to have a wider flight deck aft, making more parking space available. A third way is to lighten the first few planes so that they can launch even with a marginal wind speed over the deck. It should be added that these alternatives to those extra few knots are only necessary in very low wind conditions. As soon as there is some kind of breeze, steaming into it will provide the needed wind speed over the deck.

From a ship design point of view, every knot of speed has a huge influence on the power required. A relaxation of that requirement down to a design speed of around 30 knots enables weight to be allocated to other features, such as an armored flight deck. A slightly slower hull can also be wider, enabling hangar and flight-deck size to be maintained while having an armored deck.

All this is essentially a corollary to the maturation of the aircraft carrier and its role in naval warfare. As the new backbone of the fleet it was no longer appropriate to have a fast but flimsy scout or raider. It must now be able to take some serious hits and continue to operate, to be able stand up in a battle and to win against well-armed and armored opponents. It needed to be built more like a battleship than a battlecruiser.

Relatively slow carriers that served in World War II included the *Wasp* and the *Illustrious* class at 29.5–30 knots, plus *Kaga*, *Chitose*, *Chiyoda*, and *Shinano* at 27–28 knots. Another notch slower were *Hermes*, *Eagle*, *Hiyo*, and *Junyo* at 24–25 knots. The RN late-war *Colossus* class was also slow at 25 knots. These carriers still had reasonably long flight decks and generally operated without catapults. Most escort carriers had a design speed of 15–20 knots, and with a short flight deck needed catapults to operate heavier aircraft like the Avenger.

## AA

There is really no reason to carry heavy AA guns on a carrier. As the ship being targeted was often the best platform from which to shoot down the attacker, there were still very good reasons for an extensive battery of medium AA and perhaps light AA. With no heavy AA mounted, the flight deck could be wider.

## Centerline vs. Deck-Edge Elevator

The big advantage of the deck-edge elevator was that the fore-and-aft movement of aircraft on the flight deck was facilitated, particularly forward, during both landing and launching operations. It was also a smaller and lighter design, less susceptible to damage from explosions, did not reduce armor coverage over the hangar, and did not require an elevator well and associated drainage.

A deck-edge elevator design is limited to a single hangar for reasons of seaworthiness. A deck-edge elevator should not be placed too far forward for this reason. A centerline elevator can reach the lower hangar in a two-hangar deck ship. The centerline elevator also offered a more protected work area in bad weather, particularly on smaller carriers.

Deck-edge elevators should probably be placed on the same side as the superstructure. Both interfere with flight operations and having both on the same reduces total interference.

## Flight and Hangar Decks

Assuming that deck-load strikes are the main task, it is desirable to be able to spot the maximum number of aircraft while having enough runway length for the first plane in the strike to take off. This means a long flight deck. It should also be as wide as possible aft of the first plane in the spot.

The forward part of the flight deck can be relatively narrow, as it is used mainly as the runway while launching planes. It can be used as a deck park while landing planes but a larger portion of the length of the flight deck can be used when retrieving aircraft using arresting gears. Landings require less deck length than take offs. Being narrower, the forward part of the flight involves less deck overhangs and is therefore a natural place for AA mounts. The mid or aft portion of the flight is best suited for deck-edge elevators, as described previously. There is still a need for an elevator reasonably far forward to allow access to planes parked forward. The overall shape of the flight deck is then shaped somewhat like a bottle, seen from above, with significant overhangs aft of about two-thirds forward.

World War II carriers had flight decks with a length-to-beam ratio of about 8.3–9.1. Modern carriers have 4.0 and 4.3 (*Queen Elizabeth* and *Nimitz* respectively). The width of the flight deck is typically almost twice the beam at the waterline.

Looking at just the hull, these modern carriers also have beamier hulls compared to typical World War II designs. As an example, the length-to-beam ratio of *Queen Elizabeth* is 7.1, for *Nimitz* it is 7.8, while the *Essex* had a ratio of 8.8 and typical Japanese carrier designs had a ratio of nine or more, much like the slender hulls of cruisers and destroyers.

Building a World War II carrier with the beam and overhangs of a modern design, the available flight deck area is effectively doubled. As deck-load strikes typically involved half the air group, then in principle the whole air group can be spotted and launched as a single strike.

If deck parks are to the side, then a runway can be arranged along the full length of the flight deck, enabling take off with heavier loads. Furthermore, CAP operations can be done while a full deck-load strike is spotted, ready for immediate launch. Having planes spotted to the side of the landing area can be risky, however; a missed approach might crash into these planes and some kind of barrier probably needs to be erected while landing. Taking off is much less problematic and having planes parked along the sides less of a risk.

A wide flight deck is only really useful if deck parks are employed. Neither the British nor the Japanese used deck parks, at least not at the beginning of the war, their doctrine was to have everything in the hangar and therefore had double hangars. The Americans used deck parks and could presumably have made good use of a wide flight deck but they were also constrained by the Panama Canal. Once that restriction was removed, flight decks became much wider.

Ski jumps were tested on board HMS *Furious* in 1944 and worked as intended but needed to be integrated with the catapults. They were also a poor fit for deck parks.

With wide decks, extensive deck parks, and deck-edge elevators, it follows that a single hangar deck will suffice.

The flight deck should be armored. Carriers are vulnerable enough as they are and need to have reasonable staying power. This also reflects their changing roles, from replacing the battlecruiser as scouts and raiders, to replacing the battleship as the backbone of the fleet.

## Island

For ship navigation purposes, the island should generally be forward. For flight operations, it is generally better if the island is aft.

An island is also the obvious place for the stack. Having two stacks should make it easier to have alternating boiler and engine spaces, always a good practice to safeguard against total power loss being caused by a single torpedo hit. Having two islands also allows more space for antennas placed far enough apart to avoid interference.

The island should be outboard of the hull to avoid interference with the flight-deck traffic and to minimize turbulence. The first carriers to have the island placed clearly outboard of the hull sides was the Japanese *Hiyo* class. This was also the first time in a Japanese carrier that the stack was built-in to the island, which is probably why the island was so prominently outboard, as it now was much larger than previous designs. The later *Taiho* and *Shinano* designs followed the same pattern. World War II-era US carriers had large islands that caused a significant waist in the flight deck, not going to an outboard island until the *Forrestal* class.

## Effects of the Panama Canal

All US carriers in World War II were constrained in the maximum width of their flight decks by the need to pass through the Canal. The *Essex* class carriers were the last carriers that were able to transit. To enable passage, the deck-edge elevator on the *Essex* class was designed to be able to fold up. A second deck-edge elevator on the starboard side was considered during design but rejected as it would have made transit impossible. Some carriers had sponsons added on the starboard side, underneath the superstructure, for additional quad 40mm Bofors. These sponsons were simply removed before transit and welded back afterwards. The first *Essex* to pass through the Canal knocked down the light posts along the locks—it was a really tight fit. Having an angled flight deck or significant deck overhangs for additional deck parks was of course out of the question.

All RN and IJN carriers could presumably have transited the Canal with the exception of the *Kaga* and *Shinano*, which were both too wide. The *Midway* class of carriers were also too wide. Neither could the *Bismarck, Littorio, Yamato, Richelieu, Vanguard*, and *Montana* classes of battleships transit the Canal. After their rebuilds, the *West Virginia, Tennessee*, and *California* were also too wide.

The RN *King George V* class of battleships could transit—probably a requirement given the global nature of RN commitments. The *Iowa* class of battleships were the last battleships able to transit. Their hull lines clearly show the constraint in how the sides had to be artificially straight to fit in the locks. Had the *Iowas* not been constrained by the need to fit in the locks, they would have been built wider and probably slower and with better torpedo protection, like the classes that preceded them and the *Montana* class that followed. As it was, the only way for US battleships to evolve was to become longer and by extension faster.

An expansion of the Canal was initiated in 1940 but was canceled in 1942 as the resources were needed elsewhere. The *Montanas* were designed to pass through the new third set of locks but were canceled to make room for more carriers on the slipways.

The expansion begun in 1940 was eventually restarted in 2007 by the Panamanian government and was completed in 2016. The *Nimitz* and *Ford* classes of carriers are still too big to transit. Looking at length and beam at the waterline it should be possible but the very wide overhangs will not fit into the locks and are too close to the waterline. The *Tarawa* and *Wasp* classes of carrier-like amphibious assault ships all have their beam limited by the width of the locks before the expansion. With the elevators folded up, they fit with only inches to spare and deck overhangs are out of the question. With the expansion in sight, the *America* class was allowed to grow beyond the pre-expansion limits.

## Compared to Today's Carriers

It is quite fascinating to see that the new RN carrier *Queen Elizabeth* has a layout that is very close to what in many ways would have been the ideal World War II carrier.

# CHAPTER 26

# The Art of Carrier Operations

## Introduction

In the art of warfare, military strategists such as Sun Tzu, Clausewitz, Mahan, and Guderian are all well known. Perhaps less known is US Air Force Colonel John R. Boyd.

Boyd started out as a fighter pilot in Korea. He then served as an instructor pilot which later led him to develop the Energy-Maneuverability theory for dogfights. This E-M theory was then applied to the development of the F-16 and F-15 fighters, both very successful designs. The F-16 is the best-selling jet fighter of all time. The F/A-18, originally a competitor to the F-16 as a new lightweight fighter designed using very much of the same thinking, has seen considerable success as the backbone of US carrier-based aviation.

Boyd then went on to apply his ideas to warfare in general. One of his key concepts, and perhaps the best known, is the OODA Loop. In Operation *Desert Storm*, he was brought in as an advisor and was one of the architects behind the 'left hook' strategy that resulted in a complete breakdown of the Iraqi decision-making process followed by a quick and decisive victory.

The OODA Loop has its roots in aerial dogfighting. A carrier duel is a lot like a dogfight between fighter aircraft. It is about two technologically advanced entities that engage in a duel, striking and parrying, each trying to outwit and outfight the other.

## The OODA Loop

OODA stands for Observe, Orient, Decide, and Act. Its focus is on the decision-making process in combat (and other adversarial situations).

*Observe* is about the gathering of information of all types. When under pressure, it is easy to have tunnel vision and not see what is happening all around.

*Orient* is about the processing of that information. One can think of it as a black box or a system. This is the most important element of the loop. It is also a process that tends to suffer under pressure.

*Decide* is about the output from the black box in terms of decisions of different kinds. It is the result of a mental process, usually a set of choices that has been made.

*Act* is about the execution of these decisions, usually by issuing a set of orders and having them implemented.

The loop is actually many loops. It can more accurately be described as a process with multiple feedback loops. The outer loop is just one of them.

Bettering the enemy's decision making process is then referred to as getting "inside the OODA loop of the enemy" and the end goal is to "get the enemy to fold on himself" in Boyd parlance. Simply cycling through the loop faster is one way to achieve this but is not a goal in itself.

At the end of the day, what the OODA Loop does is force the user to think. Applying pre-packaged solutions is just not good enough. The thinking cap must be on.

## Compressing Your Own Loop

Start with making sure that you have situational awareness. Keep that situational awareness going throughout the battle and make sure to avoid tunnel vision. Try to see it from the viewpoint of the enemy. Try to understand his goals, his thinking, and his plans to achieve those goals. Try to get inside his mind and guess his actions.

Always try to gain the initiative, not only offensively but defensively. Be adaptable and maneuverable, be ready for fast changes in direction and to apply them with fast transients. Use combined arms to apply your strengths to the enemy's weaknesses, try to find the path of least resistance and flow around his strengths like water flowing downhill.

A good example of the advantage of having a better loop is the dogfights between the F-86 and Mig-15 during the Korean War. The Mig was faster, climbed better, and had better maneuverability. It had every advantage in aerodynamics. Yet the F-86 had a 10:1 kill ratio. The reason was twofold: it had a bubble canopy with excellent rear-ward visibility and it had hydraulically boosted controls. The pilot in the F-86 could both observe and act better. He could then quite easily get within the OODA Loop of the Mig-15 and that was all that was needed.

## Stretching the Enemy's Loop

The attitude here is that this is war, so anything and everything is allowed. Deny him intelligence. Disrupt his sensors. Feed him false information. Shape his views. Distract him. Use camouflage, spooks, and deceptions of all kinds. Bait his tunnel vision. Overload his nervous systems. Create a mismatch between his observations and the real threat. Get him out of his flow by forcing him into an unknown situation. The object is to create confusion and disorder resulting in paralysis and chaos.

A subtler way of undermining his decisions is to be difficult to read and predict. Use variety in everything. Do not fall into patterns. Use the indirect approach, threaten many targets at the same time, be as ambiguous as possible.

A good example of ruining the enemy's loop is the run-up to the "left hook" strike used in *Desert Storm*. Iraq had invaded Kuwait. The first stage was to deploy Allied forces on the border between Saudi Arabia and Kuwait in what amounted to a very conventional disposition. Predictably, the Iraqis put strong defenses along this very likely avenue of approach. It looked like the Allied forces would go straight up the middle into Kuwait, a fairly obvious strategy and indeed the plan at the beginning of the campaign. The enemy was now fixed in place. The second stage was to systematically knock out all Iraqi radar and communications systems, including aerial reconnaissance abilities. The enemy was now blind. The third stage was to move the main armored forces to the left flank, westward into the empty desert. This was done in secret. The fourth and final stage was a surprise armored thrust behind the Iraqis, encircling the forces in Kuwait which then fled, resulting in a quick and decisive victory. General Patton would say "hold on to him by the nose and then kick him in the rear." Adapted to what happened at Midway this would be "keep him distracted and then hit him from above."

## Applied to Carrier Operations

What happens when we apply this style of thinking to carrier operations? The main change is probably one of mental aggression, both in tactics and methods, in pushing the envelope of what the available technology can do.

At a strategic level, situational awareness is a lot about radio intelligence, such as traffic analysis and cryptanalysis. This topic has been well discussed by others and need not be repeated here.

At the tactical level, much less is known about what is really going on. There are many garbled sighting reports and it can be assumed that at least some have been interrupted by jamming. There are also various anecdotes about radio operators able to speak the language of the enemy injecting false messages. Likewise with listening on enemy tactical radio traffic—it is known that this sometimes yielded useful tidbits of information. Much more could probably have been done here, such as using more than one pre-set frequency or hidden changes in radio procedures and call signs.

Search methods have already been discussed. It is mainly a question of how much planes are to be allocated to search, to the detriment of strike capability. Putting radar and radar detectors on search aircraft is another very obvious technique.

The entire CIC concept is of course an exemplary handling of the *Orient* phase of OODA. Likewise with low-latency fighter direction. On the Japanese side, the adoption of this style of thinking was much slower. As an example, the IJN never developed anything like the CIC, they never integrated radar with the tactical plot, and they never really used fighter direction. Their decision making process stayed essentially the same throughout the war.

Flight deck and strike management are at the core of carrier operations. Faster deck operations are a given, allowing faster decision cycles. Flexible use of available flight decks pointed toward having one carrier as the duty carrier, handling search, CAP, and ASW patrols. This could well be a small carrier and does not have to be placed within visual sighting distance of the strike carriers.

A carrier with a strike on deck and ready to go is very vulnerable. A carrier with a strike ready to go inside the hangar is even more so, as it will take some time to get the strike up on deck and on its way. A carrier whose CAP is out of fuel and ammunition is also vulnerable. Small strikes might be used to disturb the enemy's deck-management plans. Strikes should be coordinated and timed to catch the enemy while most vulnerable.

Night has the effect of resetting a carrier battle. Starting at sunrise, both sides will commence a fairly predictable sequence of flight operations. An educated guess might catch the unwary with planes on deck being refueled and rearmed.

Operating carriers out of synchronization makes the threat more unpredictable, at the cost of making the strikes smaller. Surface forces can be deployed to act as a bait or as an additional factor to consider, particularly in low visibility or as a threat of a possible night action. A small carrier placed well forward can act as both bait and scout. Surprise movements and flanking attacks from an unexpected direction also help to confuse the enemy and catch him while vulnerable.

Pre-launching in the direction of the enemy, awaiting exact sighting reports is one option. Redirecting a strike is always possible but breaks radio silence, at least normally and if done from the carrier. Once a strike is launched, it generally expects to find the home carriers following a predetermined track, so the returning strike can find its way back home. Being able to communicate a new track to the returning aircraft would increase flexibility and would make it possible to evade the inevitable enemy strike once spotted.

Facing defenders with effective fighter direction, a strike can split up into many different elements, coming in from different directions and at different and changing altitudes. This will overload the fighter direction and make it ineffective.

The Japanese were quite willing to separate their carriers into more than one force. This enabled more elaborate battle plans and sometimes gave interesting results. They tried to outsmart the enemy by careful planning but having done that began to show poor adaptability. The Americans always kept their forces together, which was not as flexible but was safer. Having an airbase within the combat area gave much flexibility and many opportunities without having to split up the forces.

## Mahan and Carrier Operations

Alfred Thayer Mahan (1840–1914) was an American naval strategist whose book *The Influence of Sea Power Upon History, 1660–1783* has had a huge influence on how navies are perceived and used. However, his thinking is more about sea power in general than about carrier operations. This is only natural; he predates carriers as well as submarines. At the level of grand strategy, Mahan's principles still very much apply but his assumptions about how sea power should be applied do not agree well with how carriers fight. At that level, Boyd's principles are much more useful.

# CHAPTER 27

# Evolution of Carrier Operations

## In 1940

At this point only the British were at war and using carriers. The first air-search radar sets were in use on board selected major warships, but there was only very primitive fighter direction.

Search done by aircraft is not always done in a very comprehensive or systematic manner and there is a considerable element of luck in finding anything. With no surface search radar, there is a clear risk of bumping into enemy surface forces.

At this stage carrier-based aircraft designs were not as good as land-based designs. Aircraft were relatively slow and had short range. Biplanes armed with torpedoes were the primary attack weapon.

Carriers mostly did scouting and occasional raids. The fighters were too few in number to challenge land-based fighters but could oppose incoming bomber strikes if given enough warning.

AA gunnery was poorly developed by all nations.

## In 1942

By now air search had become pretty reliable although the Japanese were still at the primitive stage. The British pioneered fighter direction and some ships were quite good at it; the Japanese and Americans had not yet developed satisfactory methods.

Search done by aircraft was not always done in an exhaustive and efficient manner and there was an element of luck if and when something was found. Surface search radar was getting better but there was still a clear risk of bumping into enemy surface forces.

The Zero was competitive with land-based fighters and for others the gap was closing. The numbers of fighters were insufficient, there was generally not enough CAP for effective defense, and outgoing strikes suffered heavy losses if caught by CAP. Attacks were undertaken by dedicated dive and torpedo bombers.

Torpedoes launched by aircraft were not very successful as the primary means of destruction: targets maneuvering at high speed and well defended proved difficult to hit unless completely overwhelmed. Torpedo bombers were very vulnerable when attempting these attacks and suffered heavy losses.

AA gunnery was still poorly developed by all navies.

Steaming formations was a topic of intense discussion. Separating the carriers removed the possibility of having more than one sunk. Since fighters without fighter direction were relatively ineffective anyway, the cost of losing mutual support was not that great. A defenseless chap coming to the aid of another defenseless chap does not make for a strong chap: it makes for two defenseless chaps that can conveniently be killed by the same attack.

Adding another carrier increases offensive strength and enemy losses but it also raises your own losses as more eggshells are exposed. Being stronger usually means that your own losses go down but that is not what happens: *both sides* face heavier losses, even if the enemy fares somewhat worse, so from an attritional point of view it is still advantageous. However, since more carriers are more difficult to operate separately, the risk of losing several carriers rises substantially. This means that the optimum size of a carrier task force in 1942 was two carriers: one to get sunk and the other to land the survivors and launch the counterattack (and to get sunk by the enemy's counterattack).

## In 1944

Air-search radar had now matured and could be depended upon: there were many sets in the fleet including on all major warships. RN and USN fighter direction was good but still fairly leaky due to limitations in the radar and IFF systems used.

Search was still carried out by search planes but with better training and more extensive patterns; it was now as good as could be achieved visually. Fighters were starting to take over the role of scouts, with navigation aided by radar and other electronic aids.

Carrier-based planes were now equal to their land-based counterparts in performance. Generous numbers of fighters could fight for aerial supremacy, without which the bomber would not get through. Attacks against ships were still done by dedicated dive and torpedo bombers but torpedo planes had been reduced in number and were held back until defenses had been weakened.

Fighter direction was effective and those that got through the fighters were met with massive amounts of automatic AA, inflicting substantial losses. Unarmored carriers were still vulnerable but had a much higher survival rate, mainly threatened by leaks in the fighter-direction system. Facing heavy losses during the approach and the attack run itself, the Japanese resorted to kamikaze tactics.

## In 1945

The big change here was that AEW radar now provided full control over the sea, both in the air and on the surface. There was still a need for search planes to visual identify the blips but this was now done by long-range CAP. Fighter direction was now much less leaky.

Attacks were now done by fighter-bombers using shallow glide bombing and possibly rockets. The dedicated dive bomber was marginalized. Torpedoes launched by aircraft began the war as the primary weapon but had by now all but disappeared.

Guided bombs were becoming available but were quite easy to jam or disrupt in some way, once the guidance system had been analyzed. Likewise with proximity fuzes. This situation would remain in place until the late 1960s when the digital revolution began.

Massive and radar-directed AA made attacks difficult. Battleships could be attrited as they headed for a point target but not stopped entirely. On the other hand, using AEW planes the carriers no longer risked bumping into enemy surface forces.

Radar development had reached a plateau. We have also reached a plateau in AA capability, albeit at a fairly high level. Propeller-driven aircraft development had also reached a plateau with a slow transfer to jet-driven planes.

## Factors Driving Evolution

An important driver was radar technology. The first type was the air-search radar mounted on ships and was very important for carrier battles. This technology was available already at the start of the war.

A major change during the war was the evolution of effective fighter direction but this was a change in methodology and not so much in technology. Radio communications and radio navigation also remained essentially unchanged during the war.

Air search mounted on aircraft, the AEW technology, was a big step forward in that it extended range and by giving low-level coverage, removed much of the weaknesses of ship-based systems. It also effectively removed the risk of a carrier bumping into enemy surface forces.

One major factor seems to have been a widespread underestimation of the importance of defense. We can see how the need for defensive fighter direction was not well understood before the war. We also see it in the underestimation of the need for large numbers of fighters, both for CAP and for defending own strikes. We see it in the general underestimation of how much AA guns were required. We see it in the lack of armored flight decks for both USN and IJN carriers, as well as in armor and self-sealing fuel tanks in Japanese aircraft. We also see in it how torpedo bombers gradually disappeared, as it was understood just how vulnerable they were.

This could be down to the psychology of how navies operate in peacetime. Perhaps it is easier to get funding for weapons of attack than it is for defensive measures of various kinds, the need for which only became abundantly clear once the shooting had started.

Massive developments in technology during the war did not change things that much. The really important developments were much more in terms of a better understanding of the realities of carrier warfare.

The underlying driver of all carrier warfare is of course aircraft engine development. More powerful engines meant bigger bombs carried at longer range. In the early days with slow short-ranged biplanes, carriers ran a real risk of running into enemy surface ships and consequently had to have cruiser-type guns and side armor. As engines developed and surface ships could be kept at a safe distance, these guns were removed. Going further into the jet age, the ships underneath the guns were removed, as battleships and gun cruisers no longer were viable for anything more decisive than shore bombardment.

## Epilogue

Doing the research for this book has been quite a journey. As someone who first read Morison and Roskill some 40 years ago, it has been quite surprising how much there was still to learn and understand about the great carrier battles of World War II.

Two things stand out. The first is how much deep thought went into these ships and forces and how they trained and fought. At a more strategic level, how carefully thought out the strategies of these navies were. Much of the standard criticism levied against certain aspects turned out to be mostly based on a limited understanding of what actually went on. The author has come to appreciate how much skill went in to these battles, on many levels. All in all, deeply impressive.

The second is the skill and courage of the pilots and aircrews. It has been fascinating to get insights into what these men did, what risks they faced, and the unforgiving conditions they operated under, on both sides. This book begins by describing life in the cockpit. It is altogether fitting and proper that it ends with paying them homage.

# Postwar Developments

## Carrying Atomic Bombs

As soon as the atomic bombs had been dropped, carriers had to be able to employ the new weapon or face irrelevance.

Little Boy and Fat Man each weighed 4–5 tons, slightly less than a Tall Boy and about half of a Grand Slam bomb. Much of the weight of the Little Boy gun-type design was due to the fact that it had to be exceptionally strongly built, as it effectively was a cannon that shot itself as the firing mechanism. Fat Man was an implosion design depending on explosives to compress the fissile material to criticality. This involved a sphere of about 2 tons of TNT and made the bomb rather rotund. Little Boy was the only bomb of its kind ever built, as far as is known, a very simple design but also a very inefficient use of the fissile material. All future designs were based on Fat Man.

To protect these bombs against AA fire, they were built with a 3/8-inch steel casing. In the case of Fat Man, this casing weighed about a ton. The USAF had no problems with this armor as they used the B-29 to carry it, but the requirement was later dropped. Removing the armor also increased the effect of the bomb (steel slows down neutrons). As implosion technology improved, devices were built that required less and less explosives, eventually reducing the size and weight of the atom bomb to that of an ordinary bomb.

The B-25 Mitchell, famous from the Doolittle Raid, could carry 1,360kg of bombs. A single-engine carrier plane like the Avenger could carry about 1,000kg of ordnance. The de Havilland Mosquito could carry 1,800kg of bombs and could land back at the carrier. All these planes could in principle carry a heavier bomb load at the expense of fuel load.

The first carrier-launched aircraft that could carry a nuclear bomb was the Lockheed P2V Neptune. It first flew in May 1945 and could take off with rocket assistance but could not land back on the carrier. The North American AJ Savage was the first carrier-based aircraft built to carry an atomic bomb, first flying in 1948.

## Angled Flight Deck

Angled flight decks had been considered before the war and rejected. The American and Japanese doctrine of using deck-load strikes was a poor fit for angled flight decks. The cost in weight and complexity was simply not worth it. The RN doctrine of smaller ships operating alone, in close proximity to land-based aircraft and with smaller air groups, was a better fit for continuous operations offered by angled flight decks. Still, it was a big change in carrier design for a relatively marginal increase in efficiency until the advent of the jet more or less forced it.

The stacked flight-decks solution tried on *Akagi*, *Furious*, and *Courageous* in the 1920s were similar attempts to offer continuous operations but became impractical as faster monoplane aircraft required longer take-off runs; it was then better to have a single large flight deck and to use the lower flight decks as enlarged hangar space. Stacked flight decks were an even worse fit for deck-load strikes.

The key reason behind angled flight decks was the higher landing speeds of jet aircraft, increasing the danger inherent in missing the arresting wires. The faster speeds did not necessarily require more room; arresting wires were still used, but the consequences of ending up in the barrier were more serious. Attempts were made to adapt the crash barriers to faster jets but the basic problem remained. Some kind of barricade was still needed for emergencies, for example, to land a plane with a non-functioning tail hook or landing gear. Not having a crash barrier on an axial flight deck was possible, but it meant that there could now be no deck parks, as the flight deck had to be empty when landing operations were under way. Another advantage with the angled flight deck was that it allowed the use of planes with larger wing spans, an important consideration at a time when carriers were expected to operate bombers that could carry the heavy nuclear bombs.

Jets forced another change in carrier operations: the slow acceleration of early jets made the catapult the normal way of launching such aircraft. Using a catapult, there was no need to have the entire flight deck available for launching. Angling the flight deck gave each landing aircraft the option to accelerate away after a missed landing but still left enough room for concurrent launches using catapults. Simultaneous landing and launching had by now

IJN carrier *Akagi* in her early configuration with three flight decks.

also become more important with the increase in AEW and ASW operations, both being continuous in nature. The short endurance of early jets also added to this need.

The slower launch cycles when using catapults meant that multiple catapults were required, including parking spaces behind each catapult. The wider-angled flight deck made it natural to have the elevators at the deck edge instead of along the centerline, which allowed for a more compact flight-deck layout.

The slow acceleration of early jets was only partly due to lack of thrust; static thrust was roughly comparable to that of propeller-driven planes but jets were built for higher speeds and minimum take-off speeds tended to be correspondingly higher, requiring more thrust for a constant length of the flight deck. A related problem was the time it took for a jet engine to spool up to full power. A jet engine is built around a thermodynamic balance and if too much fuel is pumped into it, it will simply choke. The temperature of the engine core has to be maintained which meant that thrust could only be increased slowly, in the order of many seconds. This problem can be circumvented by using stop chocks to hold the aircraft in position while the engine is spooled up to full power but this assumes that there is only one plane on the deck or that jet blast deflectors can be used. The same problem, but in reverse, applied when landing. After cutoff it takes a short while until the jet engine ceases to produce thrust. In short, jets could well be operated without an angled deck and indeed without catapults, but the combination of an angled deck and catapult launches was simply a more robust and versatile solution.

## Mirror Landing System

With faster landing speeds came the need for faster reaction times for adjusting to the correct glide slope. The faster reaction time was achieved by eliminating the LSO (Landing Signals Officer). Instead of the LSO judging the approach and then signaling what he felt was right to the pilot using paddles and body language, the pilot could immediately see for himself where he was in relation to the intended glide slope. Speaking in terms of feedback-control systems, latency was reduced (and as any control-systems engineer will testify, latency is always the bane of any feedback system).

## Steam Catapults

An early type of steam catapult was available in the 1930s but hydraulic catapults were much more common. The hydraulic catapults on the *Essex* class carriers could launch a 7 ton aircraft to 105 knots in 1.7 seconds with a cycle time of 33 seconds. The hydraulic pumps were driven by electric motors. As planes got heavier, hydraulic catapults began to show their limitations, however. Increasing power meant increasing working pressure, risking an explosion of the hydraulic fluid.

Rocket-Assisted Take-Off (RATO) was used for some of the early jets but this is by nature a very unreliable solution. Another problem was that the exhaust plume contained substances that got deposited on aircraft windscreens and control surfaces and was difficult to remove. In aerial combat, pilots depend on excellent vision and are quite fastidious about having a clean windscreen—any fouling there is a definite handicap. On land the area to the rear of the plane taking off can be kept clear but that is not practical on a carrier. Should RATO have been a workable solution, it would have had the advantage that it did not slow down flight operations as much as the catapult did.

In the early 1950s, despite the cost and complexity, steam catapults came into general use with the British leading the way. On a steam catapult, a force is produced by applying steam at high pressure to a piston. Steam is taken from the ships main machinery. Compressed air was used in some early catapults but had problems with oxygen at high pressure igniting the oil lubricating the piston. The big advantage with steam is that it taps into the raw power of the ship's main machinery. Controlling that power is a challenge, however, requiring a complex installation with lots of piping and valves. The cycle time for a catapult launch remained the same, about 45–60 seconds, about the same as the cycle time for an elevator.

The use of power taken from the ship's main machinery has led many to believe that catapults require that kind of massive power to operate. The power exerted by the catapult during a 3-second launch is certainly considerable but the average power is actually pretty low. Operating at a launch rate of one launch every 40–50 seconds, average power required for one catapult is about the same as that delivered by the diesel engine of a heavy truck. If the ship does not have steam machinery, then steam could in principle be provided by what is known as a "donkey boiler."

Steam catapults are now being replaced by electromagnetic types. These use linear electric motors similar to those used in public transportation and in some amusement park rides. The first such EMALS (Electro-Magnetic Aircraft Launch System) catapults were used in the USS *Gerald R. Ford*, lead ship of the new generation of US carriers. The required launch energy of 122 MJ is stored in a flywheel and as these installations go, ranks as a fairly average industrial application. The energy to spool up the flywheel is taken from the on board medium voltage distribution network. The next generation of EMALS catapults will probably use supercapacitors for energy storage, simplifying the design by doing away with the mechanical flywheel.

Getting an aircraft into the air using a catapult is much more energy efficient than using a runway. With a launch energy of 50 MJ, the electricity would cost about $3 which is much less than the cost of the jet fuel used in a standard take off. Extending that to commercial airliners, Airbus has therefore proposed to use EMALS catapults for commercial passenger jets, where the catapult would pay for itself by the jet fuel it saves.

All catapults can in principle be integrated with ski jumps. The easiest one to integrate is the electromagnetic type. With a catapult, however, there may not be much point in having a ski jump except maybe as a fallback mechanism or to handle aircraft that are not built for catapults. As electromagnetic catapults can be expected to come down in price, the business case for ski jumps becomes marginal.

## Short Take offs

The basic formula for constant acceleration take offs is $v^2 = 2ad$ where "v" is take off speed, "a" is acceleration and "d" is the length of the runway (SI units).

This makes a low stall speed the most important parameter for unassisted take offs. Good acceleration with a high thrust-to-weight is also a factor but a low stall speed makes everything much easier. A low stall speed requires a generous wing area and suitable aerodynamics for good handling at high angle of attacks. The wind over the deck also helps—the more wind is available the heavier load can be carried.

The stall speed for the Zero is about 60 knots, for the Hellcat it is around 70 knots. Static thrust from these prop-driven machines can be estimated to be about half their weight, accelerating them at about 0.5g on take off. Assuming no wind over deck we get about 100 yards necessary for take off or about a third of the flight deck of a fully-grown carrier. Assuming 30 knots of wind over deck, the speed required is about half, and distance becomes about a quarter or about 25 yards. Steaming at full speed into a good gale, we can have 60 knots of wind over the deck and the Zero could in principle do vertical take offs and landings (and sometimes did if not lashed down). The Swordfish biplane actually did semi-vertical take offs and landings as a matter of routine, having a landing speed of 40 knots. Come in too slow with a Swordfish and you actually have to accelerate to keep up with the carrier, but fortunately, having a top speed of a blistering 120 knots, it was able to keep up with the even the fastest carriers in the windiest conditions! Joking aside, no wonder the Swordfish was so popular and stayed in production right toward the end of the war. It was the V/STOL aircraft of the day and was very well suited to operations from small and slow carriers.

Would ski jumps work on World War II era carriers? Yes. The British carrier *Furious* had a type of ramp fitted in 1944 to make it easier for its Barracudas to take off. The main problem with a ski jump was that it hindered spotting forward.

## Landing

The classic method is to use arresting wires sprung over the deck. The tail-hook on the plane catches one of these wires and a connected hydraulic machinery absorbs the energy. It is fairly simple and does not add much to the cost of the carrier. The plane must have a tail-hook, however, and the airframe must also be able to withstand the rather rapid deceleration.

The energy to be absorbed is proportional to the square of the landing speed relative to deck. Landings were notoriously prone to accidents and the best way to reduce the risk was to reduce speed relative to deck, that is, to have the carrier steaming at full speed into whatever wind was available. The faster the carrier the safer the landings.

World War II style "taildraggers" had their center of gravity aft of the main landing gear, making them inherently unstable when braking hard, resulting in a ground loop if not careful.

Modern jets have "tricycle" landing gear and are much more stable under heavy braking conditions. When depending on brakes, like on a racing car, downward force is required to stop the plane from just skidding along the deck. One way to get the downward force is to use some kind of air brake like canards. Brakes do depend on the wheels having enough friction with the landing surface and cannot slow down a plane in the same short distance, and with the same authority, that arresting wires can.

In the absence of arresting wires, the plane can simply apply its brakes. Now the brakes have to absorb the kinetic energy of the plane. Assuming that carbon brake disks have a specific heat of 1.0 kJ/kg*K, weigh a total of 20kg and that we allow them to heat up to 1,000°C (at which temperature they will glow bright orange), these brakes can then absorb about 14 MJ of energy. This is equivalent to a 14 ton aircraft landing at 90 knots of speed relative to the flight deck. In short, it is theoretically possible for the brakes alone to absorb the kinetic energy of a landing plane.

## Aircraft Carried

With the sinking of the *Yamato* in 1945, an era had come to an end—not only the era of the battleship but also in how a major warship was attacked. It was not known at the time but there would not be an attack on a major warship again until the sinking of Israeli destroyer *Eilat* by missiles in 1967.

Radar-directed automatic AA had made torpedo bombing too dangerous. Losses had always been high for torpedo bombers but with the new methods of defending, this attack method had become impractical. There was also the very simple fact that for the USN and its allies, there was nothing left to torpedo.

The highly specialized art of dive bombing, the art of placing a large bomb on a small high-value target by means of a near-vertical dive, was being replaced by guided bombs. For the general ground-attack role, dive bombing was being replaced by rockets and napalm carried by the new breed of fighter-bombers. These could not only provide effective ground support but also successfully defend themselves by tangling with enemy fighters. Both methods of ground attack were also relatively easy for pilots to learn.

The new category of AEW aircraft as the eyes in the sky of the carrier task force was just coming into service. In a few short years then, all the elements of carrier warfare as practiced today had come into existence. A quite remarkable series of developments. The only major development that had not yet happened in 1945 was the introduction of jet aircraft.

## The Carrier of the Future

In his book *The Better Angels of Our Nature: Why Violence Has Declined*, author Steven Pinker reasons that we are seeing a decline in wars simply because they are no longer profitable. He is effectively using Operations Research to show that today even the winner of a war has more to win by not going to war in the first place. From this one can surmise that war between major powers is unlikely. During the Cold War there were a few relatively limited proxy wars between the major powers but since the end of the Cold War, the remaining wars have been highly asymmetrical, without the major powers coming in direct confrontation with each other. These asymmetrical wars, usually involving a failed state of some sort, are the only wars that are likely to occur within the coming decades. Which of course is excellent news.

For these type of conflicts, the modern super-carrier is an overkill. Without an enemy air force and in the absence of sophisticated air defenses, jets and stealth are no longer needed, nor are the ASW and AEW functions normally provided by the carrier. Amphibious assault is also irrelevant. The super-carrier will still be needed as a "fleet in being" to discourage major conflicts, but the trend is clearly toward major wars being a thing of the past.

What might actually be needed is something more like the CVEs of World War II, something that can provide ground support and do that at minimum cost. We know that an asymmetric war will be won, eventually; it is mainly an exercise in patience until the nation-building effort has reached some minimum semblance of good governance. With that requirement for patience comes a need to do it as cost-effectively as possible lest the voters lose faith in the slow and frustrating task of nation-building. One can think of it as a step above fighting drug smugglers. It is not about winning a war at all cost; it is about winning at the lowest cost possible. Maybe it should not be seen as a war at all, maybe it should be seen as a type of (world) policing.

The air group would consist of drones and manned aircraft, all subsonic. For ground operations, moving fast just makes observation and attacks more difficult—flying low and slow is much better.

With more need for endurance than speed, turboprop engines are probably the best choice as they are more efficient than jets at low altitude. The Reaper is a well-known drone powered by a turboprop engine. The Beechcraft Texan II and the Embraer Super Tucano are similar in size and weight and are used for both training and/or counter-insurgency operations.

With lower landing speeds, an angled deck is no longer necessary and we can go back to the simpler axial deck layout. Arresting gear would probably need to be fitted, as well as barriers. A catapult might be useful but is perhaps not needed, depending on loadout and ship speed.

The principal threat to this carrier will probably be land-based anti-ship missiles, of varying degrees of sophistication. To defend against these, automatic AA guns would be fitted. Something like a 20mm CIWS might not turn out to be sufficient to achieve definite kills on anti-ship missiles, and multiple 40mm mounts are therefore added along the sides of the axial flight deck. At the end of the day there is no substitute for raw firepower and it is still a relatively small investment in terms of cost and weight.

And by now we are of course back to what is effectively a World War II carrier. As the French put it: "plus ça change, plus c'est la même chose." The more things change, the more they stay the same.

The above analysis was written somewhat tongue-in-cheek, structured in a way that would lead us back to the carriers of World War II, the topic of this book. Nevertheless, it does show how flexible the basic carrier concept is.

The two major drivers for the economics of a future carrier appear to be drones and cheaper catapults. Another major factor is how supporting an asymmetrical war has emerged as the most common task of a carrier, if not the main task. These developments point toward smaller carriers as being able to be cost-effective, opening up new "markets" or "ecological niches" for carriers.

The basic carrier concept can also be completely re-invented. One line of thought is that since the Dolittle raid, fleet carriers have essentially only operated in support of landing sites. In 1942 and 1944 there was the odd spoiling attack that had to fended off, but since then carriers have been doing nothing but providing ground support being stationed off some coast. The days of the fast carriers scouring the oceans are long gone. Naval superiority is now largely taken for granted and what remains is mainly an exercise in logistics, a reasonably mobile airbase that can be set up at sea where needed. Lily and Clover were two such small floating airstrips, built by the RN during World War II using technology borrowed from the Mulberry floating harbors. They had runways of about 1,000 feet and were intended to operate 48 Spitfires. They were built and tested but were not ready in time before the Japanese surrender. Another example is the Mega-Float airfield anchored in Tokyo Bay. The USN has looked into the very ambitious Mobile Offshore Base (MOB) concept, using semi-submersible technology to construct a very large floating base for a variety of logistics functions, including a mile-long airfield capable of handling C-17s. The main problem seems to be what the requirements should be and what it will be allowed to cost. These floating airbases are of course as unglamorous as a carrier will ever get, but again we see the flexibility of the basic carrier concept.

## Carriers of World War II vs Today

An *Essex* class carrier had a unit cost of about $75 million. With a GDP of $220 billion, the US could build 3,000 *Essex* class carriers for the GDP of one year. A *Ford* class carrier had a unit cost of about $10 billion. With a GDP of $18 trillion, the US could build 1,800 *Ford* class carriers for the GDP of one year. This means that a modern carrier costs roughly twice as much as a World War II carrier in terms of percentage of GDP. On the other hand, that cost should really be compared to the more expensive World War II battleship instead of a World War II carrier. Furthermore, the sticker price of a nuclear-powered carrier includes the fuel. In short, today's carrier costs about the same as a capital ship of World War II. Considering the much longer service life of today's carriers, reflected in the slower building tempo, they actually cost much less.

The container ships of the *Maersk B* class are almost the length of a *Nimitz* class carrier (294 vs 333m) and are capable of 30 knots. Each such container ship cost about $60 million fully completed. One *Ford* class carrier costs about the same as 170 such container ships. If a World War II carrier cost about $50–75 million and a *Liberty* class transport cost $2 million, then the carrier cost the same as 30 *Liberty* ships. This means that a modern transport costs about a sixth of what it did in World War II, relative to a carrier. The basic carrier, as in the hull and the machinery, is cheap. It is the accessories that are expensive. Putting it differently, the physical size of the carrier has only a limited effect on system cost, at least directly.

Carriers have not kept pace with the growth in size of merchant vessels. During World War II, a large transport was smaller than a fleet carrier. Today's oil tankers, bulk carriers, container ships, and cruise ships are often much bigger than the biggest carrier. Converting the latest generation of container ships would yield escort carriers dwarfing fleet carriers.

In deciding on the optimum size of the air group, there are "buy-in costs" to take into consideration. An ASW patrol will have to be kept going 24/7 which means that a certain number of helicopters are needed. A plane guard helicopter needs to be in the air during flight operations. Likewise with AEW, another few planes are needed there. It takes about a dozen helicopters and/ or aircraft just to set things up. It does not make sense to do this for just half a dozen fighter-bombers. Then we have simple scaling effects. Given that modern aircraft have a certain size and minimum requirements that do not really scale, not even for drones, then the number that can be carried drops faster than the size of the carrier. Going the other direction, ship volume increases faster than flight deck area. As ship volume and the number of aircraft increases, the flight deck then becomes a traffic jam which puts an upper bound on useful ship size. The most cost-effective size of the air group then comes in at around 60 aircraft, about the same as in World War II, for largely the same reasons.

A Hellcat cost about $50,000 and the GDP of one year would buy 4.4 million of them. An F-35 costs about $150 million and the GDP of one year would buy about 120,000 of them. Aircraft unit cost has risen about 35–40 times relative to GDP and today's air forces employ far fewer of them. As today's carriers operate about the same number of aircraft as in World War II, while costing about the same in relation to GDP, this means that carriers today are about 35–40 times more efficient at being carriers. Putting it differently, the cost of providing mobile bases for a nation's air power has fallen by about 97 percent. That mobility is highly useful for a variety of reasons, both offensively and defensively.

Nevertheless, carriers still have to earn their keep and be cost-effective. Missiles certainly threaten carriers. Missiles threatens all warships, indeed sea power in general, as did aircraft of World War II.

Lacking the pilot of a World War II bomber, a missile is bad at targeting. Against such a threat, a carrier task force is like a school of fish—there is safety in numbers. The task force might be hard to hide but it is very possible to hide from a missile inside the task force.

Lacking the wings of World War II bomber, a missile is bad at maneuvering. Without a pilot it would not know what to do with it anyway. Instead, the missile depends on raw speed to reach a target. With an effective AEW capability the missile will be detected at long range and without the "leakage" that was such a problem against kamikazes. The small carriers used by the RN during the Falklands War did not have an AEW capability; thus the task force did not receive adequate warnings about incoming missiles and paid the price for it. After the war, a very modest AEW capability was quickly added, based on a small radar carried aloft on a helicopter. Their next carrier design is much bigger and will have a proper AEW capability.

The task force protects the carrier and the carrier protects the task force. If a missile is to have any chance of penetrating a strong defense, that missile will have to be equipped with some type of intelligence. That EW intelligence will be matched against the EW intelligence of the task force. It will have to be expensive and each unit will only be used once. Missiles also have to earn their keep and be cost-effective.

The carriers of World War II started out as raiders, as eggshells armed with hammers. Over the course of the war, defensive capabilities increased dramatically through a combination of radar, fighter direction, and close-in automatic AA fire. Striking power, as well as staying power, initially matured into "power projection" through increases in numbers coupled with the relative weaknesses of the enemies. From that starting point of World War II, the aircraft carrier has then benefited greatly both from the increased importance of air power in general but more specifically from the dramatic reduction in the number of aircraft required for the projection of that air power. Today a single carrier can dominate an entire country. Responding to any international crisis by asking "where are the carriers?" was not done back in the 1930s. It was not relevant. Today it is.

# Notes on Sources

Researching for this book has been in a sense frustrating but also tremendously rewarding. This book lays claim to be unique in its approach. The problem with that is that there are essentially no books that covers the same set of topics. The source material is hence very scattered and fragmentary in nature, often also contradictory. Many sources yielded a few nuggets of information or understanding but few sources contained a definitive treatment of some sub-topic.

These notes include the author's feelings on what sources were actually useful and in what way. In some cases, critical for the discussion, the exact sources are given and discussed as part of text.

## Navigation and Communication

King (2012) provided some important insights to how Japanese naval aviators navigated. Both USN and RN navigation was easy to research. Bowditch is a classic on navigation and always useful for information on navigational techniques and equipment in general. The author's own experience as a private pilot and as a navigator in professional yacht racing also helped.

Friedman (1981) had standard but still useful information on HF and VHF radio properties. How radios were set up and used in combat, particularly early forms of electronic warfare, proved difficult to research. The text here is based on fragmentary sources and some educated guesswork with the USN CIC Bulletins being the most useful.

## Radio

Information on Japanese radio sets is from the book by Tagaya (2003). The book by Crosley (2014) had useful information on RN radios and usage. There is plenty of technical information on the various radio sets available from the ranks of museums and radio amateurs but most of that is irrelevant to how carrier operations are conducted. There is a dearth of useful sources in this area.

## Radar

The two most important sources here are the books by Howse (1993) and Brown (1999) with some additional input from Friedman (1981). The USN CIC Bulletins has extensive information on how radar was employed and on practical problems encountered. The author's own background doing design work on military radars, as well as using them under combat conditions, also proved useful.

# Flight Operations

Parshall & Tully (2005) had some useful material on flight operations. All the various memoirs published by pilots provided an overall understanding of life as a pilot on a carrier with Crosley (2014), Buell (1992) and Werneth (2008) being the most detailed and useful. USF-77 is an important reference on US carrier operations, as is the USNTMJ A-11 report on IJN practices. Several official USN and RN training films are available on YouTube. Apart from those sources, much of the information comes from discussion threads of various forums and the exact source is therefore often poorly defined.

# Scouting, Attacking and Defending

The book by Dickson (1975) is the battle account with the most detailed and consistent description of searches conducted. Belote (1975) had some useful material. Parshall & Tully (2005) also had useful discussions on these topics. The essay by Heinz (2014) on carrier defense was a most useful source. There are USN instructional videos on dive bombing and torpedo attacks in WWII that are available on YouTube (and possibly other similar sites). Again, USF-77 is an important reference.

Borrmann *et al.* from NSA contributed with a nice history of radio intelligence. They should know. The book by Prados (2001) provided information on traffic analysis and cryptanalysis as used by both USN and IJN.

# Fighter Direction

The single most valuable resource is the essay written by Woolrich and published by Navigating and Direction Officers' Association (available on www.ndassoc.net), covering RN development.

Friedman (1981) has much useful information from USN experience, the official USN CIC Bulletins also provided excellent insights on the limitations of radar and on the methods used. The book by Wolters (2013) provided useful context.

# Logistics

Data on the fuel consumption of USN ships are from the official USN document (FTP 218). Friedman (1983) had numbers on gasoline storage on US carriers. The figures for Japanese oil imports and consumption are from Evans & Peattie (1997).

# The Battles

The battles of Coral Sea, Midway, Eastern Solomons and Santa Cruz are based on the 'First Team' books by Lundstrom. Parshall & Tully (2005) was also used, being probably the best book on Midway. The account of the Pedestal operation is based on the book by Smith (2012). The battle of Philippine Sea is based on the excellent book by Dickson (1975). The battle of Cape Engaño is rather weakly covered by historians, overshadowed by the other actions around Leyte. The account is based on Morison (1963) and Woodward (2007) with additional input from the Order of Battles pages at Navweaps.com (retrieved July 2015).

# Combat Models

The basic reference here is the book by Hughes (2000). The paper by Armstrong & Powell was an important source of inspiration, as were the reports by Johns *et al.* (2001) and Beall (1990). The essay by Heinz (2014) provided useful combat statistics.

Weakly related to combat models but nevertheless very interesting is the book by Pinker (2012). In that book the author uses basic conflict models to explain why, in a globalized world, wars have simply become unprofitable. Japan in the 30s is of course a striking example of failed attitudes towards globalization.

# Armored Flight Decks vs. Size of Air Group

Stuart Slade and Richard Worth have written a piece with the title "Were Armored Flight Decks on British Carriers Worthwhile?" available on NavWeaps.com. It is well written and has been quite influential. Unfortunately, it is also rather biased in tone and makes several statements in the area of naval architecture that are highly debatable (location of strength deck, hull warping etc.). The piece has been rather comprehensively debunked over at ArmouredCarriers.com. The Wikipedia entry on "Armored flight deck" is detailed and useful but content changes over time as the contributors debate the issue.

# AA Guns & Gunnery

Statistics on kamikazes shot down are from post-war official US documents. Friedman (2014) looked like a promising book but had essentially no new statistics on effectiveness. Basic data on guns are from the NavWeaps.com web site. The author's own experience as a systems engineer in an army antiaircraft unit was also helpful.

# The Art of Carrier Operations

John Boyd gave a series of presentations on his ideas but never in the form of a book. That is unfortunate as it makes his ideas more perishable. The book by Coram (2004) is a very good book on his life and work but does not really say that much about his ideas as such. Some of Boyd's presentations have been recorded and made available on YouTube and those clips are the basis for what is said here about his ideas. In those presentations he makes some comparisons to various concepts in mathematics, physics and philosophy. Those comparisons really do not make much sense, they are essentially embellishments to impress the ignorant. What might well be going on here is that he uses them to extend the OODA loop of his audience, allowing him to then spoon-feed them his ideas (a technique that would not work as well within the format of a book). Either way, these embellishments tend to hide the essential simplicity of his ideas and that simplicity is something that should be valued.

# Post-War Developments

The data on modern fighters and carriers are from open sources (Wikipedia etc.). Regarding the physics of short takeoffs and landings, the author's own training as a theoretical physicist could finally be put to some practical use.

# Bibliography

## Official Documents

Commander Aircraft Battle Force, March 1941
*Current Tactical Orders and Doctrine U.S. Fleet Aircraft (USF-74, 75 and 76)*
*Current Tactical Orders Aircraft Carriers U.S. Fleet (USF-77)*
CO USS Lexington. *Action Report of the Battle of the Coral Sea*
CO USS Yorktown. *Action Report of the Battle of the Coral Sea*
CO USS Lexington. *Air Operations in the Battle of the Coral Sea*
CO USS Yorktown. *Air Operations in the Battle of the Coral Sea*
CO USS Neosho. *Action Report of the Battle of the Coral Sea*
CO USS Sims. *Action Report of the Battle of the Coral Sea*
CO USS Yorktown. *Action Report of the Battle of Midway*
CO USS Enterprise. *Action Report of the Battle of Midway*
CO USS Hornet. *Action Report of the Battle of Midway*
Radar Research and Development Sub-Committee of the Joint Committee on New Weapons and
  Equipment, August 1943
*U.S. Radar: Operational Characteristics of Radar Classified by Tactical Application.*  [FTP217]
Office of the Chief of Naval Operations, CIC Bulletins, 1944–1945
C.I.C. Combat Information Center vol. 1 No. 5, July 1944
C.I.C. Combat Information Center vol. 1 No. 6, August 1944
C.I.C. Combat Information Center vol. 1 No. 7, September 1944
C.I.C. Combat Information Center vol. 1 No. 8, October 1944
C.I.C. Combat Information Center vol. 1 No. 9, December 1944
C.I.C. Combat Information Center vol. 2 No. 1, January 1945
C.I.C. Combat Information Center vol. 2 No. 2, February 1945
C.I.C. Combat Information Center vol. 2 No. 3, March 1945
C.I.C. Combat Information Center vol. 2 No. 4, April 1945
C.I.C. Combat Information Center vol. 2 No. 5, May 1945
C.I.C. Combat Information Center vol. 2 No. 6, June 1945
C.I.C. Combat Information Center vol. 2 No. 7, July 1945
C.I.C. Combat Information Center vol. 2 No. 8, August 1945
C.I.C. Combat Information Center vol. 2 No. 9, September 1945
C.I.C. Combat Information Center vol. 2 No. 10, October 1945
C.I.C. Combat Information Center vol. 2 No. 11, November 1945
C.I.C. Combat Information Center vol. 2 No. 12, December 1945

Office of the Chief of Naval Operations, 1946
Radar Bulletin No. 1 (RADONE). *The Tactical Use of Radar*

Radar Bulletin No. 1A (RADONEA). *The Capabilities and Limitations of Shipborne Radar*
Radar Bulletin No. 2A (RADTWOA). *The Tactical Use of Radar in Aircraft*
Radar Bulletin No. 3 (RADTHREE). *Radar Operator's Manual*
Radar Bulletin No. 4 (RADFOUR). *Air Plotting Manual*
Radar Bulletin No. 5 (RADFIVE). *Surface Plotting Manual*
Radar Bulletin No. 6 (RADSIX). *Combat Information Center Manual*
Radar Bulletin No. 7 (RADSEVEN). *Radar Countermeasures Manual*
Radar Bulletin No. 8A (RADEIGHTA). *Aircraft Control Manual*

Headquarters of the Commander in Chief, United States Fleet, September 1945
*War Service Fuel Consumption of U.S. Naval Surface Vessels.* [FTP218]

Headquarters of the Commander in Chief, United States Fleet, 1945
COMINCH P-009: *Antiaircraft Action Summary Suicide Attacks*
COMINCH P-0011: *Anti-Suicide Action Summary*
Information Bulletin No. 22: *Battle Experience Battle for Leyte Gulf*
Information Bulletin No. 24: *Battle Experience Radar Pickets and Methods of Combating Suicide Attacks Off Okinawa March–May 1945*
Information Bulletin No. 29: *Antiaircraft Action Summary · World War II*
CO NAVAER 08-5S-120, February 1944
*Pilot's Operating Manual For Airborne Radar AN/APS-6 Series For Night Fighters*
Air Technical Intelligence Group, FEAF, November 1945
*ATIG Report No. 115: A Short Survey of Japanese Radar Vol. I & II*
Office of Naval Intelligence (ONI), 1946
*Naval Aviation Combat Statistics – World War II*
*The Battle of the Eastern Solomons 23–25 August 1942 – Combat Narrative*
*The Battle of Santa Cruz Islands 26 October 1942 – Combat Narrative*
U.S. Naval Technical Mission to Japan, 1946
A-11      *Aircraft Arrangements and Handling Facilities on Japanese Naval Vessels*
E-02      *Japanese Airborne Radar*
E-05      *Japanese Radio and Radar Direction Finders*
E-07      *Japanese Radar Counter-measures and Visual Signal Display Equipment*
E-08      *Japanese Radio Equipment*
E-17      *Japanese Radio, Radar and Sonar Equipment*
O-30      *Japanese Anti-Aircraft Fire Control*
O-44      *Effectiveness of Japanese AA Fire*
U.S. Strategic Bombing Survey (Pacific) Naval Analysis Division, 1946
*Interrogation of Japanese Officials OPNAV-P-03-100, Vol. I & II*
*The Campaigns of the Pacific War*

# Books

Adam, John A. *If Mahan Ran the Great Pacific War: An Analysis of World War II Naval Strategy* (Indiana University Press, 2008)
Adams, Douglas. *The Hitchhiker's Guide to the Galaxy* (Random House, 1995)
Adlam, Henry. *On and Off the Flight Deck* (Pen and Sword, 2010)
Belote, James H. and Belote, William M. *Titans of the Seas: The Development and Operations of Japanese and American Carrier Task Forces During World War II* (Harper & Row, 1975)

Bowditch, Nathaniel. *American Practical Navigator* (National Imagery and Mapping Agency, 2002)

Boyd, William B. and Rowland, Buford. *U.S. Navy Bureau of Ordnance in World War II* (Bureau of Ordnance, Department of the Navy, 1953)

Brand, Stanley. *Achtung! Swordfish!* (Propagator Press, 2011)

Brown, David. *Carrier Fighters* (The Book Service Ltd, 1975)

Brown, Louis. *A Radar History of World War II* (IOP Publishing, 1999)

Bruce, Roy W. and Leonard, Charles R. *Crommelin's Thunderbirds* (Naval Institute Press, 1994)

Buderi, Robert. *The Invention That Changed the World* (Simon & Schuster, 1996)

Budiansky, Stephen. *Blackett's War – The Men Who Defeated the Nazi U-Boats and Brought Science to the Art of Warfare* (Vintage Books, 2013)

Buell, Harold L. *Dauntless Helldiver* (Dell Publishing, 1992)

Coram, Robert. *Boyd: The Fighter Pilot Who Changed the Art of War* (Back Bay Books, 2004)

Crosley, R. 'Mike'. *They Gave Me a Seafire* (Pen and Sword, 2014)

Dickson, W.D. *The Battle of the Philippine Sea* (Ian Allen Ltd, 1975)

Dull, Paul S. *A Battle History of the Imperial Japanese Navy, 1941–1945* (Naval Institute Press, 1978)

Ellis, John. *World War II: A Statistical Survey: The Essential Facts and Figures for All the Combatants* (Facts on File, 1993)

Evans, David C. and Peattie, Mark R. *Kaigun: Tactics and Technology in the Imperial Japanese Navy 1887–1941* (Naval Institute Press, 1997)

Fahey, James J. *Pacific War Diary 1942–1945* (Houghton Mifflin Company, 2003)

Fletcher, Gregory F. *Intrepid Aviators* (NAL Caliber, 2013)

Friedman, Norman. *Naval Radar* (Conway Maritime Press Ltd, 1981)

Friedman, Norman. *U.S. Aircraft Carriers: An Illustrated Design History* (Naval Institute Press, 1983)

Friedman, Norman. *Naval Anti-Aircraft Guns & Gunnery* (Seaforth Publishing, 2014)

Friedman, Norman. *Fighters over the Fleet: Naval Air Defence from Biplanes to the Cold War* (Seaforth Publishing, 2016)

Goralski, Waldemar. *IJNS Aircraft Carrier* Taiho (Kagero, 2016)

Hone, Thomas C., Friedman, Norman and Mandeles, Mark D. *Innovation in Carrier Aviation* (Naval War College Press, 2011)

Hopkins, William B. *The Pacific War* (Zenith Press, 2009)

Howse, Derek. *Radar at Sea* (Naval Institute Press, 1993)

Hughes, Wayne P. *Fleet Tactics and Coastal Combat* (Naval Institute Press, 2000)

Jefford, C.G. *Observers and Navigators: And Other Non-pilot Aircrew in the RFC, RNAS and RAF* (Grub Street, 2014)

Kennedy, Paul. *The Rise and Fall of the Great Powers* (Vintage Books, 1989)

King, Dan. *The Last Zero Fighter: Firsthand Accounts from WWII Japanese Naval Pilots* (CreateSpace Independent Publishing Platform, 2012)

Lamb, Charles. *War in a Stringbag* (Weidenfeld & Nicolson, 2001)

Lundstrom, John B. *The First Team and the Guadalcanal Campaign* (Naval Institute Press, 1994)

Lundstrom, John B. *The First Team: Pacific Naval Air Combat from Pearl Harbor to Midway* (Naval Institute Press, 2005)

McWhorter, Hamilton and Stout, Jay A. *The First Hellcat Ace* (Pacifica Military History, 2009)

Morison, Samuel E. *History of United States Naval Operations in World War II* (Little, Brown & Co., 1963)

Parshall, Jonathan and Tully, Anthony. *Shattered Sword* (Potomac Books, 2005)

Peattie, Mark R. *Sunburst* (Naval Institute Press, 2001)

Pinker, Steven. *The Better Angels of Our Nature: Why Violence Has Declined* (Penguin Books, 2012)

Porter, Bruce and Hammel, Eric. *Ace! A Marine Night-Fighter Pilot in WWII* (Pacifica Press, 1985)

Prados, John. *Combined Fleet Decoded* (Naval Institute Press, 2001)

Reynolds, Clark G. *The Fast Carriers* (McGraw-Hill, 1968)

Roskill, Stephen. *The War at Sea* (HMSO, 1956)

Sakai, Saburo. *Samurai!* (Naval Institute Press, 2010)

Shaw, Robert L. *Fighter Combat* (Naval Institute Press, 1985)

Smith, Peter C. *Dive Bomber!* (Stackpole Books, 2008)

Smith, Peter C. *Pedestal* (Crécy Publishing Ltd, 2012)

Tagaya, Osamu and White, John. *Imperial Japanese Naval Aviator 1937–45* (Osprey Publishing, 2003)

Werneth, Ron. *Beyond Pearl Harbor: The Untold Stories of Japan's Naval Airmen.* (Schiffer Publishing Ltd, 2008)

Wildenberg, Thomas. *Gray Steel and Black Oil – Fast Tankers and Replenishment at Sea in the U.S. Navy, 1912–1995* (Naval Institute Press, 1996)

Woodward, C. Vann. *The Battle for Leyte Gulf* (Skyhorse Publishing, 2007)

Wolters, Timothy S. *Information at Sea* (John Hopkins University Press, 2013)

Zimm, Alan D. *Attack on Pearl Harbor* (Casemate Books, 2011)

## Articles, Papers, Reports, Theses, and Essays

Armstrong, Michael J. and Powell, Michael B. *A Stochastic Salvo Model Analysis of the Battle of the Coral Sea*

Arora, V.K. *Proximity Fuzes: Theory and Techniques* (Defence R&D Organisation, Ministry of Defence, India, 2010)

Beall, Thomas Regan. *The Development of a Naval Battle Model and its Validation Using Historical Data* (Thesis submitted to Naval Postgraduate School, Monterey, California, 1990)

Blondia, Amarilla. "Cigarettes and their Impact in World War II," *Perspectives: A Journal of Historical Inquiry*, 37, 2010

Boslaugh, David L. "Radar and the Fighter Directors" (Published on the Engineering and Technology History Wiki; available at www.ethw.org)

Borrmann, Donald A., Kvetkas, William T., Brown, Charles V., Flatley, Michael J. and Hunt, Robert. *The History of Traffic Analysis: World War I – Vietnam* (NSA, 2013)

Caravaggio, Angelo N. "Winning" the Pacific War – The Masterful Strategy of Commander Minoru Genda," *Naval War College Review*, Winter 2014

Carey, Cristopher T. *A Brief History of US Military Aviation Oxygen Breathing Systems* (Aeolus Aerospace, retrieved September 2016)

Coleman, Kent S. *Halsey at Leyte Gulf: Command Decision and Disunity of Effort* (Master's Thesis, Marquette University, 2002)

Darwin, Robert L., Bowman, Howard L., Hunstad, Mary, Leach, William B. and Williams, Frederick W. *Aircraft Carrier Flight and Hangar Deck Fire Protection: History and Current Status* (Naval Air Warfare Center Weapons Division, 2005)

Donovan, Patrick H. "Oil Logistics in the Pacific War," *Air Force Journal of Logistics*, vol. XXVIII, no. 1, Spring 2004

Friedman, Hal M. "Strategy, Language and the Culture of Defeat: Changing Interpretations of Japan's War Naval Demise," *International Journal of Naval History*, October 2013

Gray, James Seton. "Development of Naval Night Fighters in World War II," *Naval Institute Proceedings Magazine*, vol. 74/7/545, July 1948

Hanyok, Robert J. "Catching The Fox Unaware – Japanese Radio Denial and Deception and the Attack on Pearl Harbor," *Naval War College Review*, Autumn 2008

Heinz, Leonard. "Aircraft Carrier Defense in the Pacific War," essay published 2014 on fireonthewaters.tripod.com, retrieved July 2015

Heinz, Leonard. "Japan's Oil Puzzle," essay published 2014 on fireonthewaters.tripod.com, retrieved July 2015

Hodge, Carl C. "The Key to Midway – Coral Sea and a Culture of Learning," *Naval War College Review*, Winter 2015

Hone, Thomas C., Friedman, Norman and Mandeles, Mark D. *American and British Aircraft Carrier Development 1919–1941* (Naval Institute Press, 2009)

Hone, Thomas C., Friedman, Norman and Mandeles, Mark D. "The Development of the Angled Deck Aircraft Carrier," *Naval War College Review*, Spring 2011

Hone, Thomas C. "Replacing Battleships with Aircraft Carriers in the Pacific in WWII," *Naval War College Review*, Winter 2013

Hone, Trent. "U.S. Navy Surface Battle Doctrine and Victory in the Pacific," *Naval War College Review*, Winter 2009

Hore, Peter. "The Fleet Air Arm and British Naval Operations over Norway and Sweden: Part 1 – Autumn of 1940," *Forum Navale* 68, 2012

Hore, Peter. "Operation *Paul* – The Fleet Air Arm Attack on Luleå in 1940," *Forum Navale* 70, 2014

Jennings, Ed. "Crosley's Secret War Effort – The Proximity Fuze," article published February 2001 at www.navweaps.com/index_tech/tech-075.htm, retrieved July 2015

Johns, Michael D., Pilnick, Steven E., Hughes, Wayne P. *Heterogenous Salvo Model for the Navy After Next* (Institute for Joint Warfare Analysis, Naval Postgraduate School, 2001)

Levy, James P. "Was There Something Unique to the Japanese That Lost Them the Battle of Midway?," *Naval War College Review*, Winter 2014

Llewellyn-Jones, Malcolm. *Operation Pedestal Convoy to Malta August 11–15 1942* (Naval Historical Branch, 2012)

Low, Lawrence J. "Anatomy of a Combat Model," essay published 1995 on www.militaryconflict. org, retrieved August 2015

Mably, John R. *The Effectiveness of Merchant Aircraft Carriers* (Thesis in Master of Philosophy, University of Brighton, 2004)

MacDonald, Scot. "Evolution of Aircraft Carriers," *Naval Aviation News*, September 1962–October 1963

O'Neil, William D. *Military Transformation as a Competitive Systemic Process: The Case of Japan and the United States Between the World Wars* (CNA, 2003)

Parshall, Jonathan B., Dickson, David D. and Tully, Anthony P. "Doctrine Matters – Why the Japanese Lost at Midway," *Naval War College Review*, Summer 2001

Pearson, Lee M. "Naval Aviation – Technical Developments in WWII," *Naval Aviation News*, May–June 1995

Prados, John. "Solving the Mysteries of Santa Cruz," *Naval History Magazine*, October 2011

Quinn, D. and Holland, R. D. *C.W Radio Aids to Homing and Blind Approach of Naval Aircraft* (Admiralty Signal Establishment, 1947)

Reilly, John C. "Organization of Naval Aviation in WWII," *Naval Aviation News*, May–June 1991

Sackett, Larry. *Steering the Battleship* North Carolina (Scuttlebutt, 2010)

Sheehy, Chris, *USS* Robin: *An Account of HMS* Victorious' *First Mission to the Pacific* (Masters Thesis at University of New Brunswick, 1998)

Snow, Carl. "Japanese Carrier Operations: How Did They Do It?," *The Hook*, Spring 1995

Tritten, James J. *Doctrine and Fleet Tactics in the Royal Navy* (Naval Doctrine Command, 1994)

Tully, Anthony and Yu, Lu. "A Question of Estimates – How Faulty Intelligence Drove Scouting at the Battle of Midway," *Naval War College Review*, Spring 2015

van Tool, Jan M. "Military Innovation and Carrier Aviation – An Analysis," *Joint Force Quarterly*, Autumn/Winter 1997–98

van Tool, Jan M. "Military Innovation and Carrier Aviation – The Relevant History," *Joint Force Quarterly*, Summer 1997

Vego, Milan. "Major Convoy Operation to Malta, 10–15 August 1942 (Operation *Pedestal*)," *Naval War College Review*, Winter 2010

Weitzenfeld, Daniel K. *Fleet Introduction of Colin Mitchell's Steam Catapult* (The International Research Institute of McLean, 1970)

Woolrich, R. S. *Fighter-Direction Materiel and Technique, 1939–45* (Navigation and Direction Officers' Association, available on www.ndassoc.net, retrieved July 2015)

# Index